An Improbable Journey

An Improbable Journey

THE LIFE AND TIMES OF

EUGENE JELESNIK

GERALD M. McDONOUGH

Shadow Mountain, Salt Lake City, Utah

Library of Congress Cataloging-in-Publication Data

McDonough, Gerald M., 1945–
    An improbable journey : the life and times of Eugene Jelesnik / by Gerald M. McDonough.
       p.   cm.
    Includes bibliographical references.
    ISBN 1-57345-269-6
    1. Jelesnik, Eugene, 1914–   . 2. Conductors (Music)—Utah—Biography. 3. Violinists—Utah—Biography. 4. Television personalities—Utah—Biography. 5. Impresarios—Utah—Biography.
ML422.J39M45   1997
780'.92—dc21
[B]   97-13244
                                       CIP
                                      MN

Printed in the United States of America

10 9 8 7 6 5 4 3 2 1   72082

CONTENTS

FOREWORD

My wife, Carleen Hall Jelesnik, encouraged me to commission the writing of this book. She spent many days and hours with my author giving him facts and information about many aspects of my life. But above all, Carleen found my father's will from Russia and immediately called President Thomas S. Monson of The Church of Jesus Christ of Latter-day Saints to ask for his assistance in getting the document translated. President Monson graciously responded to Carleen's request, and, as you will read, the results are illuminating, factual, and interesting.

Eugene Jelesnik

PREFACE

When Eugene Jelesnik first approached me to propose I write his biography, I was deeply immersed in teaching drama fulltime and had to turn him down. The task was also daunting. There were many thousands of documents to sort through, read, and catalogue. There were hundreds of concert programs and piles of photograph albums to pore over. Eugene Jelesnik has had an extremely long and complex career, which spanned most of the century and the entire globe. When I told him I couldn't possibly take on such a task, I had no regrets. Ivan Lincoln, a staff writer for the *Deseret News* came to Eugene's rescue. Ivan began the task of organizing Eugene's papers, began conducting interviews, and started to write Eugene's story. Unfortunately, Ivan could not free himself from his other obligations, and Eugene, once again, asked me to write his book—a task I undertook in August of 1996.

An Improbable Journey is a personal history, and it is safe to say that it could not have been written at all without the continuous assistance of Eugene Jelesnik. I met with Eugene twice weekly from September of 1996 through February of 1997. Over that time, more than sixty hours of taped interviews were conducted with Eugene and his wife, Carleen. These were added to the more than twenty hours compiled by Ivan Lincoln. The bulk of the text comes from these two sources. Carleen's contribution was crucial in many areas relating to Eugene's home life, and the final work would have been incomplete without her invaluable suggestions.

Much of the early history of Eugene Jelesnik was originally filled with gaps and misinformation. I am deeply indebted to President Thomas S. Monson of The Church of Jesus Christ of Latter-day Saints who arranged for the translation of the Russian, Hebrew, and German documents relating to the Jelesnik family. I am indebted also to Dr. Donald W. Parry of the languages department of Brigham Young University and Margarita Choquette, the Russian language specialist and reference consultant with the Family History Library of the LDS church who both worked on the Jelesnik documents. Elizabeth L. Nichols, senior reference librarian and certified genealogist with the library, was responsible for compiling the genealogical materials, which eventually comprised the eighty-eight-page "Jelesnik Family Study." This work provided a wealth of detail about the Jelesnik family's life in Russia and Germany as well as details of the family's immigration and their early years in New York City. This material was made available to the author in October of 1996. Without these materials, the early chapters of this biography could not have been written.

I am deeply appreciative to Ivan Lincoln for the many hours of work he put into this project. While I chose to write Eugene's life in a linear, chronological fashion, Ivan had organized his draft chapters by topic. His work was a handy reference library in itself on the career of Eugene Jelesnik. The chapter on Eugene's USO tours in particular owes a great deal to Mr. Lincoln. I am grateful to "Saliva Sister" Rebecca Terry Heal for her willingness to share her many memories of working with Eugene over the years. I am thankful also to Jenny Boyer for her recollections of her brother Ed Allem and the early days at the Cinegrill restaurant.

The author is grateful to his sister Anne Moore who proofread the early drafts and offered many suggestions, including the subtitle of the work, "The Life and Times of Eugene Jelesnik." I am grateful for the suggestions made by my brother, Roger J. McDonough, a onetime *Talent Showcase* performer, who provided numerous clarifications on historical matters—particularly the military histories. I am grateful also to Robert Woody for his insights on the Italian campaign and the contributions of the 10th Mountain Division of which he was a distinguished member.

A special thanks goes out as well to the management and staff of the Utah State Historical Society: Max J. Evans, Director; Patricia Smith-Mansfield, Assistant Director; and staff members, Philip F.

Notarianni, Linda Thatcher, Susan Whetstone, Janet Smoak, and Doug Younkin. The Society has been made the custodian of nearly all of the memorabilia from Eugene's long career and has assembled "The Jelesnik Archive." Without the cooperation of these helpful people, this would have been a much thinner volume.

The author also gratefully acknowledges the help and assistance of the many people at Deseret Book who encouraged and supported this project from the start. I am particularly thankful to Ronald Millett, who insisted that the real story of Eugene Jelesnik be told, and to Karen Peery and Pat Williams who helped keep the project on track in Mr. Millett's absence.

I acknowledge the fine work of Kent Ware who was responsible for the jacket cover and book design and Richard Peterson who was given the difficult task of editing the entire manuscript.

I thank my wife, Ronni, who lived with the clutter of Jelesnik programs, papers, and photos for the better part of six months. She worked on countless research, reference, and text problems and typed draft after draft of the manuscript. And, finally, I thank my children, Molly Bridget and Roger John, both of whom provided research and typing assistance. Without the help and understanding of my family, *An Improbable Journey* could not have been written.

AN UNLIKELY SURVIVOR

In a darkened room on the second floor of a large house in the city of Alexandrovsk, in the Soviet Ukraine, the small boy sat quietly and listened. Occasionally, he could hear muffled voices from the floors below, or the sounds of the soldiers in the courtyard outside. It had been many hours since his mother had slipped silently out of the house, and he was beginning to worry that this time she might not return.

It had been more than a year since the little family had gone into hiding. A neighbor had first brought the warning the day the Bolshevik authorities finally arrived on Nikolaevskja Street. They were confiscating the properties and evicting all the tenants. Worse, they were asking about the family of Yakov Zheleznykov. Yakov, the boy's father, had been a rich member of the bourgeoisie. He had died in the Crimea several months before. Ever since her husband's death, the boy's mother, Jennie Zheleznykov, had been preparing for the day the authorities would arrive. She had anticipated with dread the moment that the knock would come. She had bribed local officials and secured forged documents. She had coached her family on what to do and say, and she had secreted away jewels and other valuables. And so, when the Bolsheviks finally came, the family of Yakov Zheleznykov ceased to exist, and the Ukrainian peasants who had squatted on the property for the past few weeks knew nothing about them.

When the soldiers occupied the house and all the outbuildings on the grounds, the peasant woman had persuaded them to let the family stay in the small room on the second floor. The room was only accessible from the back of the house, and the woman promised that the soldiers would never notice they were there. The ruse would succeed only as long as no one recognized that the peasants were in fact the Zheleznykovs. From that day on, the family seldom left the confines of the little room on the second floor, and if they spoke at all, it was in whispers. Only the mother ever left the home, and that was after dark in order to buy food from the neighbors. But now there was no food to buy, and many of the neighbors who had helped feed the Zheleznykovs had either died or had fled.

The widespread starvation that swept through southern Russia and the eastern Ukraine in 1921 and 1922, after the final victory of the Red Army in the Russian Revolution, was one of the greatest famines in all history. Before it was over, more than two million people would starve to death. But the little family had lived through the First World War, the Ukrainian Civil War, the Russian Revolution, and the Russian Civil War. Alexandrovsk had been occupied by four different armies during the fighting and had endured a series of vicious pogroms. Although the father was now gone, the remaining Zheleznykovs had already survived one of the most brutal periods of modern history. They simply refused to become victims of the famine. Somehow the boy knew that his mother would return. He had no doubts about his survival. He had already made great plans for the future, and he was certain that those plans would be fulfilled. This is the story of the life of that small boy. It is the untold story of Shurachka Yakovlevich Zheleznykov, whom the world would come to know as Eugene Jelesnik.

It is impossible to have lived in Utah at any time over the last fifty years without knowing something about Eugene Jelesnik. No more recognizable profile ever appeared on television, or on the street. The tiny maestro with the big nose and the impish grin was on television longer than *Gunsmoke* and *M*A*S*H* combined. His *Talent Showcase* brought momentary fame to more than ten thousand aspiring performers, and introduced us to the Osmonds, Robert Peterson, and Tanya Tucker, to name only a few. His annual

Pops Concerts drew tens of thousands, and whether we went to the circus, the Days of '47 Rodeo, The State Fair, a concert in the park, or had dinner at The Cinegrill, Jelesnik was always there. He seemed to be everywhere, and yet he still left us wondering. Who is he? What is he doing here? How did he get here? Why did he stay?

It was not until September of 1996 that Jelesnik's origins would be brought sharply into focus by a fortuitous gift. President Thomas S. Monson, First Counselor in the First Presidency of The Church of Jesus Christ of Latter-day Saints, arranged for the languages department at Brigham Young University to translate a folder of Russian and Hebrew documents that Eugene had acquired on the death of his mother in 1963. The translations provided a wealth of information about Eugene and his family, some of which he only vaguely knew about, and some things that he had never known. He would learn for the first time of another Zheleznykov family, of half brothers and half sisters he had never known existed. He would learn details of his parents' wedding, of his father's business dealings, and particulars about his mother's large family. He would examine deeds to his father's estates and the records that itemized their systematic destruction. He would read for the first time his father's last will and testament and pour over the official reports of his father's death.

But more than providing the details he had never known, the documents gave context and meaning to things he did remember. They provided proof of things he had long claimed and solid evidence for things he had only suspected. The documents, personal papers, and memories are clear and compelling, but when they are set against the historic record of what was going on at the time, they reveal an almost unbelievable story of struggle, hardship, terror, and triumph. Collectively they are a testament to one family's will to survive. They also go a long way toward explaining what made Eugene Jelesnik the man he eventually became.

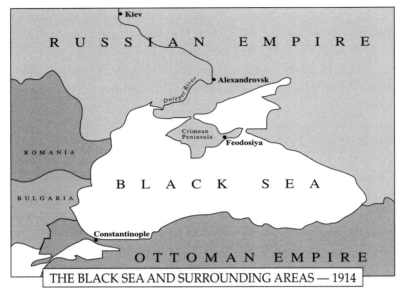

THE BLACK SEA AND SURROUNDING AREAS — 1914

Eugene Jelesnik's wealthy father, Yakov Zheleznykov, once owned a large dacha (country house) on the cliffs overlooking the Black Sea in the resort town of Feodosiya. Eugene's earliest childhood memories are of Alexandrovsk, the city where he was born, and of the many bridges spanning the Dnieper River.

THE BLACK SEA AND SURROUNDING AREAS — 1997

Alexandrovsk is now known as Zaporizhzhya and due to industrial waste is one of the most polluted places on the planet. Until he was eighty-two years old, Eugene Jelesnik was under the false impression that Alexandrovsk was located somewhere north of Moscow.

CHAPTER ONE

RUSSIA

The man who would one day be known as Eugene Jelesnik was born in the southern Ukrainian town of Alexandrovsk, Russia, on 19 March 1914. Shurachka Yakovlevich Zheleznykov was the son of Yakov (Jacob) Israelevitch Zheleznykov and Zhenya (Jennie) Rothaus Zheleznykov. Eugene's long name was shortened to "Srul" by his father; his mother called him "Shura."[1]

The Zheleznykov family had lived in the regions bordering the northern coast of the Black Sea for generations. Indeed, local tradition held that people bearing the appellation "Israelevitch"—literally Son of Israel, or Jew—had first arrived in the area shortly after Noah's ark landed on Mount Ararat.[2] As the story went, the sons of Noah—Shem, Ham, and Japheth—set out from Ararat to repopulate the earth. The Caucasus Mountains to the east of the Black Sea were said to be the first home of Japheth's descendants, from whom sprang the Gentiles. The descendants of Shem (the Jews) first settled in the Transcaucasus and along the coast of the Black Sea in what is now Georgia.[3] One version of this genealogy has the descendants of Japheth reuniting with the wandering sons of Shem, following the destruction of the first temple in 722 B.C.E. (Before the Common Era). Other Shemites must have come later, after the destruction of the second temple in the year 70 of the Common Era. Yet another account claims that one of the lost tribes of Israel escaped from their Assyrian captors and took refuge in the vast interior of eastern Europe. Whatever their origin, and however they came to settle in the region, Jews have lived in southern Russia and the Ukraine for millennia. There were large Jewish populations along the northwest coast of the Black Sea in the thirteenth century, and Jewish settlements in the Kievian Rus region on the Dnieper River in the tenth century.[4] The eighth-century Khazar rulers of the lower Volga were Jewish, and the remains of Jewish synagogues dating to 500 B.C. have been excavated both north and east of the Black Sea.[5] On the Crimean Peninsula, Hellenized Jewish inscriptions have been found on a number of ancient ruins. One such site is found on the southeastern coast in the town of Feodosiya. Founded by militant Greeks in the seventh century B.C., the seaside community is one of the most ancient settlements in all of Europe. Feodosiya was also the home of Eugene Jelesnik's father, Yakov Zheleznykov, and it was here, too, that Yakov met and courted Eugene's mother.[6]

Born in the Crimea in 1857, Yakov was the eldest child of Rabbi Israel Zheleznykov. Yakov had two younger brothers: David and Leiba, and a sister, Pasha.[7] Although tradition may have dictated that Yakov would also take up rabbinical studies, he must have decided early on that he preferred a career in commerce and industry. Eventually he became a sugar and molasses broker.

There is little doubt but that Yakov was following in the footsteps of another Russian Jew, the brilliant industrial mogul Israel Brodsky who pioneered the development of Russia's sugar industry.[8] Molasses, a by-product of sugar refining, is a vital foodstuff that is used in baked goods, alcoholic brews, confections, chemicals, pharmaceuticals and in animal fodder. Prior to Brodsky, Russia had to import much of its sugar and molasses. But Brodsky introduced modern milling technology, which not only refined sugar but economically separated the commercially valuable by-products. These innovations, coupled with improved transportation by rail and steamship, made large-scale farming of sugar beets profitable for the first time. By the late 1800s sugar beets were one of the major crops of the Ukraine, and imperial Russia had become one of the world's largest sugar exporters. Israel Brodsky became not only a millionaire, but the first great merchant prince of Russian Jewry. The Brodsky family fortune would spawn other enterprises including son Lazar Brodsky's large industrial, banking, and financial empire.

As a broker it was Yakov Zheleznykov's business to arrange for the sale, shipment, and export of molasses and other sugar by-products. Brodsky's great sugar mills were in the central Ukraine, but Zheleznykov's customers were scattered throughout south-eastern Europe. Yakov had to travel extensively in his occupation, not only to the mills but frequently to Istanbul and even Greece. The hardships that Yakov had to endure as a Jewish commercial entrepreneur in the Gentile business world were considerable. Anti-Semitism in Russia had been on the rise for decades. From the time of Catherine the Great, Jews had been confined to an area in the extreme west and south of Russia known as "The Jewish Pale."[9] Laws proscribing where Jews could live, work, and travel were enacted in 1795 and again in 1835.[10]

Following the assassination of Tsar Alexander II in 1881, and the discovery that one of the conspirators was a 16-year-old Jewish girl, a series of anti-Semitic pogroms swept over Russia.[11] In the Ukraine the attacks were particularly brutal. In town after town mobs of people roamed the streets, looting Jewish businesses, burning homes, and attacking synagogues. Several hundred Jews were beaten to death in sporadic mindless outbursts throughout the Ukraine.[12]

In 1882, more anti-Jewish legislation was enacted limiting educational opportunities for Jews and further restricting their movements. Jews were forbidden from conducting business on Sundays or on Christian holidays. Certain occupations were closed to Jews entirely, and exorbitant taxes were levied against Jewish-owned businesses. Even some towns within "the pale" were officially off-limits to Jews including: Nikoleav, Yalta, Sebastopol, and, for a time, Kiev.

Although there had been a number of pogroms through the early decades of the nineteenth century, until 1881 there was a general feeling among Russian Jews that things were getting better. But after 1882 there was no question that anti-Semitism was getting worse. One observer, Pauline Wengeroff, wrote of the pogrom and anti-Semitic laws of 1881: "The sun which had risen on Jewish life in the 1850s suddenly set. Anti-Semitism erupted; the jews were forced back into the ghetto. Without ceremony, the gateways to education were closed."[13]

Moses Lieib Lilienblum, the founder of modern Zionism, was another contemporary who noted the change in Russia following the pogroms of 1881: "We are aliens, not only here, but in all of Europe, for it is not our fatherland. . . . We are Semites among Aryans, the sons of Shem among the sons of Japheth."[14]

Nor was it any consolation that some Jews had succeeded in spite of the persecution. Working class and peasant Ukrainians resented successful Jews such as the Brodskys most of all. They pointed to Lazar Brodsky's growing industrial empire as proof of an international Zionist conspiracy. The peasants were also alarmed by the increasing Jewish population. By 1897 there were 5.2 million Jews in the Russian Empire, all but 300,000 in the pale. Within the pale they made up eleven percent of the total population, but Jews comprised more than thirty percent of the people in the Ukrainian cities.[15] While truly wealthy Jews were rare, they were always the first targets of anti-Semitic pogroms. Looting the homes of rich Jews was a common practice of nearly every political faction and ethnic group in Russia. Throughout eastern Europe, the successful Jew had always been in greater danger from pogroms than his less-well-off neighbors.

In 1882, Yakov was only twenty-five. He had married a young woman (last name Sheifeld) and had started a family. Three children would be born of this union: a son, Gidalij, and two daughters, Fenia and Maria. Yakov's first wife would die in the Crimea about 1906. The anti-Semitic laws enacted in the early 1880s were in force through most of Yakov's business career, which lasted through the first turbulent decades of the twentieth century. In light of the restrictive conditions forced on Jewish commerce in Russia, it is something of a miracle that Yakov survived at all—let alone prospered. And while he must have suffered many hardships and indignities, there was a degree of consolation: by 1908 Yakov Zheleznykov had become a very rich man, rich enough to purchase a large dacha on the cliffs overlooking the Black Sea in the ancient Crimean resort town of Feodosiya.[16]

Eugene Jelesnik's mother, Zhenya Haimovna Rothaus (Jennie), was born in Latvia on 15 January 1887. Until the First World War, Latvia was a Russian possession. Some official documents list her place of birth as "Dublin, Kurland." Through the nineteenth century, Kurland was the Russian province named for the seventeenth century "Duchy of Kurland," which once ruled the area around the seaport of Riga. The improbable "Dublin" may have been a suburb of Riga or a misprint of "Durben," a town in the western part of Latvia near the Baltic Sea. Wherever she was born, she was raised in the capital city of Riga.[17]

Jennie was the daughter of Rabbi Aaron Rothaus and Riva Fedler. It is believed that she was the third eldest girl in a very large Jewish family. Although Jennie was the offspring of a rabbi, her education could not be considered traditional. During the nineteenth century two distinct forms of Judaism arose in eastern Europe—the conservative and traditionalist "Hasidism," and a progressive form called "Haskala," or "the enlightenment." Both were natural reactions to the pogroms and the institutionalized brutality of virulent anti-Semitism. The advocates of Hasidism believed that the only hope of the Jewish people was in the restoration of the ancient traditions and customs and strict adherence to Jewish law. The proponents of the Haskalah movement—called the Maskilim—believed that the survival of the Jewish people was only possible through "modern education, free inquiry, and the love of knowledge." The original goal of the Maskilim "was the re-creation of Jewish character—an enlightenment that would help bring the Jewish people into the modern world and make them part of society at large. To traditionalists, this sounded a lot like assimilation, or worse, conversion. But to the Maskilim, the Hasidic Jew was an anachronism with no hope of survival in the modern world. Although theoretically in diametric conflict, both groups influenced Jewish thought in the nineteenth century, and Rabbis might hold various shades of both traditionalist and progressive positions.[18]

Rabbi Aaron must have held with some Maskilim tenets. While Jewish education was general, it was also distinctly parochial. Women—when they were educated—were not expected to read much more than the scriptures. But Jennie Rothaus was not only well-educated and well-read, but was instilled with a love of music, particularly French and Italian opera. This would have been unheard of for all but the most elite classes of Russian Jews, but Riga was one of the centers of the Haskala "enlightenment," and Jennie must have benefited accordingly.

Unlike the communities around the Black Sea or the Ukraine, Riga—on the coast of the Baltic—did not have a long history of Jewish settlement. The first mention of Jews in Riga does not come until 1536, and by 1594 the Jews had been expelled.[19] Sweden ruled over Latvia from 1621 to 1710, and during this occupation Jewish residence in Riga was strictly forbidden by Swedish law. It was not until the nineteenth century that Riga had any significant Jewish population. Most of these new arrivals had emigrated from Germany. The Rothaus family were probably among this number since Eugene's mother spoke fluent German. Although Jewish residence was never officially legalized, by the first decades of the twentieh century, Riga held over 20,000 Jewish inhabitants. A number of synagogues had been established, and several Hebrew and Yiddish schools were in operation.[20] By the middle of the twentieth century, the entire Jewish population of Riga had been murdered.[21]

Some patterns of behavior span cultures. One frequently observed phenomena is the tendency of children of very large families to leave home at an early age; another is the tendency to scatter widely before settling down. Both were certainly true in the case of the Aaron Rothaus family.[22] One son, Samuel Rothaus born in the Kurland area of Russia in 1878, left Riga at the age of fifteen and emigrated to the United States in 1893. His brother Abraham arrived in America soon afterward. Abraham in turn was followed to America by two daughters, Cilia and then Johanna. Another son (possibly Aaron) also left home at an early age, eventually settling in South Africa. In 1904, when Jennie Rothaus was sixteen years old, she too left home and took a job as a live-in governess with a family in rural Russia. When Jennie left, only one child remained at home, Jennie's younger sister, Rallya Haimovna Rothaus, who Eugene Jelesnik would know as Aunt Ruth. As things would develop, the early scattering of the Rothaus clan would play a small but vitally important role in the life of Eugene Jelesnik. Had the family—especially Samuel—not emigrated when they did, it is safe to assume that this history would never have been written.

Jennie's first position was not a particularly favorable one. But by 1908 she was in a much better situation as governess to three handsome Russian children who resided with their parents in wealthy splendor on the southeastern coast of the Crimea. Photos taken of Jennie and the Baronowskys[23] in 1908 show a well-dressed and happy family boating on the Black Sea, enjoying the beaches, or otherwise having a good time. Jennie was in the employ of the Baronowsky family when she met a distinguished local gentleman, a widower who quickly fell in love with the attractive young governess. The gentleman was Yakov Zheleznykov.

The South Coast of the Crimean Peninsula has been the playground of the rich since the colonies of the Greeks. The area is favorably compared to the French Riviera both in climate and beauty.[24] The steep, rocky coastline is shrouded in vineyards and olive groves. On the cliffs above are the turrets of castles, the courtyards of luxurious palaces, and the private gardens of dachas. Dense mantles of flowers—magnolias, roses, and lilacs—line the stone walkways leading down to the sea. Below the cliffs, in sheltered bays, the warm, clear waters of the Black Sea splash on protected beaches.[25] In Russian literature, the South Coast of the Crimea is the quintessential fairy-tale setting. Chekhov, Gorki, and Tolstoy, among others, used the Crimea as the backdrop for romantic interludes. And so it seems particularly appropriate that the mother of the ever-romantic Eugene Jelesnik would be courted among the floral scented terraces of the Crimea.

Considering that both Jennie and Yakov were the offspring of rabbis, it seems more than likely that their courtship was traditional. If so, it was also extended. Jewish law would dictate not only the course of their romance, but the relationship of their respective families as well. Rabbi Aaron and Riva Rothaus must have been very pleased that their daughter had landed such a prize as successful businessman Yakov. But a marriage between the children of rabbis was not something to be taken lightly, and nothing in a Jewish wedding—even the most ordinary of Jewish weddings—is ever left to chance. This was not an ordinary wedding. It certainly must have been a grand occasion. Relatives and friends would have been invited from distant cities. Yakov's sister, two brothers, his nieces and nephews would be in attendance, as would his own children: Gidilij, Fenia, and Maria. Jennie's cousins, nieces, and nephews would have been invited, and Jennie's younger sister, Ruth, would certainly have been an honored member of the wedding party.

In celebration of the occasion, special quilts and hand-embroidered linen would have been prepared by family members including the bride's mother. The rabbis would have readied special blessings and toasts. The preparation of the wedding feast alone would have gone on for three days prior to the Sabbath.[26] And then there were the matters of the marriage contract and the dowry. At the time of their marriage, Yakov was fifty-four years old, more than twice the age of Jennie who was only twenty-four. Stipulations would have to be made in the contracts for the provision and care of the young bride in the event of Yakov's death. Many of the details in the wedding of Yakov (Jacob) Israelevitch Zheleznykov and Zhenya (Jennie) Rothaus must be left to conjecture. But a remarkable amount of vivid and telling detail of that celebration held so long ago is found in the marriage contract and ceremony, documents written in Hebrew and Russian and only recently translated by Brigham Young University. The translations are as follows:

MARRIAGE CONTRACT
(translated from Russian)

This the seventh day of the week, in 21st day of the month of Sabeth in the year five thousand six hundred and seventy eight from the creation of the world by the calendar used here. The son of Rabbi Yakov Zheleznykov, said to Zhena the daughter of Rabbi Aaron Rothaus "Be my wife under the law of Moses and Israel who worked, respected, fed and supported their wives in a good manner. I will give you wine to drink and call mine all that belongs to you by the law. Your food, clothing and support I will give you and live with you compatibly according to the customs of the world." So agreed, Zhena became his wife. Dowry was brought to him by Zhena: money, gold, jewelry, dresses, household accessories and bedding was accepted by Yakov (the groom of her with the sounds of pure silver). The groom Yakov agreed to add to it from his own with the sounds of pure silver. Then the groom Yakov announced: "The responsibility under this wedding contract for the existing and for the added he accepts upon himself and his heirs, so it is all paid in full from the best and the most beautiful properties and acquisitions, that I have under the skies, from the properties that I already have in my possession and also the properties that I will acquire, movable and immovable property, all this will serve as a guarantee for the penalty in this wedding record of the dowry and everything added to it, even the clothes off my shoulders, during my lifetime or after, after my death until forever."

The responsibility according to this wedding record for the dowry and the added was accepted upon himself by the groom Yakov according to the power and the strictness of all the wedding contracts practiced with the daughters of Israel and developed by the rule of the wise men, not in the sense of anything conventional or any document. We completed the ceremony by the touching of the handkerchief between the groom Yakov and the bride Zhena the daughter of Rabbi Aaron Rothaus in the commencement of the above which is written and explained. The handkerchief was used to conduct the ceremonies and everything is for sure and forever.

The handkerchief is brought before the bride and the groom by the witnesses. They touch it and give it back, after which the relationship is commenced. December 26th, I the one that is writing below, promise to pay the sum established in the marriage act.

I will pay the agreed sum of five thousand rubles to my wife Zhenya Rathaus to whom I am about to be married.

Signature—Yakov Zheleznykov

WEDDING CEREMONY
(translated from Hebrew)

GROOM: On the Sabbath of the twenty-first of Tebeth of the year five thousand and six hundred and seventy and eight since the creation of the world and before the requisite number of males for congregational worship that we do now designate— which is ten males, Rabbi Yitzhak, under the authority of Rabbi Israel, came to join us together as one. Zhena Haimovna Rothaus daughter of Rabbi Aaron Rothaus (is) to be a wife for me in matrimony, in accordance with the law of Moses and Israel.

I will cleave unto her; I will make her precious; I will bless her with plenty; I will provide a place for her to dwell; according to the traditional laws of Jewish husbands who are worshipers of the LORD, and those who honor, and those who give sustenance and support to their wives in righteousness. I will give her coins of silver, sufficient food and clothing, ornaments, jewelry, a permanent dwelling, and the promises connected with the bed. This covenant is made with Rabbi Yakov, father-in-law, with the pledge of pure and splendid gold and silver coins.

This covenant is made into a written document which may be resorted to in case of nonpayment, including my property, the property of the guarantor, and even the cloak that is upon my shoulders, if necessary. This contract is binding throughout my lifetime, and after my life from this day and forever, and the property identified in this written document; this dowry and this additional pledge is an obligation that is accepted by me. This document is sealed with rabbinical authority by the undersigned, including Yakov, and Zhena and Rabbi Aaron. All is proper and established.

Signed by Yakov and Zhenya Zheleznykov.[27]

The couple would have stood under a ceremonial canopy called a "Chuppah" and festooned with flowers. Jennie would have been dressed in a silk gown with gold gilt embroidery. Special Blessings would have been read by Rabbis Aaron and Israel, as well as by the presiding Rabbi Yitzhak. Then the wedding glass would have been wrapped in the handkerchief used in the ceremony. It would be broken underfoot to symbolize the destruction of the temple and to remind the bride and groom of the sufferings the Jewish people had endured since the diaspora.[28] As in other traditions, the ceremony would have ended with a kiss. According to the Eastern Gregorian calendar then used in Russia, the marriage date was 26 December 1912. On the modern calendar the date would have been 3 January 1913.

How long the couple remained in the Crimea is unknown, but the Zheleznykov dacha in Feodosiya was never sold. It would be used as a stopover by Yakov during his many business trips, which resumed shortly after their marriage. The dacha was probably also used as a vacation retreat during the summers. Some early family photographs appear to have been taken in the city of Melitopol, a Ukrainian town north of the Sea of Azov.[29] So it is possible that the Zheleznykovs may have resided there for a short time. What is certain is that by the spring of 1914 the family was firmly established in Alexandrovsk on "The Great Dnieper," Europe's third largest river. The Dnieper drains a huge section of western Russia, Belarus, and the Ukraine and stretches more than 1,400 miles from its headwaters near Smolensk west of Moscow to Kherson on the Black Sea. The most important cities of the Ukraine are located on the Dnieper, including the capitol city of Kiev. For the Molasses broker Zheleznykov, the Dnieper was a highway that transported his goods from the central Ukraine to the Black Sea ports of Kherson and Odessa, where they were then sent by ship to the markets of southeastern Europe.

The decision to live in Alexandrovsk must have been an easy one. The port was not only a regional shipping, rail, and transportation hub, convenient for Yakav's business travels, but a cultural and administrative center as well. The city boasted a fine theater, which mounted local dramatic productions, and also played host to touring opera companies from Odessa, Kiev, and even Moscow. While Yakov was away on business, there would be many performances that Jennie might attend, and if she were occasionally lonely in Alexandrovsk, she at least would not suffer for lack of entertainment.

Returning from one of his trips, Yakov presented his wife with the gift of a pair of opera glasses. They were crafted in Paris in 1911 and were inlaid with mother-of-pearl and trimmed with gold. Few Jewish Russian immigrants to America would have memories of such an obvious extravagance. But for Eugene Jelesnik the opera glasses remain a prized possession linking him to another time and place. The glasses are also mute testimony to the privileged status that the Zheleznykov family held in prerevolutionary Russia.[30] Another Russian Jew, Saul Elman, father of the great violin prodigy Mischa Elman, described in his *Memoirs* the rigid class

В   день недѣля
дня мѣсяца пять тысячъ шестьсотъ
                                                                          года отъ
сотворенія міра по лѣточисленію принятому здѣсь

сынъ г.   сказалъ сей   дочери
              Будь мнѣ женою по закону Мойсея и Израиля, а я буду
работать на тебя, почитать, кормить и содержать тебя по обычаю сыновъ Израи-
левыхъ, работающихъ, почитающихъ, кормящихъ и содержащихъ женъ своихъ
прилично И дамъ я тебѣ вѣно   зузовъ
слѣдуемыхъ тебѣ по закону, пищу твою, одежду твою, содержаніе твое и буду
жить съ тобою совмѣстно по обычаю всего міра. И согласилась г-жа
                      и стала его женою. Приданное, принесенное ею ему отъ
            деньгами, золотомъ, драгоцѣнностями, платьями, хозяйственною принад
лежностью и постелью принялъ все это на себя г.
женихъ сей въ   звуковъ чистаго серебра. Женихъ г.
            согласился добавить ей изъ своего еще   звуковъ чис-
таго серебра, всего,   звуковъ истаго серебра. Далѣе
женихъ   заявилъ: отвѣтственность по сему
брачному акту: „За   ное и добавочное я пр
себя и на наслѣдниковъ моихъ послѣ меня, чтобы было уплочено со всѣхъ наи-
лучшихъ, и прелестнѣйшихъ имѣній и пріобрѣтеній, которыя есть у меня подъ
небомъ, какъ съ того, что уже пріобрѣтено мною, такъ и съ того, что мною
пріобрѣтено будетъ, движимую и не движимое имущество, все это служитъ обез-
печеніемъ и порукою для взысканія съ нихъ по сей брачной записи приданнаго
и добавочнаго, даже съ мантіи, что на плечахъ моихъ, какъ при жизни моей, такъ
и по смерти моей отъ нынѣшняго дня вовѣки".
      Отвѣтственность по сей брачной записи за приданное и добавочное принялъ
на себя женихъ г.   по силѣ и строгости всѣхъ брачныхъ
актовъ, практикуемыхъ въ отношеніи дочерей Израиля составленныхъ по поста-
новленію блаженныхъ мудрецовъ, не въ смыслѣ чего то условнаго или бланка до-
кумента. И мы совершили обрядъ чрезъ прикасаніе къ платку*) между женихомъ
г.   и невѣстою г.   дочерью
г.   въ потвержденіе чего писаннаго и разъясненнаго вы-
ше платкомъ, годнымъ для совершенія имъ   орядовъ, и все твердо и вѣковѣчно.

_____

*) Свидѣтели подносятъ жениху и невѣстѣ платокъ, ти касаются его и возвращаютъ его назадъ, чѣмъ
сдѣлка освящается.

КСУБА т. е. брачный актъ.

Перевелъ съ еврейскаго, Переводчикъ А. Дзиканскій.

Типографія Бр. Блетницкихъ Одесса улица Кондратенко, 21

MARRIAGE CONTRACT

This marriage contract, only recently translated from Russian, reveals the legal details of the union of Eugene Jelesnik's parents, Yakov (Jacob) Israelevitch Zheleznykov and Zhenya (Jennie) Rothaus. The marriage was performed 3 January 1913. (The translation of this document appears on pages 12–13 of this book.)

בְּ... בְּשַׁבַּת ... שְׁנַת חֲמֵשֶׁת אֲלָפִים וְשֵׁשׁ
מֵאוֹת ... לִבְרִיאַת עוֹלָם לְמִנְיָן שֶׁאָנוּ מוֹנִין כַּאן ...
אֵיךְ מוֹ"ה ... אָמַר לַהֲדָא ...
... בַּת מוֹ"ה ... הֲוֵי לִי לְאִנְתּוּ כְּדַת מֹשֶׁה וְיִשְׂרָאֵל וַאֲנָא
אֶפְלַח וְאוֹקִיר וְאֵיזוֹן וַאֲפַרְנֵס יָתִיכִי לִיכִי כְּהִלְכוֹת גּוּבְרִין יְהוּדָאִין דְּפָלְחִין וּמוֹקִירִין
וְזָנִין וּמְפַרְנְסִין לִנְשֵׁיהוֹן בְּקוּשְׁטָא וְיָהֵבְנָא לִיכִי מֹהַר ... זוּזֵי
מָא ... דַּחֲזֵי לִיכִי מִדְּ ... וּמְזוֹנַיְכִי וּכְסוּתַיְכִי וְסִפּוּקַיְכִי
וּמֵיעַל לְוָתִיכִי כְּאוֹרַח כָּל אַרְעָא וּצְבִיאַת מָרַת ...
דָא וַהֲוַת לֵיהּ לְאִנְתּוּ וְדֵין נְדוּנְיָא דְּהַנְעֲלַת לֵיהּ מִבֵּ...
בֵּין בְּכֶסֶף בֵּין בְּדַהַב בֵּין בְּתַכְשִׁיטִין בְּמָאנֵי דִלְבוּשָׁא בְּשִׁמּוּשֵׁי דִירָה
וּבְשִׁמּוּשֵׁי דְעַרְסָא הַכֹּל קַבֵּל עָלָיו מוֹ"ה ... חֲתָן דְּנָן
בֵּ... וְצָבִין חֲתָן דְּנָן וְהוֹסִיף לָהּ מִן דִּילֵיהּ עוֹד ... וּקְנוֹקִים כֶּסֶף צָרוּף אַחֵרִים
כְּנֶגְדּוֹ סַךְ הַכֹּל מָא ... וְכָךְ אָמַר מוֹ"ה ...
חֲתָן דְּנָן אַחֲרָיוּת שְׁטַר כְּתוּבְּתָא דָא נְדוּנְיָא דֵין וְתוֹסֶפְתָּא
דָא קַבִּילִית עָלַי וְעַל יָרְתַי בַּתְרַאי לְהִתְפְּרַע מִכָּל שְׁפַר אֲרַג נִכְסִין וְקִנְיָנִין דְּאִית
לִי תְּחוֹת כָּל שְׁמַיָּא דִקְנַאי וּדְעָתִיד אֲנָא לְמִקְנָא נִכְסִין דְּאִית לְהוֹן אַחֲרָיוּת
וּדְלֵית לְהוֹן אַחֲרָיוּת כֻּלְּהוֹן יְהוֹן אַחֲרָאִין וְעַרְבָאִין לְפָרוֹעַ מִנְּהוֹן שְׁטַר כְּתוּבְּתָא
דָא נְדוּנְיָא דֵין וְתוֹסֶפְתָּא דָא מִנַּאי וַאֲפִילוּ מִן גְּלִימָא דְעַל כַּתְפַּאי בְּחַיַּי וּלְבָתַר
חַיַּי מִן יוֹמָא דְנָן וּלְעָלַם וְאַחֲרָיוּת שְׁטַר כְּתוּבְּתָא דָא נְדוּנְיָא דֵין וְתוֹסֶפְתָּא דָא
קַבֵּל עָלָיו מוֹ"ה ... חֲתָן דְּנָן כְּחוֹמֶר כָּל שְׁטָרֵי כְּתוּבּוֹת
וְתוֹסְפוֹת דִּנְהִיגִין בִּבְנוֹת יִשְׂרָאֵל הָעֲשׂוּיִין כְּתִקּוּן חז"ל דְּלָא כְּאַסְמַכְתָּא וּדְלָא
כְּטוֹפְסֵי דִשְׁטָרֵי וְקָנִינָא מִן מוֹ"ה ... חֲתָן
בְּמוֹ"ה ...
דְּנָן לְמָרַת ... בַּת מוֹ"ה ... דָא עַל
כָּל הָא דִכְתוּב וּמְפוֹרָשׁ לְעֵיל בְּמָנָא דְּכָשֵׁר לְמִקְנְיָא בֵּיהּ
וְהַכֹּל שָׁרִיר וְקַיָּם.
נְאוּם ...
וּנְאוּם ...

בהוצאות בית מכהר הספרים של האחים בלעטניצקי בארענבא

WEDDING CEREMONY

This document, written in Hebrew, was signed by Yakov and Zhenya, and details the obligations accepted by Eugene Jelesnik's parents as they were married in a traditional Jewish ceremony. (The translation of this document may be found on pages 13–14 of this book.)

distinctions that permeated every aspect of Russian life before the Revolution. It is significant that those distinctions were adhered to in the Jewish community as strictly as they were in Russian society at large. It is also significant that they applied in equal measure to the young Jewish girls who worked twenty hours a day, six days a week in Israel Brodsky's sugar mills, and to the boy who was soon acclaimed as the world's greatest violinist. Mischa Elman's father wrote:

> The Jewish Ghettos of Imperial Russia had their class distinctions too. . . . The wealthy Jew because of his education was a patrician. After him came the middle class, the merchant, grocer, and vendor, who had generally received a proper Hebrew education and was versed in the "small letters" such as the Talmud or the Bible. This class spent a number of hours each day in study—unlike the despised working class and artisans. There was no intermarrying among the classes until after 1910. . . . Consequently, although the son of an intellectual, my father found himself by reason of his profession [a musician] in a lower class, and although people praised his art, the applause was the kind given to a skillful tailor. He would often say to me bitterly: "When two people are discussing any subject, I am not allowed to take part.""Be off," they tell me. "This is not for you. A musician does not understand such things." They are above him. "Only yesterday," my father would continue, "this same person applauded my playing! Today he meets me in the street and ignores me. He draws the line."[31]

Considering the low esteem of musicians in class conscious imperial Russia, it is little wonder that so many sought refuge in the United States. It is also ironic that the same musical talent that made them little more than servants in the Old World would bring them both status and independence in the New. The list of European Jews whose genius has enhanced the rich fabric of American music is impressive. Serge Koussevitsky would flee Russia to become conductor of the Boston Symphony Orchestra. Simeon Bellison, who as a boy played in his father's Jewish band in Yelna, Russia, would become first clarinetist of the New York Philharmonic Orchestra. Violinists Mischa Elman, Josef Szigeti, Nathan Milstein, Isaac Stern, Jascha Heifetz, and Yehudi Menuhin were all European Jews, as were the pianists Rudolf Serkin, Vladimir Horowitz, and Arthur Rubinstein. George and Ira Gershwin were the sons of Russian Jewish emigrants.[32] Russian-born Irving Berlin (Israel Baline) immigrated to the United States in 1893, the same year as Eugene's uncle Samuel Rothause. American music benefited greatly from the Jewish exodus from eastern Europe. In return, America has given Jews more than simple refuge. Freedom of religion, freedom of speech, and freedom from fear were the hard currencies America bartered for their talents. It was a fair trade, which would one day be well-understood and especially appreciated by Eugene Jelesnik.

Shurachka "Shura" Zheleznykov (Eugene) was one of two children born to Yakov and Jennie Zheleznykov. The second child, Boris Yakov Zheleznykov ("Sasha"), would die in infancy.[33] At the time of Eugene's birth (19 March 1914) the world's great monarchies were in the final throes of their gaudy declines. In a little over four months, the complacent gilded age would be gone, and the whole fabric of European society would unravel in a war of unbelievable destruction and unimagined cruelty. And yet, as Winston Churchill wrote in his memoirs, "The old world in its sunset was fair to see." The golden-domed palaces, the jeweled coaches, the royal coronations and weddings, the regattas, polo matches, the carefully staged hunts, the countless royal balls and parties, all contributed to an image of unlimited wealth and reckless excess. It was a top-heavy and often corrupt society, doomed as much by its own blind greed as its military ambitions. Nowhere was that blindness more complete than in imperial Russia.

The reign of Tsar Nicholas II was marked by an almost unbelievable inability to see beyond the palace walls. Russia's great nineteenth-century writers had all recognized and described the growing gulf between the rich and poor. Gogol accurately portrayed the desperate plight of Russia's lower classes, and damningly satirized the insensitivity of the imperial bureaucracy. Dostoyevsky chronicled the empty materialism of Russia's rising middle class, and Chekhov dramatized the decline of the aristocracy as well as the rise of ardent revolutionary idealism. Even Tolstoy, himself a second cousin to the Tsar, saw, as few of his class had, the shallowness of the ruling elite and the extravagant excesses that would eventually lead to its downfall. Sweeping changes were taking place in Russia, and the Tsar could not understand them, direct them, or stop them. Russia in 1914 had the highest growth rate of any economy in the world, and yet the standard of living and working conditions for the average Russian had actually declined substantially in the previous decade. In the first five months of 1914, the country was rocked by over 2,000 strikes. The fact was that Russia had become too large and too complex a society to be run by an autocratic, hereditary ruler.

There was something of the nature of a Greek tragedy about those final days before the world fell apart. Many observers of that time commented in retrospect on the fatalism and sense of inevitability that characterized the age. Moral paralysis seemed to prevent politicians from taking any action that might have averted the disaster. Military preparations for war had been going on for decades, but few saw that war and disaster were actually at hand. One observer who probably did recognize the immediacy of the danger was an American diplomat who sent a frantic note to his superiors in Washington in the spring of 1914: "European militarism has gone stark mad."

The colorful ceremonial armies of the nineteenth century with their plumed hats, rattling sabres, and galloping lancers remained. But now there was the added dimension of modern weapons: the machine gun, the railroad gun, the zeppelin, and mustard gas. No one really understood what those weapons could do, and so no one did anything to prevent their use. In the last year before the war finally came, the governments reshuffled their alliances, and the militaries tinkered with their new weapons, while the plumed horsemen paraded before cheering crowds of patriotic citizens. The people of Europe watched all the martial preparations with the same distracted curiosity that they might have had were they to have observed the Kaiser hunting deer in Bavaria, or the Tsar's family sleigh riding in St. Petersburg. It was the last scene of a macabre costume drama. But once Europe had started down the slippery slope to war, there was no way to stop the slide. It was impossible to see where it would lead and so Europe simply

watched. The ride finally ended just four months after Eugene
Jelesnik's birth. On 28 July 1914, the Austrian archduke, Franz
Ferdinand, was assassinated in Sarajevo, Bosnia, by a Serbian
nationalist. By August the 4th, Europe was at war. In less than four
years, the Tsar, his family, and all that he represented would be
swept away by forces he never fully understood. Within six years
the map of eastern Europe would be rewritten, erased, and rewritten twice again. The First World War, the Russian Revolution, the
Ukrainian Uprising, and the Russian Civil War were only part of
the horror. Disease, famine, plague, mass murder, and the brutal
expulsion of whole populations repeatedly swept through the
Ukraine. Over this same period, the city of Alexandrovsk would
be placed under martial law by one army, occupied by another,
overrun by a third, and sacked by a fourth. It all had disastrous
consequences for the Zheleznykov family. Everything that Yakov
had built would be lost by degree: his markets, his business, his
properties, his freedom, his home, and finally his life.

Eugene Jelesnik lived through all this turmoil, but he was only
a child at the time and knew nothing of the titanic forces that
would eventually drive him from Europe. What he did understand was that March of 1914 was not a very good time to be born
a Jew in the Russian Ukraine.

Eugene Jelesnik's earliest memories were of Christmas in
Alexandrovsk. The town square was not far from his family's
estate, and he remembered driving there in a four-horse carriage
with his parents to see the festive lights and decorations set up for
Christmas. The occasion was important for another reason. It was
the only time that he remembers ever seeing his father's brother,
Uncle David, who had come to Alexandrovsk for the holidays.
Eugene was not the only Jewish child who marveled at the magic
of the season. Irving Berlin, another Russian Jew, had similar memories and would one day pen the classic song "White Christmas"
to capture the childhood wonder of the Christian holiday.[34]

Eugene also remembered the Dnieper River and some of the
bridges in the city. He recalled many of the details of the family
home in Alexandrovsk. It was a large two-story structure with
a courtyard separating the main house from the carriage house,

stables, and sheds. Not far from the home was a public park where as a child Eugene would be taken for strolls or on weekend picnics. The layout of the home was standard for the period. The bedrooms were upstairs. The dining room, kitchen, parlor, and servants quarters were downstairs. Swinging doors separated the kitchen from the dining room. There was a small entrance hall in the front. The center of family life was the parlor, and all attention in the parlor was on the phonograph. This was not something that many Russian families had even seen, but the Zheleznykovs had an excellent machine and a large collection of phonograph recordings. The collection was added to over the years as Yakov brought back new recordings he acquired during his extensive travels. Most of the recordings were arias from Jennie's favorite operas, but there were also selections of violin solos, some by the great Hungarian violinist and stylist Yeno Hubay.

Hubay was a classically trained concert violinist. He had studied under the great Joachimin Berlin and was himself a renowned professor of music who taught violin at both the Brussels Conservatory and Budapest National Academy.[35] But Hubay was also an avid collector and interpreter of traditional folk themes, particularly the music of the Hungarian gypsies. The richly romantic gypsy music with its lyrical themes and complex improvisational bridges, fired the imagination of little "Shura" Zheleznykov. He would spend many hours sitting in front of the phonograph listening to the haunting strains that seeped out amid rhythmic scratches. Even the best recordings, on the best machines, sounded like music heard from a great distance through a long pipe. But it was good enough. The Gypsy music had captured his soul. From that time on, the boy knew exactly what he wanted to do with his life. He would be a violinist. Shura's only knowledge of the violin came from the phonograph recordings and a photo of Hubay playing his instrument. To inform his parents of his heart's desire he got two sticks, placed one under his chin and fingered it with his left hand. He drew the other stick across the first as if it were a bow. The mime show was his way of telling his parents that he wanted a violin. It would be many years before he actually got his wish.[36]

The early life of young Eugene Jelesnik was sheltered in the extreme. His parents tried to make his childhood as happy as possible, but to do so they had to insulate the boy from the reality of wartime in eastern Europe. He was never aware of huge battles raging to the west; nor was he ever told of the pogroms and massacres that occurred at the very doorstep of Alexandrovsk. Nor did the adults ever talk about these subjects in his presence. The Zheleznykovs had somehow decided that if their boy was to survive in the modern world, he had to be protected from it. To help with the job of raising the child, the Zheleznykovs hired two governesses. The first was Eugene's private tutor. It was the job of the second governess to wash, dress, and groom "Little Shura." His father made it the law that Shura was never to leave the house unless he were immaculately dressed. It was a proscription that would become a lifelong practice and characteristic trait of the always well-attired Eugene Jelesnik. Improbable as it may seem, it would also go a long way in saving the boy's life. Eugene recalled that his father gave incredibly detailed instructions to the governesses regarding his care and education. His bath water was not to be checked by hand, it had to be tested with a thermometer to make certain that the temperature was just right. Yakov may have been motivated by love for his child, but having lost one son, he was determined that he wouldn't lose a second. Every care and precaution would be taken to protect Shura from harm. It also seems that Yakov wanted to instill in his boy an aristocratic bearing. Eugene recalled the great respect that others showed his father and the demeanor that Yakov always maintained in public places. He recalled that when his family would go out to eat at one of the fine restaurants of the city, they were always given the very best table. He remembered that the waiters stood at attention four feet behind each chair to cater to the Zheleznykov family's every need. In the restaurant business, it is still known as "The Royal Treatment," and it is only extended to those who can command it. Young Shura was duly impressed. The loving protection that Yakov exhibited for his son would be long remembered by Eugene Jelesnik; so much so, that although Eugene only knew his father during his first seven years, he would always maintain that his father was the most dominant figure in his life.[37]

Eugene also remembered the watchful hovering of his mother. He specifically recalled that she did not want him running out of the house or leaving the premises. The restrictions placed on him by his parents must have seemed oppressive. Because he didn't know the reason for their rules and knew nothing of the very real dangers outside, "Shura" began to explore the limits of his protective surroundings. His very first venture outside the gilded cage nearly ended in disaster.

The Jewish folktale character called "The Khapper," or kidnapper, first appeared in European lore in the 1830s. The character was an evil tempter who lured little children away from their parents with music, candy, lies, or other enticements and then sold them into slavery. Unfortunately, the Khapper had basis in fact. In 1827, Tsar Nicholas I initiated a policy of conscripting Jewish children into special military schools. The Tzar hoped to "reform Russian Jewry" by drafting children young enough to make them susceptible to Christian conversion. The schools were supposedly for boys twelve years old and above, but children much younger were to be found in the institutions. These "schools" were brutal places, often run by hard-bitten drill sergeants. Each village and town was required to provide a certain number of conscripts for the Russian army. As draftees of the time were required to serve for a period of twenty-five years, few who entered Russian military service had any hope of leaving. Unscrupulous recruiting agents would sometimes broker deferments and exemptions to villages that paid high enough bribes. As in the American Civil War, substitutes could easily be bought at premium prices for the children of the rich. In Jewish lore, the Khapper was a professional kidnapper hired by a village to steal children from distant towns. The children would be raised until they were needed to fill the draft quota. In this way villages protected their own.[38]

The system that gave rise to the Khapper lore was abandoned in the late 1840s, but through the nineteenth century, Jews lived in constant dread of the kidnapping of their children. Tales of the Khapper still remain in many Jewish communities. The professional kidnapper may have been more fiction than fact, but the sale of children was a serious problem in Europe in the early decades of the century, and remains so in many parts of the world even today. Saul Elman recounts with horror how after his son Mischa—then seven—gave a recital before the Russian countess Urusova that the Countess came up to him and said: "Mr. Elman, you possess a treasure. Sell him to me! Name your price!" In spite of repeated demands to sell his child to the Countess, Elman declined and managed to avoid further contact with her.[39]

During the First World War and the Russian Revolution, thousands of Russian peasants fled their fields to escape the warring factions. During this period many children were conscripted into work gangs to bring in the harvest or to help with other farm work. Over a million refugees were on the roads of Russia during the War including many orphans.[40] It was only natural that a number of these children would find their way into the camps of wandering Gypsies where they were often "adopted." It was little wonder that the Gypsies would be suspected of practicing wholesale kidnapping. It was a widely held belief that they targeted the children of widows.

"Little Shura" (Eugene) was only three years old when it happened. He was playing in the yard beside his home when he heard the distant strains of Gypsy music. He had, of course, listened to the music of the Gypsies before, on the family phonograph. It had already become his passion. Being an aficionado of the form, he immediately set out to find the source of the wonderful music. It turned out that the sounds were coming from the public park near his home where a band of Gypsies had encamped overnight. They were just breaking camp when Shura arrived. The singing, the acrobatics, and the gaiety of the Gypsy band were all that Shura had imagined. It seemed just as natural as it could be that he would join them. And so when they asked him if he would like to be in the circus, he immediately accepted.[41]

It was not long before the governesses discovered that Shura was missing. They frantically searched the house, the yards, the barns, sheds, and other outbuildings but to no avail. Shurachka Yakovlevich Zheleznykov was gone. By the time the governesses finally realized the extent of the calamity and informed the parents, several hours had passed. The frantic parents immediately went to the police and a full-scale search was initiated for the son of one of Alexandrovsk's most prominent citizens. By coincidence, an Alexandrovsk policeman had already noticed a very well-dressed tot in the company of a large group of Gypsies on a city street. He thought that the child looked out of place, so he had stopped the band to investigate. He was in the process of questioning the child, when off in the distance, he noticed three frantic women and an irate, well-dressed gentleman in the company of some other police. The officer wondered if these might be the parents or relatives of the child he was trying to question. It quickly turned out that they were. The joyful reunion was tempered by the anger of Mr. Zheleznykov toward the governesses. Shura had never seen him so angry. He knew that his father only had his welfare at heart, but it still frightened him, and he would say eighty years later that he was glad he didn't inherit his father's temper. The very next day, "Little Shura" had two *new* governesses. Of the whole episode Eugene Jelesnik would comment wryly, "If they hadn't found me, I might have ended up in the circus a few decades earlier than I actually did."[42]

"Little Shura" had not entirely learned his lesson from the encounter with the Gypsies. The allure of the circus, the stage, and performing arts was just as great as it was before that episode. As he got older his mother began taking him to the opera and the theater, particularly when his father was away on business. On one such occasion a traveling troupe of singers and musicians was performing in Alexandrovsk. Shura somehow learned that the company was staying in a boarding house very near his home. Late at night, after his mother and the governesses were sound asleep, Shura slipped out of the house and made his way to the performers' lodgings. The troupe was asleep in a common room. Shura climbed on a tabletop amid the snoring performers and proceeded to belt out a Russian folk tune. The startled troupe was not a receptive audience, and a lot of pillows were thrown in Shura's direction. The audition was cut short, and the touring performers rolled over and went back to sleep. But Shura was exhilarated; somehow he would find a way to make it to the stage.

While the young Zheleznykov—in blissful ignorance—plotted ways to advance his career in the performing arts, his parents, particularly his father, bore the ever-increasing burdens of war. It would have been impossible for them not to have known what was happening all around Alexandrovsk, but they never revealed their private fears or terrors to their son. Eugene would live his entire life never realizing that Alexandrovsk was overrun by several armies during the war. Nor did he know that the town he remembered had become the huge industrial city of Zaporizhzhya. In fact, until he was eighty-two years old, Eugene believed that Alexandrovsk was somewhere north of Moscow. That the child never knew of his family's extremely dangerous situation is a testament to his parents' hope for a brighter future. What actually happened in Alexandrovsk between the years 1914 and 1922 is both difficult to follow and hard to imagine.

Russia had effectively lost the war on the eastern front before Shura Zheleznykov was six months old. The Battle of Tannenberg, fought August 26th through August 30th and the Battle of Masurian Lakes, fought September 6th through 15th in 1914, were two of the greatest defeats in Russian military history to that time. The losses at Tannenberg were so staggering that the Russian commander, General Alexander, committed suicide after the battle. The Russian army suffered over 140,000 killed in the two battles. An additional 100,000 soldiers were captured with all their equipment, including over 500 heavy guns.[43] The Russian army never fully recovered.

The misfortunes of war in the western section of the pale brought about the mass expulsion of Jews from their homes. In 1915 alone more than half a million Jews were made homeless by the war. Among the refugees were Rabbi Aaron Rothaus and his daughter Rallya Haimovna Rothaus who had fled Latvia just ahead of the advancing German armies. The Rothauses made their way to Alexandrovsk where they came to live with the Zheleznykovs. Eugene remembered that grandfather Rothaus was an aged man much older than his father. He had a long gray beard cut square in the manner of orthodox Jewish men, and he carried a silver-handled walking stick. Eugene also recalled that his aunt, grandfather, and mother would sometimes speak to each other in Latvian. It was obvious to the child that they did so only when they didn't want him to know what they were talking about. It is probable that they were protecting him from the horrible news of the outside world, but it only infuriated little Shura who had no idea why they would want to exclude him. The reasons were clear. The war and the trail of destruction that came with it had an immediate, lasting, and disastrous impact on the Zheleznykov family. Every newspaper brought word of another disaster. All of the news was bad, and much of it was terrifying. Some reports struck very close to home, and even distant events had consequences for the family.

After the entry of Turkey into the war on the side of Germany, the Kaiser sent two battle cruisers flying the Turkish flag into the Black Sea and shelled Russia's southern ports. By the end of October, Russia was effectively cut off from her Western allies. Yakov no longer had access to his markets in southern Europe. His trips to Istanbul and Greece were over. Worse, as the war went on, Yakov had less and less to sell. Russia's declining military fortunes had unforseen effects upon the economy. With fewer markets to sustain high production, crops went unharvested. The disruption of the fragile transportation system also contributed to the disruption of agriculture, as did the presence of warring armies. Horses that might have been used for agricultural purposes were pressed instead into military service. Rail transport was frequently commandeered by military authorities, and business travel was severely restricted. The transportation problems affected all areas of the Russian economy during the war, but were particularly acute in the sugar industry, which relied heavily on rail for its existence. By the end of the war, sugar production had declined by more than seventy-five percent. Even one year of war was a strain on the Russian economy. Agricultural production had dropped so dramatically that food shortages began to be noticed in the winter of 1914–15. During the winter of 1915–16 there were food riots in many Russian cities. By the winter of 1916–17 much of the population was in danger of starvation. More than any other factors,

food shortages and soaring prices would contribute to the unrest
that would bring about the Russian Revolution.

The Revolution was not a simple single event—the overthrow
of the Tsar Nicholas II. The Romanov dynasty was not so much
overthrown as it collapsed from its own ineptitude.[44] While revolutionaries worked feverishly to topple the Tsarist regime, the reason the Tsar accepted abdication was that he finally came to
recognize the fact that he no longer ruled. The old order then simply disintegrated, and in its place was left a chaotic hodgepodge
of constitutional democrats (Cadets), radicals, centralists,
Menscheviks, Bolsheviks, Ukrainian nationalists, rightist volunteers, anarchists, and private Cossack armies. From March of 1917
through 1921, these disparate forces would fight over the spoils.[45]
Nowhere was the chaos of those times more clearly illustrated
than in the Ukrainian city of Alexandrovsk in Ekaterinoslav
Province.

With the collapse of the Romanov dynasty, three hundred
years of Russian expansion and consolidation was brought to a
sudden end. Nationalities that had been absorbed into imperial
Russia began to reemerge and assert their right to independence.
The Ukrainians were among the first to take advantage of the situation. On 23 June 1917, the Rada (the Ukrainian Parliament)
declared the Ukraine an autonomous region. On 20 November
1917, they formally declared the complete independence of the
Ukrainian National Republic.[46] For a few short months, Eugene's
hometown was under the control of Ukrainian Rada forces. But
the Bolshevik government in Moscow was not yet ready to give
up the fertile Ukraine, which supplied most of the food for the
country. Bolshevik forces invaded the eastern Ukraine and took
over most of the upper Dnieper. With the complete collapse of
Russia's southern front in December and January of 1918, the
German armies swarmed into the Ukraine: one army captured
Odessa and Gherson, yet another plunged south through
Nikolaiev and into the Crimea, and a third army captured
Ekaterinoslav and Alexandrovsk before pouring deep into
Russia—even to the southern regions of the Don.[47] In February the
Ukrainian Rada signed a separate peace treaty with Germany, and

the German army quickly drove the Bolsheviks out. During January and February of 1918, Alexandrovsk was in the hands of the Germans.

The treaty of Brest-Litovsk between the Bolshevik government and Germany—ratified on 15 March 1918—forced Russia to surrender Poland, Lithuania, Estonia, Latvia, the Transcaucasus, Finland, and all the Ukraine to the Central Powers.[48] Both German and Austrian troops would briefly occupy Alexandrovsk during this period. In April of 1918, Germany dissolved the Rada and established its own puppet German government in the Ukraine under General Skoropadsky. While the Treaty of Brest-Litovsk officially ended the First World War on the eastern front, it did not put an end to the actual fighting. Independent Ukrainian Rada and Cossack forces attacked Germans, Bolsheviks, Russian Cadets (constitutional democrats), and sometimes each other. Revolutionaries, anarchists, and freebooters of every sort stalked the countryside. In May of 1918, Alexandrovsk and the state of Ekaterinoslav were nominally under the control of the Skoropadsky's Ukrainian government, but as Germany shifted more of its troops to the Western front, other forces including Bolshevik units took over.[49] The result was that in many areas of Ekaterinoslav—including the city of Alexandrovsk[50]—local civil administration did not exist.

While the hated Tsar still ruled, there was an easy target for every ill that befell the people. The war and its consequences were blamed on the Tsar, as were the cruelties of his regime, the inequities in society, food shortages, unemployment, and the weather. With the Tsar gone, new villains would have to be found—particularly for the famines that continued to stalk the land. The most handy scapegoat was the Russian Jew, but there were also the merchant class, the bourgeoisie, the aristocrat, the peasant landholder (Kukla), the speculator, and the industrialist. All these were convenient targets for those with radical agendas, and if the party being blamed happened to be Jewish, all the better. Typical of the hate rhetoric that inflamed the people of that time was a decree published in the Soviet newspaper *Izvestia* on 14 May 1918:

DECREE OF THE ALL-RUSSIAN SOVIET CENTRAL
EXECUTIVE COMMITTEE GIVING THE FOOD
COMMISSARIAT EXTRAORDINARY POWERS IN
COMBATING THE VILLAGE BOURGEOISIE, WHICH IS
CONCEALING AND SPECULATING WITH GRAIN
RESERVES, DATED MAY 9, 1918

The ruinous breakdown in the country's food supply, the
disastrous inheritance of four years of war, continues to spread
and to become more aggravated. While the consuming
provinces are starving, there are now, as formerly, large reserves
of grain which have not even been milled, from the harvests of
1916 and 1917, in the producing provinces. This grain is in the
hands of the kulaks and the rich, in the hands of the village
bourgeoisie. Well fed and provided for, having accumulated
immense sums of money during the years of war, the village
bourgeoisie remains stubbornly deaf and indifferent to the cries
of the starving workers and poor peasants, and does not bring
grain to the collection points.

The bourgeoisie count on forcing the government to make
new and further increases in grain prices and at the same time
sells grain in its own places at fabulous prices to grain
speculators and bagmen.

. . . There must be an end to the stubbornness of the greedy
village kulaks and the rich. . . . To the violence of the owners of
the grain against the starving poor the answer must be: violence
against the bourgeoisie.[51]

The revolutionaries did not need prodding to attack the
landed class. Back in February of 1918, sailors from the Black Sea
fleet had run amok in the Crimean city of Sevastopol, killing hundreds of "bourgeoisie" men, women, and children.[52] Landowners
were the special targets of the mobs, but anyone who owned anything of value might be murdered. For the rich landowner, Yakov
Israelevitch Zheleznykov, who owned estates in the Crimea as
well as in Alexandrovsk, the accounts of the Sevastopol massacres
must have been horrifying. So it seems peculiar that Yakov would
choose this time to purchase what amounted to an entire city block
of Alexandrovsk. The translation of a number of old deeds in
Eugene's possession reveals that his father purchased the property
from a rich Jew named Haim Gersh Abramovich Vaskevich. The

purchase was made on 2 June 1918, only two weeks after the notice threatening the bourgeois had been printed in *Izvestia*. The sale comprised two large tracts of land and a number of buildings. One section of property fronted Nikolaevskay, Kyznechnay, and Moskovskay Streets, then the principal thoroughfares of the city. The total sale price was two hundred and thirty thousand rubles, out of which Zheleznykov had already paid fifty thousand rubles. Forty thousand was paid on the signing of the documents, and the remaining one hundred and thirty-five thousand was to be paid in seven days. Descriptions of the property included the names of the bordering streets, the dimensions of various lots, and the names and occupations of some of the tenants. One of the buildings was rented to a watchmaker named Durbrovinsky and another to "The Alexandrovsk City Produce Committee." An entire suite of offices on one lot was leased to an attorney, Ykov Zimence. The Zimence property was described in some detail. There were seven rooms, a kitchen, two lobbies, corridors, offices, a shed, an ice-storage building, a cellar, a garret, and a garden. This was only one of the properties included in the sale. Considering what had happened in the Crimea, and what was about to happen in Alexandrovsk, it is probable that Haim Gersh Abramovich Vaskevich was selling out—most likely for his own protection. Zheleznykov was taking a big chance. In less than two weeks the city would be rocked by a vicious pogrom directed against the Ukrainian bourgeoisie. It was certainly no accident that many of the victims also happened to be Jewish.

Alexandrovsk was the traditional homeland of the Zaporozhian Cossacks. Their island fortress of Khortytsya, located just southwest of Alexandrovsk, was a center of Cossack power from the mid-fifteenth to the eighteenth century. From here they ruled southcentral and northeastern Ukraine for over 150 years until the fortress was destroyed in 1775 by the Russian army on orders of Catherine II. The name "Zaporozh ye" comes from the phrase "za porohamy," or "beyond the rapids," referring to the spot past a series of rapids on the Dnieper River where navigation was possible. The Zaporozhian Cossacks had a long history of anti-Semitic activity, as did their Ukrainian neighbors. In the seventeenth century when the Cossacks were in rebellion against Poland, Cossack Ataman (Chieftain) Bogdan Khmelnitzy systematically massacred thousands of Jews who he claimed had acted as tax collectors and stewards of rich landlords during Polish rule. In 1918 and 1919, Zaporotsian Ataman (Chieftain) Semosenko ranged throughout the Ukraine in a similar pogrom against "rich Jews." Semosenko personally executed hundreds of Jews and landowners. Either he, or someone very much like him, was probably responsible for the violence in Alexandrovsk in mid-June of 1918. The violence was sporadic but continued for the better part of three weeks. Hundreds of shootings, beatings, and robberies took place during that period.

Historian of the Russian Revolution, William Henry Chamberlin, compiled some of the events of that June from contemporary newspaper accounts. Chamberlin chose Zheleznykov's hometown of Alexandrovsk and the surrounding counties to illustrate the random violence and confusion that reigned in the Ukraine during the civil wars. He wrote:

> A single day's budget of news from the neighborhood of Ekaterinoslav (province) in June 1918, gives an idea of the violent social unrest which was seething in the country districts.
>
> The Zemstvo office in Alexandrovsk was attacked and robbed of 10,500 rubles. The landlords Kovalev and Mirgorodsky were assaulted and the latter was wounded. Seven persons were killed during an attack on the home of a certain Konko. The estate manager Ivakin was murdered. The landlord Budko was robbed of 20,000 rubles. The home of Prince Urusov, in Novo-Moskovsky County, was burned. There was an armed attack on the estate of a woman named Gersanova, in Pavlograd County; the home was blown up, two persons were killed, and three injured. During an onslaught on the estate of Livtienko, in Bkhmut County, three were killed. A man named Peretyatko and all the members of his family were killed by robbers in Verkhne-Dnieprovsk County. The Nekazanov family were robbed and shot down in Slavianoserbsk County. A bomb was thrown into the home of Vartory; his wife was killed by the explosion. Robberies and assaults were also taking place in the town of Ekaterinoslav. [52]

Since Yakov Zheleznykov was in the area on 2 June 1918, and had to complete his property purchase by the 9th, it was fortunate that he was not one of the victims. The Count and Countess Ursova, who had once tried to purchase the child prodigy Mischa Elman, were burned out of their home, as were many other members of the nobility. By the beginning of July, more than three dozen large property owners in and around Alexandrovsk had been attacked.

How the Zheleznykovs managed to escape robbery, beating, injury, or death is unknown. However, something is known of at least one stratagem that Jennie and Yakov employed to protect their son from the various marauding bands that occupied Alexandrovsk during the Russian Revolution and the civil war that followed. The ploy is well-documented in a series of remarkable family photographs. Starting in 1915 and continuing through 1921, the Zheleznykovs had periodic, formal portraits taken of their son in the photographic studio of Ber Kogan in Alexandrovsk. The earliest photos show a little boy dressed in a simple white blouse. But when photos of the child are taken six months later, he is costumed as a Ukrainian peasant. A few months after that, Shura is dressed up as a little Russian sailor. Yet another photo, taken some months later, portrays child and mother as Ukrainian peasants again. Around the age of four, a series of photographs was taken portraying the boy as a Zaporozhian Cossack, a middle-class Ukrainian, and finally as a Russian sailor again. Some of the photos show mother and son in similar costumes. At least three of these later portraits were taken on the same day, as evidenced by the photographic backdrop, lighting, chairs, and other elements, which are identical in the various photos. At least one of these later photos seems to have Shura dressed in a costume that would only be appropriate for a much younger child, and the boy clearly portrays his embarrassment and displeasure to the camera.

The order of the photographs is significant. It roughly corresponds to the occupation of Alexandrovsk by various armed forces. Whether the photos were used on false identity cards or with other documents is unknown, but their intent is clear.

Whoever was in power, "Little Shura" was going to be one of them, and photographic documentation would be on hand to support the needed identity. His clothing had once helped save him from being kidnapped; perhaps the same kind of ploy could be used to keep him from being killed.

There is one very curious element in the photographs worth mentioning. Each costume is unique with the exception of three ornamental buttons, which appear in a vertical row on the clothing in many photographs. On some costumes they had been sewn onto the boy's tunic and on others on the lower pant leg. While it may be idle to speculate on the specific purpose of these buttons, such devices were used by other Jewish families to help identify their children's bodies in the event that other forms of identification were impossible. Though this sort of precaution may seem callous, if not gruesome, it was unfortunately a common enough practice of the time.

Whether the various national costumes that he wore as a child actually played any role in saving Eugene's life is speculative, but elaborate costumes have been a trademark of Eugene Jelesnik's professional career. Over the years he would appear on stage in every possible guise—from cowboy to Gypsy. At his home in Salt Lake City, Eugene Jelesnik would one day own a collection of thirty-seven elaborate concert jackets in every color of the rainbow.

As will be evident, the life of Eugene Jelesnik was profoundly affected by his childhood in Russia. In a 1978 interview he was asked why he spent so many years of his life entertaining U. S. troops overseas. He replied that it was a direct result of his childhood experiences in Russia. He told the interviewer that he felt he owed a debt to this country for the privilege of being an American citizen. Eugene said he understood better than many, the value of freedom. He had learned about it firsthand in Russia—where he had none of it.

CHAPTER TWO

THE SIEGES OF ALEXANDROVSK

Eugene Jelesnik never gave much thought to his early years in Russia. After all, he was only a child there, and his recollections were vague and uncertain. Curiously, he had never discussed those times with his mother and had never bothered to closely examine the things he did recall, which would have kept them fresh in his mind. Eugene was therefore a little surprised the day he realized that he had actually lived under the Tsar. As he examined family papers and deeds with their imperial stamps and elaborate seals and devices, he was suddenly linked to a time that he had only half-believed existed. The documents tied him to another age—to gilded carriages and overdressed opulence. The papers also seemed to link him to the bloody cellar where it all came tragically to an end.

Tsar Nicholas II was still in power when the Zheleznykov family attended the Christmas festivities in Alexandrovsk that Eugene places among his earliest memories. The Tsar would abdicate his throne about the time that "Little Shura" first ran off to join the circus. At the time of the pogrom against the bourgeoisie in Alexandrovsk, the Tsar and his family were being kept as state prisoners in a house in the Siberian town of Ekaterinburg. A few weeks later, in the early morning hours of 17 July 1918, the Romanoff family—Tsar Nicholas, Tsarina Alexandra, and their four children—were awakened by their guards. They were told that they were going to be transferred to another location, but first an official photograph was to be taken of the family. They were escorted to a half-cellar and lined up as if for a group portrait. Then a group of Bolsheviks, members of the Cheka (special police), burst into the room. Their leader read aloud a Soviet decree ordering the immediate execution of the Tsar and his family. "What? What?" Nicholas is said to have asked in disbelief. The order was then read again, after which the executioners produced pistols and began firing into the terrified family at point-blank range. The Tsar and Tsarina died quickly, but the four daughters were wearing clothing that concealed jewels sewn into their corsets. The bullets ricocheted off their bodies. Firsthand accounts of the massacre stated that several of the daughters had to be repeatedly bayoneted and bludgeoned before they died.[1]

The execution of the Tsar and his family was to have dire consequences for the Zheleznykovs. While the Romanov family had lived, there was a pretense of civility among many of the revolutionary forces. But the execution of the Romanovs seemed to open a floodgate of horror. The brutal killings stunned the world and held horrifying implications for the former ruling class. If the Tsar could be killed, then who was safe? The answer was no one. Over the next three years the Cheka would seek out and execute, in similar fashion, more than 12,000 former members of the aristocracy, as well as landowners, rich industrialists, and others who were deemed to be bourgeois enemies of the communist state.[2] Among those marked for execution was the rich sugar broker Yakov Zheleznykov. Eugene's version of what happened next was terse: "After they killed the Tsar, all hell broke loose. My father was immediately sought by the Bolsheviks because he was rich and we were millionaires, at least according to standards there at the time. They wanted to take our property, and they were looking for my father. They wanted to kill him because of all his wealth. We were Jews, but they still considered us remnants of the czarist regime. Soldiers were always looking for him. He started traveling from city to city to keep away from them. He was in hiding the whole time—staying with friends and relatives—always on the run. But most of the time he was in Crimea, in Feodosiya."

Except for a compression of the time line, Eugene's description of the situation was accurate. To the Soviets, whose understanding of foreign trade was dubious, Yakov was not only a capitalist but the worst sort of bourgeoisie, an exporter who profited by sending vital food products abroad. The Soviet government considered such men war profiteers, and when they were found they were usually shot on sight. A series of official decrees issued by the Soviet government between April and October of 1918 could have been written with Yakov Zheleznykov in mind. The decrees would first take away Yakov's right to do business, then they would strip him of his property, and finally would seek to take his life. The decrees confirm Eugene Jelesnik's version of the history.

DECREE OF THE COUNCIL OF PEOPLE'S COMMISSARS
ON THE NATIONALIZATION OF FOREIGN TRADE, OF
APRIL 22, 1918

I. All foreign trade is nationalized. Business dealings for the purchase and sale of any products (of the mining and manufacturing industries, agriculture, etc.) with foreign states and individual trade institutions abroad are made in the name of the Russian Republic only by organizations which have been granted special powers to do so. Outside the agency of these organizations any commercial dealings for import or export with foreign countries are hereby forbidden.[3]

DECREE OF THE ALL-RUSSIAN SOVIET CENTRAL
EXECUTIVE COMMITTEE OF MAY 1, 1918

Inheritance both by law and by testament is hereby abolished. After the death of the owner, all property which belongs to him (both movable and immovable) becomes the state property of the Russian Socialist Federative Republic.[4]

In late August of 1918 a series of assassinations and bombings by anti-Bolshevik counterrevolutionaries shook the Bolshevik leadership. Lenin[5] himself was injured in one of the attacks. The response was immediate:

ORDER FOR INTENSIFIED RED TERROR,
ISSUED BY THE COMMISSAR FOR INTERNAL AFFAIRS,
OF SEPTEMBER 4, 1918

There must be an immediate end of looseness and tenderness. All right wing Socialist revolutionaries who are known to local Soviets must be arrested immediately.

Considerable numbers of hostages must be taken from among the bourgeoisie and the officers. At the least attempt at resistance or the least movement among the White Guards mass shooting must be inflicted [on the bourgeoisie] without hesitation. The local Provincial Executive Committees must display special initiative in this direction. The departments of administration, through the militia and the Extraordinary Commissions must take all measures to detect and arrest all persons who are hiding under assumed names and must shoot without fail all who are implicated in White Guard [counterrevolutionary] activity.

All the above mentioned measures must be carried out immediately. The heads of the departments of administration are bound to report immediately to the People's Commissariat for Internal Affairs any actions in this connection of organs of the local Soviets which are indecisive. The rear of our armies must, at last, be finally cleared of all White Guard activity and of all vile plotters against the power of the working class and of the poorest peasantry. Not the least wavering, not the least indecision in the application of mass terror [will be tolerated].

Confirm the receipt of this telegram.

Communicate it to the county Soviets.[6]

PEOPLE'S COMMISSAR FOR INTERNAL AFFAIRS,
PETROVSKY

Fortunately for the Zheleznykovs, the decrees were not yet enforceable in the Ukraine, which was still under the control of Germany and its puppet Ukrainian government. But on 11 November 1918, Germany capitulated to the allies in the west. Two days later, the Soviet government annulled the Treaty of Breast-Litovsk and a Civil War of unimaginable complexity immediately broke out in the Ukraine. The struggle for the Ukraine was one of the most confusing multisided battles in all history. Over the next two years, army after army swept across the landscape. The Zheleznykov family in Alexandrovsk, and Yakov, by now in hiding in Feodosiya, were caught right in the middle of it. While Yakov might have thought he was fortunate not to be in the hands of the Bolsheviks, as things developed, the Bolsheviks were the very least of his worries.

In December of 1918, Ukrainian nationalist troops under

Petlura occupied Kiev and overthrew the Skoropadsky Ukrainian government that had been installed by the Germans. The Red Army began moving west into the area formerly controlled by Germany and ran headlong into the two warring Ukrainian armies, as well as anti-Bolshevik White Armies and their foreign allies.[7] French and Greek armies landed in Odessa and Sevastopol to aid the anti-Bolshevik "White" forces of General Denikin, who had taken control of the Crimea from the Austrians and Germans. These troops pushed up the Dnieper, capturing Kherson and Nikolaiv before being forced to retreat. But it wasn't the Bolsheviks who drove them back, it was the Ukrainian partisan army of General Grigoriev that had temporarily allied itself with the Red Army out of fear that foreign interventionists would help the Whites restore Imperial Russian power in the Ukraine. For a short time in the early weeks of 1919, General Grigoriev also controlled the area around Alexandrovsk. In February of 1919, the Red Army captured Kiev, capital of the Ukrainian nationalist regime, and Kharov, the largest city in the eastern Ukraine. By April, another Red Army had captured the port of Odessa on the Black Sea, after its evacuation by French forces. By the end of April 1919, the Red Army had occupied all the Crimea, except for the extreme southeast of the Peninsula.[8]

In Feodosiya, Yakov must have watched the approach of the Reds in horror. Through most of this period, Feodosiya would remain in White Army hands, but the hold was tenuous, and fighting was taking place in the outskirts of the town. But the Red Army was now under attack by nationalist Ukrainian armies in its rear. Taking advantage of the Ukrainian nationalist's attack on the Reds, General Denikin of the Whites took the offensive against Soviet Red Army all along the southeastern front in mid-May of 1919. His attack was assisted by a former ally of the Red Army, the troops of the revolutionary anarchist General Nestor Makhno. Makhno's anarchists would help Denikin to win decisive victories over the Red Army on the lower Don. By the end of June 1919, the cavalry forces of General Denikin occupied many of the large towns of the southeastern Ukraine, including Alexandrovsk.[9]

With the surprising exception of the Red Army, all of the

warring factions in the field carried out vicious pogroms against the Jews.[10] The White Armies of General Denikin, Wrangel and Kolchak, the anarchist army of General Nestor Makhno, bandit chieftains, Cassock atamans, and partisan generals all participated in the murderous pogroms.[11] But the most fanatical instigators of anti-Semitism during the period were the Ukrainian Nationalist troops of Nestor Petlura and the atamans under his command. Large-scale anti-Jewish pogroms were initiated with the second retreat of the Ukrainians before the Red Army in early 1919. The common practice was to flog Jews, extort money, and destroy property.[12] But the pogroms gradually grew in intensity and brutality to the point where the period is now known as "the Ukrainian holocaust."[13] In the years 1918 and 1919, twelve hundred separate pogroms were carried out against the Jews in the Ukraine, a third of which have since been attributed to the Ukrainian National Army.[14] In March of 1919, Petlura forces carried out one of the most brutal massacres of Jews recorded to that time. Throughout the Ukraine, unbelievable acts of terror were carried out under Petlura's orders.[15] Cruelty was a part of the strategy. Ataman Struk dragged Jews from their homes and drowned them in the Dnieper River.[16] General Grigoriev conducted pogroms against the Jews in the town of Elizavetgrad on 15–17 May 1919.[17] Hundreds were slaughtered over the two-day period.

In Ekaterinoslav, the Ukrainian state where Alexandrovsk was located, several well-organized attacks against the Jewish population were carried out between 1919 and 1921. Over that period more than fifty percent of the Jewish-owned farms were abandoned or confiscated. In most areas, laws were enacted that sought to deny Jews the means of making a living. In other parts of the Ukraine the pogroms were simply mass murders. Thirty thousand Jews are known to have been executed outright. Estimates of Jewish dead for the period 1917 through 1921 range between 70,000 to 100,000 killed and more than a million left homeless. An unknown number would die of untreated wounds, starvation, and exposure.[18]

It probably meant nothing to Yakov Zheleznykov that the Red Army did not participate in the Jewish pogroms in the Ukraine in

1918 and 1919. Joseph Stalin, who was nearly as anti-Semitic as Adolph Hitler, would more than make up for the oversight in the not-too-distant future. Besides, the decree of the Peoples Soviet Commissar of 4 September 1918 made it perfectly clear that the Soviets would happily kill Yakov on the spot if they ever got hold of him. With as many enemies as he had, his survival to date had been nothing short of miraculous. Little is known of Yakov's years in hiding. There is only one certainty, Yakov must have had many friends, some in high places. But no amount of protection could shield him forever. Sooner or later, one of the factions was bound to catch up with him.

Shortly after 1:00 P.M. on the afternoon of 4 July 1919, Yakav Israelevitch Zheleznykov went to a public building at the corner of Dvorianskaja and Bulvarnaja Streets in the city of Feodosiya. He was accompanied by several acquaintances. They included Ilva Davydovich Pinkus, a bourgeois and neighbor from Alexandrovsk, Gavriil Abramovich Dafner, a rich bourgeois of Feodosiya, and Abram Samiulovich Sheer, a bourgeois from the city of Simpherpol. The four men climbed the steps to the third floor and entered the office of city notary Veniamin Samoilovich Panpulovsmall. They were there to meet a local magistrate, Harlamij Dmitrievich Melnikov. The men who accompanied Yakov were old friends, and they were there as witnesses to perform the solemn duty of attesting to the dictation of Yakov's last will and testament. The document read in part:

> I, Yakov Israelevitch Zheleznykov, being in my right mind and memory, would like to make the bequest of all the property I own, and that might be left after my death as follows:
>
> 1) The house I own in the city of Alexandrovsk, on the corner of Kuznechnaja, Moskovskaja, and Nikolajevskaja streets, and other immovable properties I own, no matter where they are and in what form they are I bequeath to wife of my second marriage, Zhenia Haimovna Rothaus.
>
> After my wife's death, all these properties should be shared between all my children from my second marriage in equal proportions. In case my wife Zhenia Haimovna Rothaus marries again after my death, her ownership of all properties and my bequest to her discontinues and all these properties pass into

the hands of my children from my second marriage and to my
son from that marriage, whose name is Srul Yakovlevich
Zheleznykov. [Srul is the name that Eugene was called by his
father.]

Yakov also bequeathed various sums of money to each of his
children by his first marriage: Gidalij Yakovlevich Zheleznykov,
300 rubles; his daughter Fenia Yakovlevna Zheleznykov, 200
rubles; daughter Maria Yakovlevna Zheleznykov, 200 rubles. But
Srul (Eugene) was given 15,000 rubles. Other than the real property, which he left to Jennie, it was the largest single bequest to any
of his children. The money was to be held in trust for the boy
until he was twenty-one years of age, or at the discretion of his
mother who was appointed executor. Yakov also left substantial
sums of money to his nieces and nephews: David Israelevitch
Zheleznykov's children, 5,000 rubles; Leiba Israelevitch
Zheleznykov's children, 5,000 rubles; Pasha Izraelevna Gin's
children, 3,000 rubles; and nephew Shleila Borukhovich Sheifeld,
3,000 rubles. One other bequest of note stands out. Yakov left
20,000 rubles to his wife's sister, Eugene's Aunt Ruth. The rest of
his money and all movable property, he left to Jennie.

At the signing of the statement, the witnesses testified that the
testator, Yakov Israelevitch Zheleznykov, was in his right mind
and memory, and that the text of the bequest he made by his own
(Yakov Israelevitch Zheleznykov's) hand. The will was signed by
Yakov and notarized by H. Melnikov at exactly 2 P.M., 4 July 1919.
Until the translation of the will in September of 1996, Eugene
Jelesnik had no idea that his father had another family by an earlier marriage. He and his mother were to be the principal benefi-
ciaries of the will. The token amounts left to Yakov's other children
indicate that they had been otherwise provided for. It also seems
probable that Yakov's siblings were already dead since money is
left to his nieces and nephews, but no mention is made of his
brothers and sister.[19]

The Soviet decree of 1 May 1918 abolished all inheritance. So
unless the White Army was successful in overthrowing the
Bolsheviks, the effect of the will was moot.

The day that Yakov chose to draw up his will also seems

historically significant. Not because it was the fourth of July, but rather because the day before, General Denikin, commander of the White Army, issued his orders for a final drive on Moscow, and July 4th was the beginning of the offensive. The two attacks had multiple objectives, too many to succeed. One army was to drive north toward Moscow, along the Dnieper, and another was to drive south and capture the ports on the Black Sea:

DENIKIN'S ORDER FOR THE DRIVE ON MOSCOW,
OF JULY 3, 1919

> The Armed Forces of South Russia have smashed the armies of the enemy, have captured Tsaritsin and have cleared out the Don Territory, the Crimea and a considerable part of Voronezh, Ekaterinoslav and Kharkov Provinces.
> General Mai-Maevsky is to move on Moscow in the direction: Kursk, Orel, Tula. In order to safeguard himself to the West he is to move to the line of the Dnieper and the Desna, occupying Kiev and the other crossings on the sector Ekaterinoslav-Briansk.
> General Dobrovolsky is to come out on the Dnieper from Alexandrovsk to the mouth of the river, having in view the future occupation of Kherson and Nikolaev.

It might be supposed that Yakov's hopes were riding on the success of the offensive, but if he knew anything at all about General Denikin, he probably would not have wished him well. In August of 1919, General Denikin's White anti-Bolshevik forces moved deep into the Ukrainian interior and immediately began large pogroms against the Jews. Denikin, like many other White commanders, mistakenly believed that the Jews were in league with the Bolsheviks.[20] During his offensive, bloody pogroms were carried out in nearly every community in the Ukraine. By the beginning of August 1919, one of Denikin's armies striking south out of Alexandrovsk met with White forces of the Crimea and captured all the principal ports on the lower Dnieper. By October they were threatening Odessa.

But further east, Makhno's anarchist army was already harassing Denikin's supply lines. Makhno, whose alliances were as temporary as they were frequent, was one of the oddest figures of the entire period. Like Pancho Villa in Mexico, Makhno had a large following among the peasant class. He often sacked large towns, and gave part of the plunder to the rural peasants. A baby-faced, twenty-three-year-old general, Makhno was both a born leader and a killer.[21] Operating against both the Red Army and Denikin's White volunteers, Makhno captured Berdiansk on the Sea of Azo on 11 October, then Maritapol and Nikipol. On 22 October 1919, Makhno marched into Alexandrovsk.[22] Every place that Makhno went, he formally announced a reign of freedom, by which he meant anarchy. No more appropriate figure could be imagined to represent the chaos and bloody insanity of that time than Makhno. As a true anarchist, he did not believe in any government, whether it was Bolshevik, Tsarist, or constitutional democracy. The rule of the people for Makhno was just that. Makhno seemed to believe in mob rule as devoutly as others believed in communism. Even his army was run in a somewhat anarchist fashion. The official daybook of one of his brigades recorded the following: "It was unanimously resolved to obey the orders of the commanders, providing that the commanders are sober when they give them."[23] On 9 November 1919, Makhno captured the provincial capital of Ekaterinoslav.

With Makhno to his rear controlling the lines of supply, and the Red Army pushing forward out of Moscow, Denikin's offensive collapsed. Over the next two months he would retreat more than a thousand miles to the eastern shores of the Black Sea. On 30 December 1919, Red Army troops took Ekaterinoslav from Makhno and within weeks controlled the area around Alexandrovsk.

By March 1920, the remnants of Denikin's shattered army were trapped on the eastern shore of the Black Sea at the port of Novorossik. British warships assisted in the evacuation of the White Army to the Crimea. The towns along the southeastern coast of the Crimea, including Feodosiya where Yakov Zheleznykov remained in hiding, were flooded with refugees from the defeated White Army.[24]

The war should have been over. It was not. Western powers were continuing to hope that somehow the Bolsheviks could still be stopped. Huge shipments of arms poured into the Crimea. The White army was resupplied. Denikin was replaced by Baron Peter Wrangle, a former Tsarist general.[25] After reorganizing the White Army, Wrangle began an all-out offensive against the Bolsheviks on 6 June 1920. Wrangle struck north out of the Crimea and during the summer made astounding progress, recapturing much of the territory lost the previous spring.[26] By late September he had captured Alexandrovsk and was threatening Ekaterinoslav. In a period of less than a year, Alexandrovsk had been captured by three entirely different armies. The Zheleznykovs' home was in the very center of the city near the intersection of two principal streets. How the family survived during this period is unknown. Eugene, who was six years old, has no recollection of the troubles.

Baron Wrangle had vainly hoped that Makhno would join him in expelling the Bolsheviks from the Ukraine. He went so far as to send an envoy to Makhno suggesting an alliance. The envoy was promptly hung. "Makhno would fight the Communists as an anarchist peasant insurgent, but never in an alliance with a former Tsarist general and baron."[27] The Bolsheviks took immediate advantage of the situation. They released imprisoned anarchists and granted them clemency provided they would take up arms against Wrangle. Makhno then took the field against the Whites and played a small but significant part in Wrangle's eventual defeat in late October. By 2 November 1920, Wrangle was forced back into the Crimea. During the second week of November, the remains of the White Army and thousands of refugees, including bourgeoisies, Tsarists, landowners, and capitalists fled on British, French, and American ships. The war for Russia was over. The Reds had won.[28]

On 29 November 1920, the Supreme Economic Council of the Soviet Union issued a decree for all the newly captured territories including the Ukraine and the Crimea. The decree read:

> All industrial enterprises belonging to private persons or companies and employing more than five workers with mechanical power or more than ten workers without mechanical power are declared nationalized.
> All the property, business assets, and capital of the

enterprises specified in Paragraph 1, wherever this property may be, and whatever it may consist of, are declared the property of the Russian Socialist Federative Soviet Republic.[29]

For reasons that are unknown, Yakov Zheleznykov did not flee the Crimea with the defeated White Army. Thousands of bourgeoisies like him were now in hiding on the peninsula, and the Red Army was determined to hunt the fugitives down. On December 4th and 5th 1920, the Soviet newspaper *Krasni Krim* in Simferopol published the following orders:

> We need pitiless, unceasing struggle against the snakes who are hiding in secret. We must annihilate them, sweep them out with an iron broom from everywhere. The great fighter for the great future, the worker-titan, bearing peace to the whole world through a sea of precious blood, shed in the struggle for a bright future, knows neither pity nor neglect.
>
> Too many White Guards remain in liberated Crimea. Now they have become quiet, hiding in corners. They await the moment to throw themselves on us again. But no! We pass over to attack. With the punishing, merciless sword of Red terror we shall go over all the Crimea and clear it of all the hangmen, enslavers, and tormentors of the working class. We shall take away from them forever the possibility of attacking us.[30]

As with many other decrees of the period, the orders seem to apply specifically to Yakov Zheleznykov and other men of his ilk. Incredibly, Yakov would continue to evade capture. For more than a year he would elude his oppressors as he had his entire life. He would die of a cerebral hemorrhage a little over one year later, on 22 December 1921, in Feodosiya. The records show that at the time of his death he was residing in the "House of Haja" on Lazaretnaja Street. He was sixty-four years old. The records are also clear on another point. His wife Jennie was in attendance at the time of his death. She would report his passing to the authorities and would sign the official papers in the presence of the examining physician, Dr. Alekseev. Yakov Israelevitch Zheleznykov was buried in the Jewish cemetery in Feodosiya.[31]

Eugene Jelesnik does not remember ever going to the Crimea. Nor does he recall that his mother ever left their home in

Alexandrovsk. But then there were other hard facts that Eugene did not remember or was protected from ever knowing. Over the previous four years, Alexandrovsk had been under the control of the German army, two Ukrainian Armies, three different White Armies, two Bolshevik armies, and the anarchist army of General Nestor Makhno. These, too, were facts that Eugene never knew. But at the time of Yakov's death, "Little Shura" was only seven years old.

Jennie Zheleznykov had known for years that the day would eventually come. She had read or been told of the murder of hundreds of fellow bourgeoisie. She had certainly known of the anti-Semitic pogroms that swept through the Ukraine. She must have known of the death squads of the Cossack and Ukrainian atamans Semesenko and Struk—the drownings in the river, the tramplings, maimings, and the other atrocities. Alexandrovsk had been overrun so many times it must have been hard to keep track of the factions. The Jews suffered disproportionately during the Revolution and Civil War. At least seventy thousand Jews were dead in the Ukraine. It seems more than probable that she personally knew many of the victims. It is more than likely that she had witnessed at least some of the violence firsthand, and if not, had heard the screams in the night and the dull thud of distant gunshots and smelled the smoke from the fires.

Jennie had been preparing for the day from the time she was a child in Riga. Her father, Rabbi Aaron Rothaus, would have told her of the great pogrom in that city forty years before, when the synagogue was burned. She also would have been told by her husband of the persecutions of 1881 following the assassination of Tsar Alexander II. She had anticipated with dread the day that the knock would come, and she had also made preparations. For years she and her husband had placed money, jewels, and other valuables in secret and well-disguised hiding places. It is known, for instance, that Jennie had hidden diamonds in the hollowed-out heels of her shoes.[32] The Zheleznykovs had been very rich, and there may have been many other concealed reserves.

But money and jewels were only good if you were alive to use them. Yakov and Jennie had discussed in detail how they were to act toward the invaders when they finally came. She must have rehearsed the scene many times in her mind. What she could not rehearse were the reactions of the others in her household: her son, her father, and most especially her younger sister, Ruth.

Eugene remembered the night well. The scene is his most vivid memory of life in Russia. It took place just a few weeks after his father's death. A group of mounted soldiers arrived suddenly at the house—the hooves of their shod horses clattering noisily on the cobblestones of the courtyard outside. The front door flew open, and they burst into the parlor. Eugene remembered: "They barged in and acted like gangsters! That's just what they were too, gangsters, a bunch of gangsters!"

They demanded all the money and valuables and began to ransack the house. They opened drawers and cupboards and dumped everything on the floor. One of the soldiers grabbed Rabbi Rothaus and began to take the rings from his fingers. The old man feebly resisted and they knocked him to the ground. In the struggle, one ring fell to the floor. Eugene remembers that his Aunt Ruth saw this and ran to the place where it fell. The stone had come loose from its setting and was laying on the floor. She quickly snatched up the stone and put it in her mouth then she grabbed the gold ring. The soldiers didn't notice that she had put the stone in her mouth, but they grabbed her and twisted her hands open and took the stoneless setting. They also pulled the rings off Ruth's fingers. To Jennie and Shura's dismay, Ruth resisted the men, who threatened to cut her fingers off if she didn't remove her rings. She finally gave in and surrendered her jewelry to them. After this, they threw her to the floor and whipped her mercilessly with their riding crops. Fortunately for Ruth, the Bolsheviks were there to steal and not to kill. If they had been Petlura Ukrainians or Zaporozhian Cossacks instead of Bolsheviks, Ruth would have likely been butchered on the spot.

While this was going on, other soldiers were combing the house, tearing things up and looking for money. Eugene was panic-stricken and didn't know what was going on or what to do. He clung to his mother's dress and watched the proceedings in terror. Unlike Ruth, Jennie knew exactly how to react to them. She told the men she would cooperate and quickly showed them where the silver and jewelry were hidden, where money was stashed, and where the best shoes, boots, and other items of clothing were to be found. She did not tell them of the diamonds hidden in the hollowed-out soles of her own shoes or of other secret places where she had hidden hordes of jewelry and money. But a lot was taken: Rabbi Rothaus's silver-handled walking stick, all the visible jewelry, pocket watches, gold, silver, and currency—even the phonograph. As Eugene described it seventy-eight years later, "They took everything they could get their hands on. They were gangsters!"[33]

Then as quickly as they had come, the soldiers left. Their home may have been in shambles, but the family had survived. That night the Bolsheviks ransacked every house on the block. Most of the residents of the neighborhood were tenants or friends of the Zheleznykovs: the watchmaker, Durbrovinsky; the attorney, Yakov Zimence and his mother Ekaterina; the family of the bourgeoisie Pinkus—all suffered a similar fate. House after house was broken into, and family after family was stripped of its possessions. The ordeal of that night was only the beginning of two years of horror for the Zheleznykov family. The stone that Aunt Ruth had saved from the Bolsheviks at the risk of her own life would be reset in a new ring that would one day be worn by Eugene Jelesnik for his grandfather, Aaron, and for Ruth, and by extension for all those who defied oppression.

It was only a day or two after "the night of the gangsters" that the family was threatened with an even more dangerous situation. A neighbor brought word that Bolshevik administrative authorities—backed by police—had just appeared on Nikolajevskaja Street and were confiscating the Zheleznykov properties and evicting the tenants. While the police were nailing up the confiscation and eviction notices, the Bolshevik officials were going door to door systematically taking a residential census of the neighborhood. Worse, they were asking about the Zheleznykovs. The news of this came so suddenly that there was no time to make preparations. The officials were less than a block away. Once again Jennie kept her head and instantly devised a plan to thwart the new threat. The urgency of that moment was so vividly burned into Eugene's memory that in retelling the tale, his voice quickened: "Things were becoming chaotic. When they confiscated all the property we thought we might all be killed right then and there. Mother said everything had to be done fast . . . fast . . . fast."[34]

The repeated word must have echoed the urgent instructions that Eugene's mother gave that day. The family gathered a few of their remaining personal belongings and moved into a small second floor bedroom at the back of the house. Everyone was to remain silent. Jennie would meet with the authorities. Somehow she convinced the Bolsheviks that the family on the second floor were not the sought-after Zheleznykovs. For the next two years the family would occupy the little room under an assumed name. How this was all accomplished is unknown. She might have had help from the neighbors, or she might have bribed an official. However it was done, the whole scheme would be exposed if anyone identified them. For this reason they would have to remain in hiding. For a family as prominent as the Zheleznykovs, it seems incredible that they would be able to sustain such a deception for very long. Eugene does not remember the name that the family went by during those years, but it was a strange name, possibly Cossack or Ukrainian. Whichever it was, the most reasonable explanation for the family's survival is that they were all costumed as local peasants. Over the next two years of his life, "Shura" seldom left the confines of the little room on the second floor. It is certain that the family never went outside in the daytime.

The rest of the Zheleznykov home was quickly filled with Ukrainian peasants and local commissars. The surrounding buildings were used to billet soldiers, and for a time the courtyard was guarded by a sentry. The family took their meals in their room and only Jennie had much contact with the other residents of the house. Eugene commented: "For the whole time that we stayed up there we were so quiet that the other people in the house hardly knew we were there. We never did anything, never saw anyone. It was like being in prison, and all the time we were constantly afraid that someone would find us out."

Rabbi Aaron Rothaus died within a few weeks of the move to

the room. The death presented unique and frightening problems for the family. The logistics of arranging for burial in the Jewish cemetery were daunting. What name would be on the stone? Aaron was a Rabbi, and the thought of carrying on the deception beyond the grave was out of the question. But the death was sure to draw the attention of the authorities. Papers and official documents would have to be signed. Identity cards would have to be shown. Who would sign as next of kin? All the paperwork would give them away instantly. Though the world had turned upside down, the Russian bureaucracy of Gogol's time was still humming along as efficiently as ever. There was only one solution; the funeral would have to be carried out in secret. All solemnity would be eliminated, but Aaron would be buried under his own name, and they would just have to take their chances at being discovered. Eugene described his grandfather's funeral as "the quietest that ever occurred. It took place so that none of the neighbors or soldiers would know what was going on. It was secret. There was no ceremony, no Rabbi, nothing."[35]

It was very clear that Jennie, Shura, and Aunt Ruth could not live forever in the little room on the second floor. They had to find a way to escape Russia altogether. Jennie arranged for friends to smuggle letters out of the country. These would then be forwarded to her relatives in the United States. Direct mail communication in their present circumstance was out of the question since it would have alerted authorities to their real identities. After many months Jennie finally got word to her brother Samuel Rothaus in the Bronx of the family's desperate situation. It was some time before she got back a reply via the same tortuous route. Sam had begun making arrangements to get the family out of Soviet Russia, but it wasn't going to be easy, and it would take time. Until the arrangements were made and the exit visas were secured, they would have to stay where they were. And until they knew it was safe to do otherwise, they would have to remain in hiding. For young Shura, waiting in the silent, darkened room in Alexandrovsk, "Uncle Sam" was synonymous with the United States. He was very surprised when he later learned that there was a symbolic "Uncle Sam" associated with America.

Living under an assumed name created problems that the family had not anticipated when they first went underground. The Bolsheviks sought them out initially because they had been elite members of the bourgeoisie, but if they discovered that the family was living in hiding under an assumed name, additional charges were certain to be brought against them. Using false papers and identity cards was a serious offense, as was the bribing of officials or the hiding of money and valuables from the communist authorities. But the most serious problem was getting enough food to eat. Since Jennie could not go to the market for fear of being identified, she had to arrange the purchase through sympathetic neighbors or buy the food herself from passing street vendors. But there was precious little for sale. Food was quickly becoming unavailable. With the entire province facing hunger, the plight of the little family living in hiding was becoming even more dire.

The earlier food shortages (during the war and the revolution) were caused primarily by breakdowns in the transportation and distribution systems. Though these had not yet been restored, the great famine of 1921–22 was caused by a truly disastrous decline in production. The Bolsheviks had requisitioned the harvest of 1920 and had never paid for it. Because the Bolsheviks were still in power, the peasant farmers responded by not bothering to plant crops in 1921. This was not entirely a matter of vengeful neglect. Since they hadn't been paid for the last crop, they couldn't afford to buy seed for the next. Large-scale agriculture for profit had been wiped out in the revolution. The biggest sections of the best lands went unplanted. Actual figures for 1921 show that agricultural production for that year was less than half the tonnage of 1913.[36] The new communist state of Russia was not producing enough food to feed its people. The result was one of the greatest famines in all history. From Ekaterinburg in Siberia to Kherson on the Black Sea, famine stalked the land. It is estimated that over two million people died of starvation in southeastern Russia and the Ukraine between 1920 and late 1922.

Shura Zhleznykov knew nothing about the famine. In his isolated world, in his little room on the second floor of a building occupied by people from whom he was hiding, the world outside hardly existed. He did know that his mother had been keeping him fed by selling off her hidden hoard of jewelry, piece by piece. Eugene would later claim that he never suffered from hunger. If so, then the sheltered protection that his parents had given him during the war years continued during the famine. If Eugene knew nothing of the thousands of people starving in the streets, the same could not be said of his mother, Jennie, for it was she who had to purchase the provisions and deal with the realities of life outside the little room.

In Eugene Jelesnik's family album, in the section devoted to Russia, is one of the most poignant and puzzling photographs ever taken. A group of people—old men, women, and young children—are crowded into a narrow hallway. The photograph may have been taken in secret since there is no other explanation for the strange setting. An even more peculiar aspect of the photo is that with the exception of one woman standing by a window at the left, everyone is holding up a dinner plate and tilting it toward the camera. Only one child (front row center) has anything on her plate. What is on the plate is not clear. It may have been a scrap of bread or a potato. All the other plates are empty. The photo was obviously intended to tell someone, somewhere, that they were without food. Eugene does not recognize any of the people in the photograph and doesn't even like to look at it. But the woman standing by the window bears a strong resemblance to Jennie Zheleznykov. If it is Jennie, the photograph would go a long way toward explaining how the family managed to deceive the Bolsheviks. Jennie may have been using her jewelry and money not only to keep her family alive, but to assist her friends, neighbors, and former tenants. If so, it is likely that they in turn would be inclined to help their benefactor by keeping the family's true identity a secret. They would also be useful in helping to pass letters and other messages along to the outside world.

Because they were considered an insult to the communist government, photographs revealing the horrors of the Soviet famine had to be smuggled out of Russia. Many photos did get out, and far worse and far more damning photos than the simple hallway tableau in Eugene's family album. The sight of hundreds of skeletal figures begging for food, touched the conscience of the world.[37] Charitable groups such as the American Relief Association, the Red Cross, and the Hebrew Sheltering and Immigrant Aid Society (HSIAS) mounted large-scale relief efforts and thousands were saved.[38]

"Shura" Zheleznykov may not have gone hungry, but he remembers that one of the greatest treats he received during that time was an orange. He was at least partially aware of the sacrifices that his mother was making to keep him alive. One evening at the height of the famine, Jennie went out to get food for her boy. Somewhere in starving Alexandrovsk, she traded a large diamond ring for a single loaf of bread.

After countless prayers, two years of hiding, and an eternity of hopeful waiting, the necessary exit visas finally arrived. The papers authorized the exit of Jennie and Shura Zheleznykov and Ruth Rothaus. But these were not the names that they were living under in Alexandrovsk, so just as the other communications from Uncle Sam, they must have been delivered clandestinely.

Jennie once again took charge and told Eugene and Ruth to pack. Eugene remembered that: "We packed quickly but very quietly." There wasn't much for "Shura" to put in his small wooden box, only two changes of clothing. Jennie and Ruth each took a suitcase. In one, Jennie packed an envelope of family photographs and a few small odds and ends. The decision to take the family documents—including Yakov's will and the deeds to the family properties in Alexandrovsk—must have been a difficult one. If the Bolsheviks discovered these while inspecting their luggage, officials might assume that Jennie had hopes of one day returning to claim the property after the Soviets had been removed from power. Keeping the documents was a treasonous act, and it seems probable that they were well-hidden. The family spent most of the afternoon just waiting quietly for nightfall. They made no good-byes and said nothing to the others in the house or to the neighbors. When dusk came, they slipped out of their former home and more recent prison cell, and made their way to the train station. It was about seven or eight o'clock in the evening.[39]

The train was not scheduled to depart until many hours later, but Jennie wanted to be certain that their travel documents would be accepted. Then, too, she still had to buy tickets and make other arrangements for the trip. Arriving that early was probably a mistake. Through the evening and into the next morning, as they waited for their train, more and more passengers arrived. Eugene slept on the floor. His mother and aunt must have tried to look as inconspicuous as possible.

Finally, around three in the morning, the train they had patiently awaited for two years pulled into the station. Even then there was fear that they wouldn't be allowed to get on. The train was already overcrowded, and when they started to board, the conductors had to push the passengers into the cars like cattle. It was a confusing nightmare. Eugene remembers that the train ride was very long—at least three, possibly four days of travel. The officials repeatedly checked and double-checked the documents of every passenger. Some unfortunate travelers whose papers were found out of order would finish their trips in Soviet prison camps. Each stop was a cause for anxiety. Eugene remembered: "There was always apprehension. We were always looking back, with our eyes in the back of our head, to make sure that nobody was watching us, that nobody was trying to catch us, so that we wouldn't be stopped from leaving."[40]

The escape from Russia was another moment in time that was vividly pressed into Eugene's memory. It was the boy's first venture out of Alexandrovsk, his first train ride, and his first view of Russia's vast countryside. The Russia that rolled by as Shura pressed his face against the window was a different country than the imperial Russia to which he had been born. Gone was the private wealth of the ruling class, the public pomp of the imperial state, and the rich splendor and privilege of the Russian Orthodox Church. Everything connected with the Tsars was to be purged from the new communist state. No trace of the old system was to remain. Even the names of the cities would be changed to reflect the new order. The old imperial capital of St. Petersburg, named nominally for St. Peter, but actually honoring Tsar Peter the Great, would become Leningrad. The city and province of Ekaterinislav, which had been named for Katherine II, would become

"Dnepropetrovsk." Alexandrovsk was founded by Catherine II after her armies supplanted the Zaporozhian Cossacks in the region. Three hated Tsars bore the name Alexander, and if young Prince Alexi had ascended to the throne he would have become Tsar Alexander IV. It is little wonder that Alexandrovsk was one of the first names literally wiped from the map by Soviet authorities.[41]

Until September of 1996, when he was shown an historic atlas of Russia, Eugene Jelesnik had never seen the name "Alexandrovsk" on any maps. He had never read about the city and never heard the name mentioned in the news. Its seeming obscurity was the principal reason that he had long assumed that his birthplace was a small and insignificant town. It was anything but. Two years before the Zheleznykovs' train pulled out of the station, the Supreme Soviet had issued a decree changing the name of Alexandrovsk to its ancient name of "Zaporizhzhya." It was a wise political move, and went far to appease the local Zaporozhian Cossacks who derived their own name from the old designation. The Cossacks had fought on all sides during the war, and it was important to cement their allegiance to the new state. Less than five years later, Zaporizhzhya would become the site of one of the world's largest construction projects—the massive steel and concrete Dnipro Hydroelectric Station and Dam. The construction was undertaken with the aid of Canadian and American engineers, and was not completed until 1932. It was the USSR's first hydroelectric dam. The power plant was not only one of the world's largest, but it was most likely the only power plant to have a symphonic work composed in its honor.[42] By the mid 1930s, Eugene's hometown had become the industrial center of the entire region. Steel mills, foundries, refineries, and huge factories lined the banks of the Dnieper River. For a time, the city was known as the "Pittsburgh of the Soviet Union." The city was destroyed by the Germans during World War II, but was subsequently rebuilt and expanded. Zaporizhzhya today has a population approaching a million people and is the regional capitol.[43] The city has modern architecture and wide, tree-lined streets. It is the computer and research center for the southern Ukraine, and has an array of cultural facilities, including opera houses, theaters, ballet studios, art galleries, and museums. Zaporizhzhya State University is the educational center for the entire region.[44] But even with its scenic and cultural attractions, Zaporizhzhya's overwhelming reputation is as a dirty industrial center with a plethora of huge smokestacks spewing out black clouds of noxious fumes into the sky. It even has an aging nuclear power plant. The city that Eugene Jelesnik fled in 1923 has since become one of the most polluted places on the planet.[45]

The Zheleznykovs crossed the Russian border into Germany with the clothes on their backs, two suitcases, and a small wooden case holding all of Shura Zheleznykov's worldly possessions. Of the huge family fortune that Shura might have inherited if the civil war had gone differently, nothing remained. The only valuables that they managed to get out of Russia were the stone from his grandfather's ring that Ruth had saved from the Bolsheviks by hiding it in her mouth, a ceramic napkin ring given to Jennie as a present by a friend, and the opera glasses that Yakov had given his wife shortly after their marriage. The last of the diamonds from the secret compartment in Jennie's shoe was used to bribe officials on the train and later at the border. She might have saved the jewels for use in Germany, but she was taking no chances. She had to be certain that they would actually be allowed to leave. Of the loss of the diamonds Eugene Jelesnik would emphatically say, "It was worth it! It was worth it! If the jewels were worth a million dollars, it was worth it!"

Neither Eugene, his mother, nor his aunt ever spoke to each other of Russia again. They would never discuss any of their experiences there or the ordeals they had endured. It was all permanently behind them: The sieges of Alexandrovsk, the Ukrainian holocaust, the desperate flight of and eventual death of Yakov, the night of the gangsters, the famines, and their life in the little room on the second floor. From the time they crossed the border, they would only look to the future, to the day they would join Shura's aunts and uncles in America.

The Zheleznykovs' dreams were not easily realized. During the years the family had been struggling to stay alive in

Alexandrovsk, things had been changing in the United States. At first the Russian Revolution had been viewed by Americans as little more than a curiosity, then as a distant tragedy, and then by degrees as a horror, an abomination, and finally as a threat. In rejecting the Treaty of Versailles in 1920, the U. S. Senate had led the country back into the isolationist stance it had taken before entering the First World War. Europe was again viewed as a hopeless place full of dark intrigue, alien ideologies, and tyrannical political systems.

The years directly following the war saw a rise in unemployment and related labor unrest in the United States as the country adjusted back to a peacetime economy. In the period August to October of 1920, there occurred the largest proportionate rise in immigration from eastern and southern Europe in American history. As were aliens of a later day, the large number of new arrivals were blamed for taking jobs that many believed rightfully belonged to native sons. Eastern European Jews and Italian Catholics became easy scapegoats for labor troubles, housing shortages, falling wages, and crime. Some Americans also believed that the same forces that destroyed Russia were about to be unleashed on U. S. soil.

A few took the threat more seriously than others. In January of 1920, the Justice Department, headed by Attorney General A. Mitchell Palmer, launched hundreds of simultaneous raids in thirty-three cities and arrested suspected Bolsheviks, anarchists, communists, socialists, and other "alien radicals." Although the raids were supposedly staged to thwart a dangerous conspiracy to overthrow the American system of government, the only thing that most of those arrested had in common was that they were "aliens."[46] Palmer arrested recent legal arrivals whose only crime was traveling on forged foreign visas. Many immigrants had to have forged visas to leave their totalitarian homelands. The United States government did not have formal diplomatic relations established with some of the states and hence visas to travel to America were not even issued by some governments. Attorney General Palmer's midnight search for "alien radicals" was known as "The Red Scare," and hundreds were deported after swift and perfunctory trials conducted before specially appointed tribunals. The government's expulsion of many Jews and Italians "confirmed" the belief of certain elements that these nationalities were threats to America's well-being. "The Red Scare" had the secondary effect of igniting the most intense period of anti-Semitism in American history.[47]

Palmer was convinced that aliens were behind every radical cause, and he specifically saw a link between "radical thought" and the Jews. Jews such as Leon Trotsky[48] had helped lead the Russian Revolution. Other Jews such as Alexander Berkman and Emma Goldman were leaders of the radical left in America. Palmer and a growing number of others linked Bolshevism and Jews. It was the same sort of anti-Semitic propaganda that had caused the White Army of General Denikin to slaughter Jews by the thousands in the Ukraine. But far worse than the paranoia of the U. S. Attorney General was the rising tone of hate in the American press. On 22 May 1920, Henry Ford's personal weekly newspaper, *The Dearborn Independent*, began running a series of articles under the general title "The International Jew." The first article began:

> There is a super-capitalism which is supported wholly by the fiction that gold is wealth. There is a super-government which is allied to no government, which is free from them all, and yet which has its hand in them all. There is a race, a part of humanity, which has never yet been received as a welcome part, and which has succeeded in raising itself to a power that the proudest gentile race has never claimed—not even Rome in the days of her proudest power.[49]

The diatribe went on to blame an international Jewish conspiracy for all evils facing the country. If Henry Ford, one of the most influential and admired men in America, could lend the support of his newspaper to endorse the notion that Jews were behind America's industrial troubles, then surely Congress had to act. It was doubly unfortunate that all this was going on while thousands of Jewish immigrants fleeing tyranny in eastern Europe were flooding into Ellis Island. The United States Commissioner for immigration even lent his voice to the chorus of anti-Semitic hysteria by stating to the *New York Times:* "Something must be done to stem the tide."

Demands were beginning to be heard in Congress that "the flood of Jews from eastern Europe had to be stopped." Congress, which had succeeded in passing an immigrant literacy law in 1917, and had also banned the immigration of "political undesirables," began to consider laws to severely restrict or eliminate Jewish immigration altogether. By the end of 1920, several bills were introduced into Congress to drastically reduce immigration. Representative Albert Johnson of Washington introduced a proposal to ban all immigration for two years. On 9 December of that year, Johnson made a speech on the floor of the House of Representatives, in which he said, "The fact is that the new immigration is not of the kind or quality to meet the real needs of the country. We are being made a dumping ground. We are receiving the dependents, the human wreckage of the war, not the strength and virility that once came to hew our forests and till our soil."[50]

The debate went on in Congress until April of 1920, when the new "restrictive" quota system was adopted. The law was designed to restrict the flow of specific immigrant populations. Since the increase in Jewish immigration had only come after the war, the solution was to roll back the percentage to pre-war levels. The law read in part:

> The number of aliens of any nationality who may be admitted under the immigration laws to the United States in any fiscal year shall be limited to three percent of the number of foreign-born persons of such nationality resident in the United States as determined by the United States census of 1910.[51]

The law, which was supported wholeheartedly by the Ku Klux Klan, among others, was designed to radically restrict the immigration of southern European Catholics and eastern European Jews into the United States. Specifically targeted was immigration from Italy and eastern Europe. It was passed by the House on April 22 and by the Senate on May 3. The vote in the Senate was 78 to 1. The bill was promptly signed by President Warren G. Harding, and it went into effect 30 June 1922.[52] Less than two years later, the bill was further amended to roll back the nationality quotas to two percent of each nationality as determined by the Census of 1890. The effect of the measures can be seen in the actual immigration statistics for the period 1921 through 1924. Jewish immigration, which peaked at 120,000 in the period 1921–22, was cut in half in 1923. But in 1924, only 10,292 Jews were allowed to enter the country.[53] The gates to America, which had been a symbol of hope to the oppressed peoples of the world, were swinging shut, but they weren't closed entirely. For those who were determined enough, and who were willing to wait their turn to be included in the quota, the golden gate of freedom was still ajar. Among those lucky few who would patiently wait was a little family fleeing Bolshevik Russia, called Zheleznykov.

After the flow of immigration from eastern Europe had been slowed by the new American immigration laws, refugees began to pile up in German ports. Something had to be done to house and feed the thousands of people who were suddenly stranded in Germany. Various organizations, including the Hebrew Sheltering and Immigrant Aid Society (HSIAS) convinced the German government to expand the facilities that already existed to temporarily house American-bound immigrants. HSIAS contributed large sums of money to the project as did German and American steamship lines who were dependent upon the immigrants for a substantial portion of their revenues. One of the largest such complexes was constructed in the German North Sea port of Bremen. It was here that Jennie, Shura, and Aunt Ruth were sent after their arrival in Germany. Officials from the government or possibly HSIAS met the train and took the refugees to the place that would be their home for the next two years. Eugene remembers the facilities well:

"There were a number of big barracks-like buildings in the compound . . . and a large central courtyard surrounded by dozens of buildings. . . . We lived in common dormitories with other escapees from tyranny: Russians, Latvians, and others. . . . We were assigned private sleeping quarters, but there were communal bathrooms and dining halls. Each building housed perhaps a hundred and fifty to two hundred people. All of our meals were cooked in a large, central kitchen. Things in Germany were good, a lot better than what we had just left in Russia. I enjoyed Germany very much. We could come and go as we pleased, it was very pleasant. The experience was probably tougher on my mother than it was for me, but she never complained. I considered it just another adventure."[54]

All of the refugee children were required to attend regular school. The gymnasium, as it was called in Germany, was not in the compound, but was located in the center of the town. Eugene remembers the address: Number 12 Zwingliestrasser. Eugene also remembers his first public schoolteacher, Richard Feller, who taught him both his regular studies—German, grammar, reading, writing, and math—as well as music. Shura Zheleznykov showed an immediate and remarkable aptitude for music. He had wanted a violin from the first time he heard Yeno Hubay on the phonograph as a child. He dreamed of the day that he would actually hold the instrument in his hands. During the darkest days in Russia, his mother had often promised him that when they got out, Shura would get his violin. It was not long after he began school that his dream came true.

Eugene remembered the occasion well. "It was the happiest day of my life," he says. The instrument was three-quarter size and within weeks—under the strict tutelage of his teacher—Eugene was quickly playing tunes. The very first melodies that Eugene mastered were the German Christmas carols "Oh, Tannenbaum" and "Shille Nacht" ("Oh, Christmas Tree" and "Silent Night"). He remembers playing "Volga Boatman" and many other Russian folk tunes and melodies that his parents had sung to him as a child. Once he had learned the fingering and controlled the use of the bow, Shura could play almost anything by ear. "If I heard it once, I could play it." But his teacher knew that this would be very bad for him and worked continuously to make certain that Shura was actually reading the music. Shura practiced for many hours every day, but he also found time to play soccer and games with his schoolmates. It was the first time that he had had friends his own age.

Through the German government and steamship company,

HSIAS also made certain that there were jobs available. Jennie and Aunt Ruth worked as housekeepers in the compound to pay for their board and room. Food and clothing were provided by the German Refugee Fund. In addition, Jennie received a small allowance for some of the family's necessities. They also made extra money by doing odd jobs and sewing. Both Jennie and Ruth soon became proficient tailors. Communication with "Uncle Sam" was now unrestricted and frequent, and Jennie's brother would often send along parcels and small amounts of money to help out. The family had access to bicycles and went on rides through the surrounding countryside.

Bremen was one of the most beautiful cities in all Europe. There were many public parks, museums, galleries, and theaters. The family took every opportunity to see the sights. They sometimes went to the opera at the Stadtheater but most often spent their weekends in the beautiful surroundings of the famous Burgerpark. Here they would enjoy visiting the elaborate floral gardens, boating on the lake, or simply enjoying picnics on the grass by the Parkhaus. Eugene remembers that he heard his first crystal set radio while at the park. He recalls straining to hear the music over the earphones and wondering where it was coming from. Eugene also has a large collection of postcards from Bremen mounted in his family album. Photos of the family in Bremen confirm that their time there was a happy one.

Shura's progress on the violin was so startling that his mother was convinced he was a prodigy, and if he was not another Mischa Elman, it was only because he had gotten a late start. At one point during their stay in Germany, Shura became so proficient at the instrument that his mother took him by train to the city of Budapest, Hungary, to meet the great Yeno Hubay himself, in the hope that he might take Shura on as a student. Hubay, who had many students at the time, listened to the boy patiently, but in the end said, "He's not yet ready. He needs more study." Neither Shura nor his mother were very disappointed. The boy had barely started his study of the violin, and though his progress had been rapid, he actually knew very little about music. Shura greatly admired Hubay, so his comments were taken as constructive.

Shura made the commitment right then that he would study even harder.[55]

Finally, on 30 September 1925, Shura, Jennie, and Aunt Ruth were granted visas to immigrate to America. Their ship would sail less than a week later. For two years they had hoped and prayed that their visas would be granted. Now that their departure was at hand, the brief final wait was almost too hard to bear, and they counted down the days until their departure. Along with hundreds of fellow refugees, the little family boarded the steamship SS *America* in the port of Bremerhaven, and on the morning of 6 October 1925, set sail for New York. Many of their closest friends from Germany were sailing with them, including another Russian Jewish family: the Raconds.

The ten-day voyage was a rough one, and there were heavy seas most of the way. Shura was seasick during the entire passage but continued to practice his violin. He also began his study of English. Over the course of the voyage he would talk to American seamen, passengers, and anyone else who knew the language. Mostly, Eugene learned the common phrases of introduction, "How do you do," and the like, but by the time the ship reached American waters, Shura was certain that he had mastered English. It was his third language.

One of the passengers that the Zheleznykovs met on the ship was an elderly woman named Betty Davidoff. She was a distant relative of the screen actor Melvin Douglas. Mrs. Davidoff listened to Shura practice. He told her of his ambition to study the violin in New York and to one day become a great musician. The woman was very impressed with the youngster's determination. She told Jennie and Shura that she was a close friend of Max Schlossberg who played first trumpet with the New York Philharmonic Orchestra, and she hinted that she might be able to help Shura in some way. The Zheleznykovs gave her the address of the Rothaus family in the Bronx with whom they expected to be staying. The shipboard friendship would have unexpected results. Eugene's life in New York, and his entire future career, would be influenced by his chance meeting with Betty Davidoff.

There is a deep bond that unites all those who immigrated to

America through New York in the early decades of the century. The common experience was so profound that nearly everyone who went through it tells similar stories, as though they all shared one heart and mind. Immigrants would invariably gather on deck and strain to be the first to see their new country. Few had ever seen buildings more than four stories high, and the New York skyline was then, and still remains, the greatest in the world. It was no different for Shura Zheleznykov and his fellow passengers than it had been for another young Russian Jewish violinist seventeen years earlier. Mischa Elman's father described that arrival in 1908: "A bright day, full of sunshine, greeted our arrival in New York. I shall never forget the moment when we first beheld the skyscrapers. They stretched toward the blue sky, their gold-topped roofs bathed in radiance. We were as happy as children. Our hearts danced with joy. Only those who have ventured across the Atlantic, and for days at a stretch have seen nothing but sky and water, can realize what it is to behold land, to see the New World of which so many have dreamed, the world which to millions remains, a dream."[56]

The SS *America* arrived in New York Harbor the morning of 16 October 1925. As the ship glided through the channel between Staten Island and Brooklyn, the passengers crowded on deck to get their first real view of the New World. Suddenly, the Statue of Liberty appeared out of the mist on the port side of the ship. Tears filled the eyes of all those on deck, and a spontaneous and exuberant cry went up from the immigrants. The shouts quickly grew into a roar of cheering and clapping that overwhelmed participant and spectator alike. It was the greatest music that Eugene Jelesnik had ever heard.[57]

CHAPTER THREE

AMERICA

The Zheleznykovs had arrived at the gates of the New World, but there was one more trial to endure before they would actually be allowed in. The inspection process at Ellis Island was dreaded by all immigrants. There were shipboard stories of trick questions, arbitrary medical examiners, and corrupt officials who demanded bribes. There were also warnings about crooked money changers and a host of shills, con artists, and thieves who preyed on arriving passengers. These were the prevailing conditions that had existed during the nineteenth century at the old Castle Garden immigration station on the New York mainland. The scandals associated with Castle Garden had led to the construction of facilities on Ellis Island in 1892. But when Jennie's older brother, Samuel, entered the country in 1893, all of the old problems remained.

The original wooden buildings burned down in a fire of suspicious origin in 1897, so Jennie's other siblings, Abraham, Cilia, and Johanna, who came to the U. S. after the turn of the century, would have entered through the same imposing red brick buildings that Shura would see from the rail of his ship twenty years later. The new buildings at Ellis Island improved the handling of immigrants and speeded up the examination process, but did little to change the old system of graft and corruption. Things were so bad in 1902 that President Teddy Roosevelt appointed a commission headed by William Williams to "clean the place out." Williams was successful in removing corrupt officials and improving sanitary conditions, but the reputation of the Immigration Service had been badly tarnished, and immigrants remained deeply distrustful.[1] What finally cleaned up the corruption at Ellis Island was not any action by crusading reformers, but declining profits. The restrictive laws that gradually closed the gates and brought an end to open immigration also meant that there were far fewer immigrants to steal from; so the thieves, shills, and corrupt money changers went elsewhere.

While the inspection process remained much the same throughout Ellis Island's history, the quota system and the visa application process already weeded out most of those who might be excluded. Two full years before they were granted their visas, Shura, his mother, and Aunt Ruth were required to undergo complete physicals in Germany. On August 21, 1923, they were examined by a doctor in Bremen. The examining physician filled out the first of several medical certificates required by the U. S. Immigration Service. At the time of the first exam, Jennie was thirty-five years old, her sister Ruth was thirty-three, and Shura (by then known as Geshua) was nine. The document stated that Jennie and Ruth spoke both Russian and German; it certified than none of the three had a "contagious, disgusting or deadly disease, mental illness, idiocy, dementia, tuberculosis, heart disease, venereal or skin disease, disease of the head or nails, trachoma or any other disease of the eye." The certificate also attested that the family did not suffer from any physical disabilities, and that none was crippled or had "crippled parts." The form ended with the most peculiar question: "Is he/she pregnant?" The doctor answered "No" for all three applicants.[2]

Eugene remembered the day at Ellis Island well.[3] He remembered that the SS *America* anchored some distance off the island and that they had to take a barge from the ship to the immigration station. He remembered that there were thousands of people lined up on the dock by number. Everyone seemed to be ahead of them, and the waiting increased their apprehension. Some years before, when immigration was at its height, an immigrant in a similar cue feared "the country would be full before they got to the head of the line." The immigrants were then led to the reception building where they climbed the stairs on the side of the building to enter the great hall. Although Eugene was unaware of it at the time, the examination had already begun. The climbing of the stairs was part of the test for entry. Immigrants who seemed unusually winded or tired, or who gave any evidence of a limp after the climb were marked for further examination.[4] In fact, climbing the stairs was the only physical test that most immigrants had to take.

The Grand Hall was the largest room Eugene had ever seen. He couldn't believe how huge it was. Here they encountered the first medical examiners. These inspectors looked for any obvious mental or physical defects. The scalp and throat were checked, as were the hands and neck. The doctors were quick to recognize contagious diseases, and a once-over was usually enough to spot anyone who might be infected.[5] After the first doctors examined him, another inspector checked his eyes and pulled up his eyelids to look underneath. For a brief time he was separated from his mother and stripped for a complete examination that included an inspection for lice. A lot of time was spent waiting in line or sitting on hard benches. Some of the smaller examining rooms and hallways had murals depicting scenes from American history, one of which portrayed the driving of the golden spike at a place that Eugene would later learn was Promontory, Utah.[6]

After the physical came the part that the immigrants feared the most: the verbal examination by an immigration officer. Over the years the number of questions that immigrants were required to answer had gradually increased. In 1925 there were thirty-six items on the questionnaire, including many questions that had been added after the "Red Scare" to weed out potential anarchists and social revolutionaries. The complete transcripts of the answers given by Jennie and "Geshua" Zheleznykov, and Rhlr (Ruth) Rothaus have been located. The Family History Library in Salt Lake City contains many such records, but these are particularly revealing. The landing of the SS *America* on 16 October 1925, is contained in film roll #1755479. The SS *America* is the second ship documented on the film. The page recording their arrival has a large handwritten 7 on it, and is stamped #188. The entries for Jennie Zheleznykov and her family are the last, or nearly the last, passenger entries in the registry for that day. Eugene was correct, the Zheleznykovs were among the last processed and must have spent a lot of time waiting. It seems that Jennie, Ruth, and Geshua (Eugene) were all questioned together as a family with Jennie supplying most of the answers. This is clear from handwritten notations that frequently stated, "Same as for sister." The form also provides specific details about the new Americans.[7]

On the day she arrived in New York, Jennie Zheleznykov was thirty-seven years of age and listed her marital status as "Widow." Her occupation was listed as "Housewife," and she claimed to be able to read Russian and German. Her nationality was listed as Russian and her race as "Hebrew." She was five feet tall and had a fair complexion. Her hair was black, her eyes were brown, and her place of birth was "Doblen," Latvia. On line #12 Jennie had to name and provide a complete address of the nearest relative or friend in her native country. She wrote: "Brother-in-law, Perezman Altnz/Latvia." The visa she carried was stamped #109 and was issued at Bremen, 30 September 1925. Line #17 asked whether she was in possession of 50 dollars or less, if less, how much? Jennie answered 26 dollars. Line #19 asked if she would join a relative or friend, and to provide his name, relationship, and complete address. Jennie answered: "Brother: Samuel Rothaus, 3369 E. 169th Street, NY, NY." When asked why she had come to the United States she replied: "Freedom." When asked if she ever planned to return to the country of her birth she replied: "Never." When asked how long she intended to remain in America she replied: "Always."

The same records show that Ruth Rothaus was 36. A penciled notation said that she was the sister of Jennie. Most of the lines in the form simply say "ditto" or "same as for sister." The lines unique to Ruth reveal that she was unmarried and was five feet two inches in height, two inches taller than her older sister. On Line #7 for occupation Ruth had listed: "Tailor." Like Jennie, her hair was black, her eyes were brown, and her place of birth was "Doblen," Latvia. Eugene's form listed him as "Geshua Zeleznikoff," and a penciled note in the margin said: "Child of Jennie." He was nine years of age, had no occupation, and was 4 feet 6 inches tall. His complexion was fair, and his eyes were brown. Unlike his mother and aunt whose hair was black, Geshua's hair was listed as brown. His place of birth was Alexandrovsk, Russia.

All three forms were completed for lines 21 through 28. These were the dreaded "questions of exclusion." A wrong answer on any one of them would be cause for deportation. The questions were mandated by acts of Congress, and the only tricky question was number twenty-five: "Have you been promised a job?" Many immigrants had indeed been promised jobs by relatives and friends, but Congress had forbidden the importation of foreign contract laborers, and all immigrants knew that the only correct answer was "No." The crucial section for Jennie, Ruth, and Geshua reads:

21: Have you ever been in prison or an almshouse or institution for care and treatment of the insane or supported by a charity? . . . . No

22: Are you a polygamist? . . . . No

23: Are you an anarchist? . . . . No

24: Do you believe or advocate the overthrow by force or violence of the government of the United States? . . . . No

25: Have you been promised a job or are you here by reason of any offer, solicitation, promise, or agreement expressed or implied to labor in the United States? . . . . No

26: Have you ever been previously deported? . . . . No

27: What is your general health? . . . . Good[8]

Question 28 covered the same gamut of potentially exclusatory maladies that appeared on their visa application exam in Bremen. The questions were perfunctory, and, for the most part, were childishly transparent. The absurdity of having to ask them at all would have been comical were it not for the serious demeanor of the questioner. Still, it is hard to imagine the hapless immigrant who would openly declare that he was "an insane contract laborer and anarchist who was entering the country for the purpose of overthrowing the U. S. government, even though he was blind, crippled, and had a hideous disfiguring disease."

At the end of the questioning, the officer took a rubber stamp from a box on his desk and brought it down quickly on an ink pad and then onto the three forms in rapid succession. The stamp read: "APPROVED." They were lucky, only 10,224 eastern European Jews would be allowed to immigrate to America that year, down from over 120,000 only five years before.[9] All the immigrants were then directed to another floor where they turned in the clothes they were wearing in exchange for fresh clothing. They showered, dressed, and then returned by barge to the ship for the night. Why the inspectors confiscated their clothing is unknown. It was an unusual precaution, but occasionally the doctors would confiscate personal items when there was concern about the spread of contagion among the passengers.

It was a widely told story that the streets of America were paved with gold, but Shura's mother had told him over and over again that they would have to work hard if they were to succeed in their adopted country. The following morning on the afterdeck of the SS *America,* a photo was taken of the Zheleznykovs, the Racond family, and other shipboard acquaintances. Sometime later the photo was put in the family album and Eugene scribbled a telling note in a childlike scrawl. The inscription made it clear that Eugene had no illusions about what awaited them:

> "WE COME TO AMERICA, OCTOBER 17, 1925.
> WE ARE VERY HAPPY THAT WE ARE HERE,
> BUT NOT THAT WE HAVE TO WORK SO HARD."

The SS *America* was towed to Pier 48 in New York harbor, where Eugene's Uncle Samuel Rothaus was waiting. Sam had sponsored Jennie, Ruth, and Eugene's entry into the United States. The meeting was happy and tearful. It was the first time that Jennie and Sam had seen each other in over thirty-two years. Ruth was only three years old when Sam left Latvia, and she hardly remembered her brother. Of course "Geshua" had never met him at all, but he had dreamed for so long of the day he would finally meet "Uncle Sam" that it was almost like greeting an old friend. On the ride from the port, Samuel described some of his life. He had worked as a laborer for a time, then as a plumber, and then as a general contractor. But after his eldest son's graduation from school, he went into partnership with him in a drugstore, a business they had started just shortly before the Zhelezynokovs' arrival. Samuel took the excited new arrivals to his home in the Bronx, where he and his wife lived with their five sons and one daughter. During the ride, Eugene stared in disbelief at the towering buildings and the crowded streets of New York City. Nothing that he had imagined came close to what he was seeing.

The next few weeks were busy ones. Jennie and Aunt Ruth almost immediately began looking for work in New York City's "garment district." Eugene's mother found a job as a seamstress with one company and his Aunt Ruth got work as a tailor with another. Both were soon toiling for twelve hours a day in the shops. It was mid-October and school had already been in session for more than a month. It was important that Shura be enrolled at once if he were to avoid being kept back. Uncle Sam looked at the tiny boy in his European-style short pants and shook his head doubtfully. He knew from the experiences of his own children how cruel others could be to new immigrants. He also knew exactly what had to be done. The first thing Uncle Sam did was take the boy to a store and buy him a suit of American clothes. He then told Eugene's mother that she "was never to put her son in short pants again." Then Sam counseled his nephew on how important it was to become "Americanized" in every way as soon as possible. He would have to work on his language and his accent. Everything had to change if he were to succeed in America. Uncle Sam's wise counseling was taken to heart. Shuraska Yakovlivitch Zhelezynkov—"Little Shura"—the Russian refugee, was quickly relegated to the past. The boy who confidently walked into P.S. 40 on Monday morning, 26 October 1925, was now Eugene Jelesnik.

Eugene remembers Uncle Sam's wife, Mamie, who was self-deluded into believing that she was a great cook. Shortly after they moved in with the family, Mamie spent all day preparing her special soup. She gave Eugene a steaming bowl of the creation, which he thought was the worst stuff that he had ever tasted. But Eugene was well-brought-up and had been taught to be polite. He pretended to eat the soup until his aunt left the room. At that moment he leapt to the sink and dumped the soup down the drain, returning to the table with a spoonful that he ate with mock relish when his aunt returned. She was so pleased and flattered that Eugene had liked the dish that she served him an extra helping.

After staying with Uncle Sam Rothaus and his family for several weeks and learning the layout of the city, Sam helped the family find temporary lodgings nearby. Jennie, Aunt Ruth, and Eugene would share a small apartment in the Bronx for their first six months in America. It had at least one plus to recommend it. The flat was in the same building where another of Jennie's sisters, Aunt Johanna Hatkin, lived with her husband, Samuel, and their two boys—then nine and fourteen. The families frequently had dinner together. Eugene remembers the Hatkin family well: "Sam Hatkin was a lithographer—a printer. He was a wonderful man, very religious, and most devout in the Jewish faith. He made sure that I attended the synagogue regularly and observed all of the Jewish customs."

These were happy times for young Eugene who—as he had in Germany—quickly made friends with other boys at school and in his neighborhood. It was also an exciting time to live in New York City. It was the middle of "The Roaring Twenties," the era of the "The Charleston," "flappers," and the Ziegfeld Follies. Nineteen twenty-five was the year that the Roxy and other great movie houses were built to accommodate huge new audiences for the silent films. On the stage were many attractions including the musicals *Sally; Blossom Time; Rose Marie;* and *Showboat.* Baseball fans had three stadiums: Ebbits Field for the Dodgers, The Polo Grounds for the Giants, and the new Yankee Stadium ("The House that Ruth Built") for the Yanks. The sporting world was also excited about the completion of Madison Square Garden on Eight Avenue between 49th and 50th Streets. Though the Zheleznykovs, now the Jelesniks, never got caught up in the peculiar American mania for baseball and could not then afford the theater, Eugene remembers being taken to Madison Square Garden to see his very first circus.

Sometime in early 1927, the family moved to another apartment in a tenement house at 1436 Crotona Park East. It was a cold-water flat, on the 6th floor—a walk-up with no elevator. The only convenience was a hallway dumbwaiter for ice deliveries. In the summer, the rooms were excruciatingly hot, and in the winter, freezing cold. Through this time Eugene continued to practice his violin. The walls were thin and everyone on the floor could hear him practicing. It was an unusual compliment that no one to his memory ever told him to quiet down. The family had by this time acquired a secondhand radio, and Eugene recalled that they never missed the opera broadcasts on Sunday afternoons.

Eugene vividly remembers the morning of 13 June 1927. That was the day the city honored the man who had flown solo across the Atlantic Ocean. The entire world recognized the importance of Charles A. Lindbergh's crossing, and everyone wanted to see him. For thousands of immigrants who knew that a voyage across the Atlantic took more than a week, the feat was particularly impressive, and the Jelesniks were no different: "My mother took me down to Broadway to see the parade. It was incredible. It was amazing. I was just able to see him go by in an open car."

Uncle Sam Hatkin continued to tutor Eugene in the Jewish faith. Through the early months of 1927, Sam prepared his nephew for his bar mitzvah. At the age of thirteen, he was formally recognized by his Jewish congregation, confirming that he had entered manhood and was a member of the Jewish faith. It was a great occasion, and all of Eugene's uncles, aunts, and cousins gathered to celebrate. He was photographed wearing the prayer shawl and hat required of all Jewish men when in a synagogue. He was given his silver ceremonial confirmation wine cup, engraved with his initials and the Star of David. Eugene Jelesnik was now officially a man.

Eugene made the transition from grade school into junior high, attending New York Public School No. 61, where he began to take his music much more seriously. Mr. Wuckerer was in charge of the music and physical education programs at the school and was also the organizer of the school's orchestra. The teacher immediately recognized Eugene's drive and talent, and took him under his wing. He advised the boy to focus on his music and to avoid heavy contact sports for fear of injury. The principal of the school, Mr. Maguire, also took a keen interest in P.S. 61's new prodigy, and the two quickly became fast friends. Eugene's other memory of junior high school was of a very pretty biology teacher who sometimes helped him with his lessons after school.

Some months after the Jelesniks moved to the flat on Crotona Park East, Mrs. Davidoff, the elderly woman they had met on the ship, came by for a visit. She told Jennie and Eugene that she had arranged for him to meet her friend Max Schlossberg, who played first trumpet with the New York Philharmonic. Eugene was to bring his violin with him so that the musician could hear him play. Jennie accompanied her son to the informal audition. Schlossberg was a renowned music teacher. He was the founder of the "Schlossberg Method of Instruction" still used for trumpet by many music academies. Schlossberg had a great ear for recognizing potential. He listened to Eugene and was so impressed by the boy's drive, talent, and concentration that he suggested a way that Eugene might be able to receive first-class violin lessons. The New York Philharmonic offered a very limited number of scholarships to promising students who showed unusual musical talent. The scholarship came through the New York City school system, and Eugene would first have to apply through the schools to qualify. He would then have to undergo a formal audition before the man who selected the violin students for the program, Hans Lange, the assistant concertmaster of The New York Philharmonic Orchestra. Mrs. Davidoff helped the Jelesniks apply for the program, and with the additional help of his friends Maguire and Wuckerer, he quickly received the endorsement of the school system. Max Schlossberg then arranged for the audition with Hans Lange.

After practicing several pieces to perfection, Eugene gave his audition for Mr. Lange. Less than four years after first touching the instrument, and less than two years after arriving in the United States, Eugene Jelesnik had a scholarship to study violin under the private instruction of Hans Lange himself. The scholarship also included classes in music theory and harmony with Winthrop Sargeant, the French horn player with the symphony and later the music critic of the *New Yorker* magazine. For the Jelesniks, the scholarship was proof that America was not only the land of opportunity but also the place where dreams come true.

Hans Lange was a very strict, serious, and demanding tutor. If the boy did not know the assigned lesson perfectly, Lange would not bother to teach him, but would send Eugene home with the instruction not to return until he had mastered the material. If he made even the smallest of slips, his instructor would verbally abuse him. Many of the pieces were far more difficult than anything that Eugene had attempted before. The boy quickly realized what he was up against. In order to keep up with the formal lessons of Hans Lange, Eugene would have to have private lessons, and these he would have to pay for himself. The Jelesniks then arranged to have an additional lesson once a week from another violinist in the symphony, Morris Kreiselman.

Kreiselman's personality was the opposite of Lange's. He was a warm and generous man, as well as a brilliant musician, and Kreiselman soon became the boy's confidant and musical mentor. Eugene always felt that he learned more from the understanding and patient Kreiselman than from the quick-tempered and overbearing Lange. Eugene recalled that both Winthrop Sargeant and Hans Lange would frequently refer to the contrasting technique and styles of violinists Mischa Elman and Jascha Heifetz. While the names were familiar as great musicians, Eugene had never actually heard either of them play. Then one day Morris Kreiselman mentioned that Mischa Elman was giving a recital that weekend at Carnegie Hall and that Eugene really ought to hear him. The matinee recitals only cost fifty cents for seats way up in the back of the hall. It was high art at a bargain basement price, and so Eugene decided to go. Just as seeing Lindbergh had been impressive, hearing Elman was a thrill, and the memory of the experience was vividly impressed on Eugene's mind.

It was a Saturday, sometime in the spring of 1928. Eugene took the subway to the concert hall. He arrived early enough that he was able to get a seat in the front row of the highest balcony. From the moment that Elman began to play, Eugene recognized what a true genius he really was. So vivid was the memory of the recital that Eugene still remembered the program nearly sixty years later: "He knocked me off my feet. I was completely bowled over. He played Mendelssohn's violin concerto. I identified with his method of playing immediately. I was not as good as Mischa Elman, that was certain, but what he put into his music was something very personal. You could tell how much he loved the music, and how much he felt it. It was incredible. Elman was an excellent technician but he also had soul."[10]

After a sustained ovation, Elman returned to the stage and performed an encore. By coincidence it was a piece that was already one of Eugene's favorites, "The Meditation" from the opera *Thais*, by Jules Massenet. From that day on, when Eugene wasn't involved with three weekly violin lessons, going to school, or practicing, he was working a variety of odd jobs to earn money to attended as many concerts as he could. For a hard-earned fifty cents he would sit in the balcony week after week and hear the finest musicians of the day; and though he heard all the great violinists, including Jascha Heifetz and Yehudi Menuhin, Mischa Elman would remain his favorite. It was therefore ironic that he would meet Heifetz long before he met Elman. It was after a radio concert at NBC that Eugene went backstage and told the manager that he was a violinist and was wondering if he might ask the great Heifetz some questions. Heifetz had a reputation as being somewhat distant, so Eugene was very much surprised when he was quickly ushered into the presence of the world's most acclaimed violinist. Somehow Heifetz got the impression that Eugene was interested in how Heifetz took care of his instrument. He showed Eugene how he wrapped his violin carefully in a silk scarf before enclosing it in its case. He told Eugene that the silk not only protected the instrument from moisture but preserved the natural oils of the wood. It was a little tip that Eugene always followed from that day on, and silk scarves would become as much a part of Eugene's accoutrements as batons and bandannas.

Although Eugene was deeply emersed in the study of classical music, he never lost his passion for the Gypsy music that had first enthralled him as a child. In the Yorkville neighborhood of New York, along Eighty-sixth Street, there were a number of Hungarian restaurants. Eugene did not particularly like the food, but the music was pure Gypsy, and he frequented the establishments as often as he could. There, amid the smell of charred green

peppers, garlic, and steaming goulash, violinists in bright bandannas strolled between the tables—no doubt covered with red
and white checkered tablecloths—and poured forth their souls. Of
the music Eugene would comment: "In Hungarian Gypsy music
there are no mentors or teachers. You either have it or you don't.
Gypsy music is a unique art—it comes entirely from within. It can
be fast and exotic, slow and romantic, or, at times, even morose."

Eugene had a scholarship to study at the Philharmonic, but
the family still had to struggle to stay alive, to pay the rent, eat,
and have clothing to wear. His mother and Aunt Ruth worked
long hours at their jobs in the garment district. For most Jewish
working women it was the only place they could find employment, and the conditions in the sweatshops were notoriously bad.
Most workers huddled over sewing machines hour after hour in
poorly lit rooms amid the deafening whirl of hundreds of sewing
machines. It was not an easy life, and for many it was their doom.
In 1911, at least 125 immigrant garment workers—mostly Jewish
and Italian women—had burned to death in the infamous
"Triangle Shirtwaist Fire."[11] That tragedy had led to the adoption
of one of the strictest fire safety codes in the nation, but the wages
and working conditions in the sweatshops remained wretched.

From their earliest days in New York, Eugene had taken any
jobs he could to help out. One of his first jobs was working after
school for a neighborhood laundry. Eugene remembered: "My job
was to make coffee for the owner in the morning and to deliver
laundry to the various tenements in the neighborhood in the afternoon and then collect the money from the customers. It wasn't an
easy job, carrying heavy packages of clothing up all those stairs.

"One time I took laundry to a woman named Ethyl Kelly. She
lived on the fourth or fifth floor of a brownstone. She opened the
door, and she was in this robe. She invited me in and directed me
where to place the laundry. I put it where she told me, and when I
turned around and was about to ask her for the money . . . well,
she was nude. Completely naked! She'd taken her robe off and
was just standing there. I was so shocked I was shivering. Then
she asked me if I would like a glass of milk or something. I just
turned and bolted out of there as fast as I could."

Eugene had always enjoyed contact with people. He was fascinated by the interchange of goods and services. The art of barter, trade, and salesmanship was as much a part of his makeup as was his passion for Gypsy music. Eugene's next job was at I. Harlem Pawn Shop on 8th Avenue and 39th Street.

"I. Harlem's was in a pretty bad area, a very transient population. My job was in the used clothing department. But it was a strange clientele. I remember a guy who came in with two different colored shoes on. There were a lot of bizarre characters. I became such a fantastic salesman that I could sell anybody, anything, no matter the size. When I took customers to the mirror, I knew just how to grab the back of the suit and gather in just enough material to make it seem to fit at the front. If he was a size forty, I could sell him a thirty-eight or a forty-four. I found I had the ability to sell things to people whether they wanted them or not. I was so good at it that when I finally quit they didn't want to let me go."

But as talented as he was at hawking ill-fitting clothing and escaping the amorous invitations of lonely ladies, Eugene's real talent was music, and from his earliest days in America he found ways to make extra money with his violin. One of his first afternoon jobs was playing in small orchestras for silent movies at theaters in the Bronx. Eugene had never seen a movie until he came to the United States, but within a year he was accompanying Rudolph Valentino in "The Sheik." When the movies went talkie in 1927, the need for pit orchestras was greatly reduced, so he got a part-time job in the projection booth, synchronizing the giant transcription discs to the film running through the projector.

All during the period while he was going to school, Eugene and Gertrude Rothaus, the wife of Eugene's cousin Harry, had a weekly fifteen-minute program on radio station WGBS. Gertrude was an accomplished pianist, and she accompanied Eugene in playing selections of light classical music. The radio station was in Brooklyn, and the small stipend they received barely covered their subway fare. But Eugene never turned down any offer to play, no matter the fee or how scant the audience.

As a young musician, he would frequently perform at charity

functions. One of the more interesting characters of the time was a philanthropist named Robert Spiro. He was not a relative, but everyone knew him as "Uncle Robert." Spiro believed that the importance of the family unit was being undermined by long hours of work and the ever-increasing brutality of industrialized society. He saw that respect for the older generation was eroding as families were being torn apart by the struggle to earn a living. To counter the trend, Spiro worked to found a national holiday, which he called "Parents' Day." This was the forerunner of Mother's Day, and later Father's Day, and for three years, with the help of Eugene, he produced free summer concerts in Central Park to promote the idea. Eugene dutifully performed every year in Spiro's extravaganzas, and though he was never given a dime for his efforts, it was good exposure. Eugene was the highlight of the program, and the event often drew crowds in excess of 20,000.

While he was still in junior high school, Eugene organized and directed a small ensemble called the Continental Trio with Eugene on the violin, George Walters on the cello, and Phillip Green on the piano. They performed initially at dinner parties, bar mitzvahs, and school functions but gradually added restaurants, cabarets, and radio performances to their schedule as they got better. The International Trio continued to perform together after Eugene moved on to James Monroe High School where he also maintained his busy schedule of private music lessons. The trio performed for conventions at the Astor Hotel, and once a week for fifteen minutes on radio station WMCA. When Eugene was a senior in high school he formed "The Russian Echoes Radio Ensemble." George Walters was the only holdover. The ensemble consisted of two mandolins, cello, and violin, and they performed only Russian music. Unlike his other groups, the ensemble played exclusively on the radio—primarily for a station in the Bronx. Eugene described what was behind all the feverish activity: "I was never afraid in New York. I loved all the people. I mingled with them, I became one of them. I went about my business and began immediately the task of making a name for myself, in school, out of school, you name it. And the fact that I was active in school circles with my music gave me the chance to perform before audiences, and I was quickly performing in the professional circles as well. After establishing the Continental Trio, I began to play for bar mitzvahs, weddings, parties, anything. I did all that to help my mother. That was my primary goal, to contribute to the support of the household. Those times were hard, and it was constantly a struggle. I wasn't making much money, but I kept going and kept going. I did everything I could. I auditioned, I played odd jobs, I was constantly trying to improve, and I continued to practice, practice, practice."

When Eugene was only fifteen years old he was highlighted in a remarkable story in a Bronx newspaper. The feature-length photo article not only described his career but his hopes for the future.

IMMIGRANT YOUTH PRACTICES VIOLIN LESSONS FOUR HOURS EACH DAY AND DREAMS OF FAME

Eugene Jelesnik, 1161 Straford Ave., near Westchester Ave., someday may win world-wide acclaim as a violinist. So say teachers at school and all who have heard him draw his bow across the strings of his violin.

Eugene himself believes his dream someday will come true, for, although only 15 years old, he is already the author of "The Gypsy's Dream," a composition for the violin, which has won very favorable mention from many musicians.

Eugene was born in Alexandrovsk, Russia. His parents possessed all the Old World's love for music. His father died about seven years ago, and his mother, Mrs. Jennie Jelesnik, left Russia shortly afterwards. After spending two years in Germany, Mrs. Jelesnik and her son, now beginning to lean towards music as a career, departed for the United States.

It was not until five years ago that Eugene began to study the violin in earnest, and in six months he had definitely made up his mind about a musical career and was giving weekly concerts through a local radio station.

At the same time he did not neglect his general education, and although he has been only five years in the country, speaks English fluently and is a member of the graduating class at Junior High School 61, Charles St. and Crotona Park East.

He is now the proud possessor of a new violin, which he bought himself with the money he earned by working all last summer, and hopes some day to own a Cremona, or maybe one fashioned by Stradavari himself—but all that belongs to the future.

Recently Eugene gave the first of a series of eight concerts in the auditorium of the school for the student body and all the members of the staff. He is the concertmaster of the school's thirty-five-piece orchestra, and has organized a string trio, which makes radio and professional appearances. At the age of fifteen he organized The International Trio. He has also been the assistant director of the orchestra for three years, ever since he was singled out for his industry and his love of music.

Edward R. Maguire, principal of the school, also has taken an interest in the boy's career, and feels that Eugene is bound to succeed because his love of playing is so great and his ambition so strong.

As for the future, he plans to complete his high school course, then to play in a symphony orchestra of one of the larger theaters until he has had practice enough to make public appearances on the concert stage.

He hopes then, by the end of twelve years, to have made enough money here to complete his musical education in Europe. And then? Eugene says he will attain his highest ambition—to be a famous conductor of one of the world's greatest orchestras.[12]

Though Eugene's "highest ambition" was to be realized some years in the future, there were certain things that he wanted to accomplish immediately, and though he appreciated classical music, he was never an elitist when it came to the performing arts. He loved all forms of entertainment: the symphony, the circus, popular music, the opera, and vaudeville. He was young; his life was ahead of him; there seemed no reason why he couldn't become an accomplished artist in all of these disparate and seemingly contradictory entertainments. Eugene's real ambition was to do everything. In 1931 his chances of one day becoming an opera star must have seemed better than his chances of ever appearing in vaudeville. The same "talkies" that had helped to wipe out the orchestras in movie theaters, and had sent Eugene from the pit to the projection booth, were helping to bring down the curtain on vaudeville. By the late 1920s vaudeville was well past its prime. The advent of

talking motion pictures heralded by Warner Brothers' 1927 production of *The Jazz Singer*, starring Al Jolson, cast long shadows
across many areas of the entertainment business. The "talkies" not
only sounded the death knell of the silent film and pit orchestras,
but the whole arrangement of independent theaters throughout the
country. This in turn helped kill vaudeville. By 1932 all movies
were being produced as talkies, and by then many of vaudeville's
greatest performers had already abandoned the stage for the silver
screen. Jack Benny, Fred Allen, Sophie Tucker, Edgar Bergen, Rudy
Vallee, George Burns and Gracie Allen, plus hundreds of others
were leaving vaudeville to play in Vitaphone and Warner Brothers
"shorts." Radio also played a part in killing vaudeville. The same
performers who flocked to make movies were also regulars over
the airwaves. With the organization of the National Broadcasting
Company in 1926, and Columbia Broadcasting System in 1928, the
audience for radio increased fivefold in less than two years.[13]

The stock market crash of 1929 and the Great Depression that
followed brought about theater failures, corporate consolidations,
and sell-offs. As the unemployment rate climbed to twenty-five
percent, the audiences dried up. Eugene Jelesnik seems to have
been largely unaffected by the stock market crash and its devastating consequences: "I didn't understand any of it. We didn't
have any stocks, and so we didn't lose any money. There was no
reason for us to jump out of any tall buildings. We were already
on the bottom rung. I remember the soup lines and the trouble
people had finding work, but as a musician I wasn't affected by
the depression very much. Wages were low but there always
seemed to be work. Besides, I never had any doubt that I would
one day succeed."

In 1930 and 1931, movie studios and their subsidiaries began
to produce unit shows and tour them to the ever-growing list of
failed theaters they acquired after the crash. RKO, Warner
Brothers, and Paramount Publix began producing vaudeville as
packaged shows. It was the last gasp of the art form and ultimately was its doom. But Eugene Jelesnik desperately wanted to
become a part of it before it was gone entirely, and in 1931 and
1932, he made two extensive East Coast tours with Paramount

1. Eugene's father, the prosperous sugar and molasses merchant, Yakov (Jacob) Israelevitch Zheleznykov

2. Eugene's parents, Jacob and Jennie Zheleznykov.

3. Eugene's little brother, Boris Jacob Zheleznykov.

4. Eugene with hobby horse about 1916.

5. The Zheleznykovs in Alexandrovsk, March 1917.
Jennie, Aunt Ruth (standing), "Little Shura" (Eugene), and Jacob.

6. Eugene in Ukrainian peasant garb.

7. Eugene and Jennie in merchant class costume (note buttons).

8. Jennie in rich furs with her little Cossack.

9. Eugene seated between Aunt Ruth (left) and one of his governesses (right). Jennie is in chair, behind "Little Shura."

10. Eugene on picnic in Burgerpark, Bremen, shortly after their arrival in Germany. Eugene is standing (left). Aunt Ruth and Jennie are 2nd and 3rd from right.

11. Eugene (front right) and his first friends. Bremen, Germany, 1924.

12. Aunt Ruth, Eugene, and Jennie. Bremen, Germany, 1924.

13. Eugene and his first violin. Bremen, 1924.

14. Eugene and Jennie. Bremen,
14 January 1925.

15. The Jelesniks arrive in New York harbor aboard the SS *America*, 17 October 1925.
Eugene is in front row, left, holding life preserver. Inscription on back of photo reads:
"We came to New York and we are happy that we are here, but not that we have to work so hard."

16. Eugene in his Bar Mitzvah prayer shawl at his
Uncle Sam Hatkin's house, 1927.

17. Eugene performing in Central Park for
"Parents Day." The man standing, left, is
"Uncle Robert" Spiro, the event's founder.

18. Eugene's first orchestra: the Continental Trio. Left to right: Jelesnik, George Walters, and pianist Phil Greene.

19. Eugene in the early thirties. Belmont Bar, New York City.

20. Eugene's first marquee, Loew's Ziegfeld Theater, 1933.

21. One of Eugene's early radio orchestras, the "Russian Echoes,"
played European folk music from a Bronx station.

22. In 1935. Eugene Jelesnik and his Continentals performing live over WHN Radio
from the Holland Hotel shortly before his "discovery" by Sophie Tucker.

23. Jennie Jelesnik poses before portrait of her son shortly after he became an "MCA Artist."

24. Marquee at the Hollywood Restaurant when Eugene opened with Sophie Tucker, April 1935.

25. Eugene and Sophie Tucker at entrance way to Hollywood Restaurant.

26. A suave and debonair Eugene, c. 1935.

27. Marquee at Café Venezia where Jelesnik played for the "3 Racketcheers."

28. Milton Berle and Eugene at Hollywood Restaurant, 1935.

29. Jelesnik's Continental Orchestra in publicity shot in Western attire, atop the Hotel Utah, March 1938.

30. The Continentals back up Eugene as he and Virginia take their vows into the telephone at the Ambassador Hotel in Salt Lake City, 1938.

31. Eugene's NBC television program *Gypsy Moods* broadcasting live from Rockefeller Center, Studio 8-H, 1940.

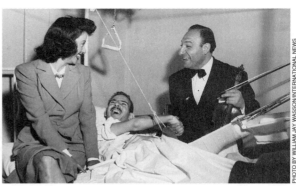

32. Eugene and Virginia during the period of his USO tours to Italy at the close of World War II.

33. Jelesnik entertaining wounded soldier at bedside, during a domestic tour, 1943.

34. Red Skelton sees Eugene off for his first USO tour, at Camp Patrick Henry, November 1944.

35. "The Three Abroad," Eugene's USO unit in Italy. Left to right: Irish folk singer and guitarist Bob Gilchrist, Jelesnik, and mind reader Jack Ber-Mar.

36. Eugene and sailors entertaining troops aboard ship bound for Europe. December 1944.

37. Gilchrist and Jelesnik entertain group of soldiers near the front, February 1945.

38. Eugene standing in front of army ambulance shortly before his encounter with the minefield.

39. Frank Sinatra, Eugene Jelesnik, and Phil Silvers in Venice, Italy, with the USO tour, June 1945.

40. Jennie, Eugene, and Aunt Ruth celebrate Eugene's return from Italy, August 1945.

41. Mrs. Vallee, Sid Fox, Rudy Vallee, and Eugene at KDYL, 1946.

42. Rep. Clare Booth Luce signs autograph on Eugene's violin. KDYL studios, 1946.

43. Gloria Swanson signs autograph on back of Eugene's violin at KDYL studios.

44. The two noses: Jimmy Durante and Eugene Jelesnik.

45. Dale Evans and Eugene exchanging copies of "The Nadocky" at Days of '47 celebration, July 1949.

46. Jelesnik and Jack Benny perform a violin duet at V.A. Hospital benefit.

47. Lowell Thomas delivers the news from KDYL Radio, 1950.

Publix as "Eugene Jelesnik, Wizard of the Gypsy Violin." Eugene loved touring and took to it immediately:

> It wasn't easy, but it was always exciting. I roomed with the other musicians who played in the acts. We usually spent a week in a town, but sometimes just three or four days on what was called a split week. We were booked out of New York but mostly played Pennsylvania, Ohio, and down the coast. When we got out of the theater it was usually late. We always ate dinner after midnight, and never went to bed until two or three in the morning. I loved it. It was always very exciting because each new audience was a challenge. And having to work a new audience every night teaches you a lot about what people like. My mother wasn't too pleased with my touring, but I knew that vaudeville in New York was dying off. I knew it was going under, and I wanted to be a part of it. In fact, I wanted to be a part of every facet of show business and learn as much as I could. In my vaudeville days I toured with a number of acts and even played background music for acrobats, jugglers, and balancing acts who used chairs and high ladders. Most of the time I played solo as my own act. I remember that they always had a number of old silent movie stars on the road. I toured with Vilma Banky, Charles Ray, and Agnes Ayers, who back in 1921 had starred with Rudolf Valentino in "The Sheik." A lot of actors and actresses from the movies toured on the Paramount Publix circuit making personal appearances. They didn't do anything, they just appeared.[14]
>
> I don't remember many of the towns. I do remember big floods in Stubenville, Ohio. It was one of the only times we ever canceled a performance. The streets were full of water.

By the spring of 1932, only New York's famed Palace Theater remained of the city's great two-a-day vaudeville houses. After several seasons of long runs, special shows, big bands, offbeat personalities, and gimmicks of every kind, the Palace added two extra daily shows and dropped prices for most seats to fifty cents.[15] But cheap vaudeville wasn't going to make it any better, and adding shows only split the tiny gate into ever-smaller portions. The competition was offering not only a better price, but a better product. At the Paramount Theater, just down the street from the Palace, audiences could not only see a film, but also Fred Astaire in a live version of his hit *The Band Wagon.* At the Capitol Theater, for one dollar, you not only got a movie but Burns and Allen, Arthur Tracey, and Cab Calloway's band. Loew's State Theater had a film, plus Smith and Dale, and a selection from the Broadway hit *Girl Crazy.* In the fall of 1932, the great vaudevillian and radio comic Fred Allen observed: "Vaudeville is dead. The acrobats, the animal acts, the dancers, the singers, and the old-time comedians have taken their final bows and disappeared into the wings of obscurity. For fifty years vaudeville was the popular entertainment of the masses. Nomadic tribes of nondescript players roamed the land. The vaudeville actor was part Gypsy and part suitcase. With his brash manner, flashy clothes, capes and cane, and accompanied by his gaudy womenfolk, the vaudevillian brought happiness and excitement to the communities he visited. [Now he's gone.]"[16]

Shortly after returning to New York following his last vaudeville tour, Eugene Jelesnik was invited to conduct the overture at the Paramount Theater. The guest appearance was a great honor. After all, that's where the great performers seemed to be going.

Sometime in 1931, after one of Eugene's radio broadcasts, someone mentioned something called "visual radio," or television. Eugene had never heard the term before, but was always interested in new developments in the industry. Mostly out of simple curiosity he began making inquiries about the new medium.

Utahn Philo T. Farnsworth had drawn the first schematics of the system that would make television possible while he was still a high school student in Rigby, Idaho, in 1923. By the mid-1920s he had secured patents on the working components of television cameras, transmitters, and receivers. In 1926, Farnsworth demonstrated his invention in San Francisco by transmitting and receiving a film loop of Mary Pickford and Douglas Fairbanks from the silent movie *The Taming of the Shrew.* It was a public relations coup. This was more than a year before the release of *The Jazz Singer,* and since radio was already a nationwide fad, many anticipated that sound and sight would quickly be linked. Overnight, Philo T. Farnsworth was a celebrity.[11]

By the late twenties, General Broadcasting Corporation, NBC, CBS, RCA, ABC, and Bell Labs were all convinced that "radio talkies" were the wave of the future and that huge profits were waiting for the first company to successfully overcome the enormous technical problems involved. Television was in its infancy, and teams of scientists from the competing networks were working feverishly to be the first to offer practical transmitters and sets.

Sam Pickford, vice president for CBS, was one of the far-sighted and imaginative pioneers who recognized both the potential and the problems of television. In an interview in the *New York Times* he outlined the coming age:

> Sam Pickford has returned from a survey of stations in the CBS network. He reports that the one question upon which all others hinge deals with television. The station owners all wonder what effect television will have on broadcasting? What will it cost to change over to television? Where are the programs going to come from? Mr. Pickford believes that television is destined to cause one of the most revolutionary scientific changes in entertainment and education that the world has ever seen. Television is expected to thrill the world, and he foresees the day when New Yorkers at home will watch pearl divers at work off the coast of Asia under the glare of an Indian sun.
>
> The broadcasters are wondering if they will all be tied together by wire lines to get television scenes from some central headquarters as they do with radio programs . . . or if they will be supplied with films mailed in advance—the way electronic transcriptions are now handled. This might be a boon to the film industry because it would take many a reel daily to entertain the invisible audience from coast to coast.[17]

But before Indian pearl divers could be seen clearly by viewers in Manhattan, there were huge problems to overcome, and the first was to make the thing work on a commercial scale. On 21 July 1931, CBS went on the air with its first experimental station W2XAB. Eugene Jelesnik's growing reputation in radio, and his expressed interest in the possibility of broadcasting "visual radio" over the airways soon brought him to the attention of the men at CBS who were then conducting experiments in their primitive television studio. One day in the late summer or early fall of 1931, Eugene received a call from one of the engineers at CBS who asked him if he would be interested in participating in a series of programs over W2XAB. Eugene told the engineer that of course he was interested. The engineer then told him the catch: "Well the first thing we want you to know is that we don't pay any money. We are just experimenting. We don't know what, if anything, is going to come out of it."

Eugene agreed to participate and they scheduled a time for him to perform from the W2XAB studio which was on the eighteenth floor of the CBS building. He was also told that if he wanted to invite anyone to the historic broadcast that they were welcome to attend. Eugene was very excited and invited his mother and Aunt Ruth to be his guests at his debut on television. When Eugene arrived in the studio, he was stunned to find that he was going to be performing in a tiny cubical. The room was only sixteen by eighteen feet, and if there were more than three people in the studio with instruments no one could even turn around. It was also impossible at that time to show more than one performer at a time as there was only one camera in the studio. Worse, Eugene's face had to be painted with dark purple makeup just to create an image on the screen.

The program was broadcast all the way from the eighteenth floor down to the sixth floor of the CBS building where a small audience of about twenty people including Eugene's mother and aunt stared at a tiny luminescent screen. The images were indistinct with big lines rolling through the picture. If the camera were moved back at all, the figure on the screen receded to little more than an indistinguishable dot. Up close, all that could be seen was the shadowy movement of Eugene's arm across the screen as he bowed his violin. At best, the broadcast occasionally showed half an arm and half an instrument. The visual and audio portions were broadcast on separate frequencies and there were occasional breaks where one or the other would go out entirely. Jennie and Aunt Ruth were confused by the whole exhibition and kept asking, "What is it? . . . What is it?" No one was certain.

Over the next couple of months Eugene Jelesnik gave other performances over W2XAB. By January, many of the initial problems had been ironed out. Transmissions could be clearly picked up as far away as Albany and focal length problems and imagery had been greatly improved. CBS felt confident enough about their system that they began to advertise their television programming in the newspapers. Since very few people actually had television-receivers, the advertisements routinely plugged the radio portion of the program separately. The ads promoted Eugene Jelesnik as much as they did the new novelty:

> On Thursday, January 7, 1932, over W2XB 9:30 Eugene Jelesnik Program.

> On January 17, 1932, TELEVISIONIST Eugene Jelesnik will appear Thursday evening, and will conduct a concert orchestra in a program of Gypsy music which will emanate from station WABC in a television broadcast. The program will be from 9:30 to 9:45. The moonlight sleepy time program over WHN will also be under the direction of Eugene Jelesnik, and on Friday night another program will also be under his direction.

> Saturday, January 23, 1932, Eugene Jelesnik, the Russian violinist who conducts the Internationalists as an instrumental ensemble will have as his guest artist Leonid Martor, Russian baritone, who will be seen and heard in a presentation of Russian and Gypsy songs on Thursday at 9:30 P.M. over W2XAB Television.

> Jan 28th 1932, over W2XAB Television Eugene Jelesnik and his Gypsy violin. 9:30 P.M.[18]

By April of 1932, the station could be clearly received in Chicago. Many of the makeup problems had also been solved—at least for the time being. The engineers found, for instance, that the complexion of performers greatly affected the clarity of the picture. Redheads seemed to come through best. Brunettes had to be treated with a heavy foundation of white, then cream, and finally the lips and eyes had to be shaded a dark brown. They found that some of the imaging problems could be solved by greatly increasing the intensity of the lighting. This would later cause enormous problems for performers, as the heat from the lights made studios unbearably hot. Early television musicians found their instruments going out of tune during performances, a problem that would plague television for decades to come. Eight years later Eugene would find that his ability to play the violin by ear was a major plus. As the instrument went out of tune under the heat of the studio lights, he was able to adjust his fingering to keep the melody in pitch. It was a talent that would serve him well when television became more than an experimental medium. Until then, Eugene was through with working like a lab animal in a tiny box for no pay. The experiments would continue, but the deepening worldwide economic depression was making it more and more unlikely that television would ever show a profit. In mid-1933, William Paley, president of CBS, was as sick of working for nothing as Eugene Jelesnik, and pulled the plug. His announcement on the cancellation of public broadcasts was terse but spoke volumes: "Further operation . . . offers little possibility of contribution to the art of television. It is however, our intention to resume our experimental transmission as soon as we are sufficiently satisfied that advanced equipment of a broader scope can be installed."

Eugene's role as one of TV's early guinea pigs has been largely forgotten. Philo T. Farnsworth would sell most of his important patents in order to finance his continuing research, and for many years David Sarnoff and others took the credit while the inventor of television went unrecognized for his achievement. In 1957 Farnsworth appeared on the TV hit show *I've Got a Secret* with host Garry Moore. None of the panelists could guess who he was or what he had done. For stumping the panel he was awarded fifty dollars.[19]

Each of Eugene's musical ensembles were formed with specific musical styles in mind: classical music, Gypsy music, Russian folk music, and light popular music. But it was not until he founded "Eugene Jelesnik's Continentals" that he had an orchestra versatile enough to play everything. The orchestra was first formed in late 1932, and quickly became Eugene's pride and joy. One of the elements that made Eugene's new orchestra so unique was the addition of Dick Marta and his cymbalom. The strange Hungarian instrument was a kind of horizontal harp and was played with hammers like a mountain dulcimer. The cymbalom was the perfect compliment to Eugene's Gypsy violin arrangements and became a permanent addition to the orchestra.

In early 1933, the new orchestra was booked at Loew's Ziegfeld

Theater in midtown Manhattan. The marquee sign promoted the film *One Sunday Afternoon* starring Gary Cooper and Fay Wray. The bottom of the marquee touted Eugene Jelesnik's Continentals as the featured live stage attraction. It was one of the first big performances of the band that would serve as Eugene's principal instrument for the next seven years. A flyer touting the event said:

> "Loew's Ziegfeld, 6th Ave. at 54th St.—
> Extraordinary Engagement!
> Friday, Saturday & Sunday, Oct. 13–15,
> the Dynamic Musical Sensation . . .
> JELESNIK AND HIS CONTINENTAL ORCHESTRA
> . . . playing nightly at 8:30 P.M. on the stage.[20]

During the summer of 1933, Jelesnik's Continental Orchestra was heard over a CBS hookup from the Show Boat Garden in Atlantic City. The ensemble then began playing weddings and other single bookings while it built its reputation with frequent radio performances. From April to November of 1934, Eugene and his new orchestra were featured at the Belmont Hotel in New York City, and in December at the Ritz Carlton Hotel's "Merry-Go-Round" in Atlantic City. The *Atlantic Evening News* of 31 December described the orchestra and the unusual setting:

JELESNIK'S GYPSY BAND POPULAR
AT THE RITZ CARLTON

The Merry-Go-Round bar, larger, gayer, and more entrancing than ever, is assuming new popularity in Atlantic City. Here Eugene Jelesnik and his orchestra hold forth for supper dancing. Not only does the popular maestro, well known to radio fans, play excellent dance music, but his greatest forte is his brilliant rendition of classical melodies, Gypsy songs, Hungarian, Italian, and Russian folk songs. His music adds new atmosphere to the Merry-Go-Round bar, which takes nine minutes to complete a revolution while a concealed hurdy-gurdy plays tinkley old barroom favorites.

Eugene continued to perform at the Ritz Carlton until the end of January. In February he was back in New York City playing a four-night-a-week booking at the dining room of the Holland Hotel in midtown Manhattan. The group also made frequent guest appearances at other venues. On 27 March 1935, his orchestra appeared at the Ziegfeld Theater for the "Midnight Follies," a huge musical review promoting some of the city's best orchestras and popular singers.

By April of 1935, Eugene Jelesnik and his Continental Orchestra were being broadcast live from the Holland Hotel over WHN radio. One evening, Sophie Tucker, the famous cabaret singer and the "last of the red hot mamas," came to the hotel to have dinner with some friends. Tucker (born Sophie Abuza), was, like Eugene, a Jewish Russian immigrant. One biography described her as "loud, lavish, brash, brassy, sexy, sassy, and just a little bit naughty."[21] Everything that Sophie did was on a grand and exuberant scale. Her costumes were always extravagant, and she had hundreds of them. She was one of the first female singers to demand and get huge fees for her performances, often claiming that she needed the money just to pay for her wardrobe. One of her costumes consisted of a 24-carat-gold-cloth gown, a white mink coat, and a diamond headdress. She boasted that she spent $50,000 for each new act, $25,000 alone on her dresses.[22] Her previous year had been a busy one and included a triumphant European tour, a divorce from her husband, her real-life rescue of a child from a runaway automobile, and a command performance before the King and Queen of England. Sophie was nothing if she wasn't newsworthy, and in that spring she was at the peak of her very public career.

Eugene and his eight-piece society orchestra were playing their usual set of dinner selections when Eugene decided to insert one of his more romantic Gypsy numbers. When the piece was finished, Eugene was summoned to the table of Sophie Tucker. She asked if he took requests, and when he replied, "Of course," she asked him to play "Come back to Sorrento" for her. Eugene obliged. After the orchestra had played several other requests, Miss Tucker asked Eugene his name, background, and a number of prying questions about the band and their bookings. After the gentle grilling she said: "You don't belong here. You should be playing at the Hollywood Restaurant on Broadway."

Eugene thanked her for the compliment. The Hollywood Restaurant was one of the most prestigious and largest cabaret venues in the city. It was a haunt of New York's most celebrated actors, singers, and performers as well as politicians, writers, and sports figures. But Miss Tucker was not making an idle compliment. She was serious about getting the orchestra booked at the Hollywood. She gave Eugene the number of the restaurant's owner, Joe Moss, and made Eugene promise her that he would call him the following day. "Tell Mr. Moss that Sophie Tucker asked you to call," she said.

That next day, Eugene called on Joe Moss, who told him that he had already been contacted by Miss Tucker. Moss said they were making arrangements and that he would get right back to him. Later that afternoon Eugene received a telegram from Joe Moss.

> APRIL 5, 1935 (Telegram)
> To: Eugene Jelesnik
>
> Be ready to play tomorrow night with the boys at 9 O'clock. Be in at 8:30. Please call Nat Moss when you receive this telegram.[23]
>
> (Signed) Joe Moss.

Eugene and his orchestra auditioned in front of a live crowd at the Hollywood Restaurant, during the nine to midnight slot that very evening. "We played our hearts out," Eugene said. "We played some light classical music and a lot of Hungarian tunes and Gypsy melodies by Ubay and others that I had picked up in Yorkville." The arrangements were perfect and the choice of music could not have been better. Mr. Moss was of Hungarian descent, and he was a great lover of Gypsy music. He recognized Eugene as a great artist of the form.

Eugene Jelesnik always insisted that he was discovered by Sophie Tucker. While it is probably true that Sophie Tucker opened the door to his successful professional career, it would not be accurate to say that it was a lucky break. There was nothing lucky about it. Eugene Jelesnik's early success came from continuous practice, exertion, struggle, and hard work. Behind that effort was a character trait that would serve Eugene throughout his life. Betty Davidoff had noticed it during their Atlantic passage. His jr. high school principal, Mr. Maguire, had noticed it and made a point of commenting about it in the newspaper interview. Max Schlossberg had seen it, as had his teachers, Richard Feller in Germany, Mr. Wuckerer at P. S. 61, Morris Kreiselman, Winthrop Sargeant, and even Hans Lange. They had all seen it.

Eugene Jelesnik was imbued with a fierce determination to succeed. That drive was behind the long hours of practice, the ceaseless auditions, the formation of a half-dozen musical ensembles, and the continual stream of small jobs. His determination coupled with his work ethic made success inevitable. Sooner or later Eugene was bound to be discovered, and if Sophie Tucker happened to be the one who brought his talent to the fore, she was the lucky one. At the Hollywood Restaurant, Eugene Jelesnik and his Continentals would bask in the limelight of the musical and entertainment capital of the world.

On 14 April 1935, two years after publishing his first composition, "My Gypsy Melody," Eugene Jelesnik and The Continentals opened a twelve-month engagement at the Hollywood Restaurant on Broadway between 47th and 48th streets. They were featured as part of the second edition of the cabaret's "Hollywood Revels of 1935," along with Estelle Taylor (soon to become the wife of boxer Jack Dempsey), Cass Daley, and Phil Nealy. The booking would lead to other engagements and close professional friendships with not only Sophie Tucker, but Ozzie Nelson, Jimmy Durante, Milton Berle, Rudy Vallee, and many other notable performers who would assist him in building his reputation and his career. It had been just over ten years since Eugene had first set foot on American shores, but Eugene Jelesnik had finally "arrived."

CHAPTER FOUR

THE HOLLYWOOD RESTAURANT

Eugene Jelesnik and his Continental Society Orchestra opened at the Hollywood Cabaret Restaurant the week of 14 April 1935. His band alternated playing sets with Rudy Vallee and his orchestra in three nightly shows at seven, midnight, and two A.M. They were featured as part of the second edition of the cabaret's "Hollywood Revels of 1935," which also showcased Sophie Tucker with pianist Ted Shapiro.[1]

The Hollywood, on Broadway between 47th and 48th streets, was a New York institution. Owner Joe Moss had been a pioneer of the city's cabaret theater scene. Fifteen years earlier he got the idea of combining musical revues from the Broadway stage with large-scale floor shows, à la the Ziegfeld Follies and acts from vaudeville. He took the shows out of their traditional theater settings and placed them in a large open arena surrounded by tiers of tables where he served patrons dinner and drinks. This was the age when movie stars frequently toured the country promoting their latest releases. Hollywood, California, was already the movie capital of the world, and its biggest stars were frequent visitors to New York. Moss recognized the potential draw of inviting the touring celebrities to the restaurant where they could enjoy a night on Broadway and at the same time promote their latest features. The name of his restaurant was in keeping with its movie star image. To keep the stars coming he packed his shows with beautiful women, dancing girls, and comely ingenues. The marquee out front unashamedly touted the attraction: "50 Gorgeous Girls, 50!"[2] The number of bachelor celebrities who met their match in the chorus lines of The Hollywood was legion. Moss took great pains to keep his acts fresh, and frequently changed his lineup of head-liners. By 1935 he was mounting four entirely new productions a year, each more extravagant than the last.

The European-style cabaret setting was a big part of the Hollywood Restaurant's attraction. For a very reasonable price ($1.50 on regular weekdays), patrons could eat dinner, enjoy a lavish show, and rub shoulders with some of the country's most well-known celebrities. Anyone who was anyone went to the Hollywood: politicians, sports figures, stars, starlets, gangsters, and journalists. The restaurant was a mecca for theater and movie reviewers, but it was particularly attractive to the gossip columnists and entertainment writers who made the Hollywood a regular part of their weekly beats. Then as now, "who was seen with whom" was the grist of the writers. The most notable columnists of the day: Ed Sullivan, Walter Winchell, Louis Sobol, Ted Friend, and Nick Kenny all had their own tables permanently reserved to view the comings and goings of the ever-changing cast of luminaries. The nightly clientele at the Hollywood was a living "Who's Who" of the entertainment industry, and the seating arrangement of the various celebrities was a major headache for the owner and particularly the headwaiter. In order to stay on top of the revolving social register, Joe Moss and his staff had to know not only who was in town on any given day, but their relative standing in the social pecking order. Ed Sullivan described a typical scene at the Hollywood Restaurant in his popular "Broadway" column in the *New York News*:

> The beamers and the mutterers and the mumblers were out in full force. In case you don't know, the beamers are those who sit at the ringside tables, the tables which really are pages in the social register of Broadway. They beam because they are in row A. The mutterers are those who miss the ringside tables and land in the second row. The mumblers are the occupants of all the tables beyond rows A and B, and the drone of their anguished voices can be heard in the stilly atmosphere. The mutterers and mumblers mutter and mumble for years at the injustice of the seating diagrams, which place them out in right field. Then overnight a mutterer or a mumbler writes a hit song, produces a hit play, or in some other way jimmys his body into

the spotlight. At the next big opening at the Hollywood the headwaiter seats the ex-mutterer or ex-mumbler at a ringside table, and immediately he becomes a beamer with all the privileges, rights, and honors due his newly acquired exalted station.[3]

In addition to the regular floor shows and quarterly revues, each Sunday was celebrity night at the Hollywood. These special evenings of entertainment were usually hosted by the headliner of the show. The first week that Eugene's orchestra appeared at the Hollywood they were included as part of a celebrity showcase hosted by Sophie Tucker. On hand were George Raft, Mary McCormic, George Bancroft, Bernice Claire, George Givot, and boxer Jack Dempsey. Dempsey, himself a prominent New York restauranteur, was one of the many Hollywood regulars who had fallen victim to the allures of the establishment's well-developed attractions. He married one of the cabaret's principal stars, Estelle Taylor. The *New York Times* noted that celebrity nights were becoming compulsory in the highly competitive nightclub scene, and that a number of New York clubs were offering star-studded evenings. The very week Eugene opened at the Hollywood the newspaper pondered the dilemma of patrons torn between competing establishments:

> Tomorrow night, the irrepressible Sophie Tucker, who probably has as many friends as anyone in the business, will play host to several of them—and will show them off in fact, under the beam of a baby spot at the Hollywood Restaurant. . . . Jimmy Durante, too, will give another—the fourth—of his "Hollywood Parties" but at the Casino de Paree—which means that the blushing bigwigs will be tossed on the horns of a dilemma. An enterprising taxi driver might do well to set up a shuttle service between the two spots.[4]

The second week of Eugene's run at the Hollywood featured another Sophie Tucker-hosted celebrity showcase, this one with Helen Morgan, Rex Webber, Dave Appleton, the Ritz Brothers, and Milton Berle. In less than two weeks, Eugene had met or performed with more leading vaudevillians, movie stars, and top entertainers than he had even seen during his previous career. Moreover, the parade of stars would continue to pass through the Hollywood throughout Eugene's long engagement at the restaurant. It was a golden opportunity. Most of the cabaret's star performers, including the big-name bands, were only engaged for three months in the seasonal revues. A few performers, including Jack Waldron, Marion Martin, Gloria Cook, and Terry Lawlor were part of the core group about which the visiting stars and bands were arrayed. During 1935 and much of 1936, Jelesnik and his Continentals were the equivalent of the Hollywood's "house orchestra." Star after star came and went, and Eugene got to know and work with them all. The personal contacts that he would make during his year at the Hollywood would serve him through his entire career, and the friendships would last a lifetime.[5]

Of more immediate importance to Eugene's career were the notices that he began to get in the pages of the newspapers. Ed Sullivan placed his seal of approval on the orchestra, calling Eugene "the fiery little leader of the symphony band at the Hollywood." Walter Winchell was also quick to praise and raved that "Eugene's crew of music makers were the best in the town." Gerald Griffin of the *New York Inquirer* dubbed Eugene "The Wizard of the Violin"; Louis Sobol called him "Impressive"; and Nick Kenny in the *New York Mirror* hailed Eugene as the town's "Big Credit Man" and targeted him for quick stardom:

> We've picked a lot of winners in the mad race for popularity over these last few years. They've included Kate Smith, Morton Downey, Phil Regan, George Hall, and Baby Rose Marie. . . . Our most recent selection for stardom is Eugene Jelesnik, the violinist. This boy has something different.[6]

But as Eugene's star rose ever higher, there was one person who was becoming increasingly skeptical about his success, and it was the one person that Eugene wanted to impress the most. From his earliest years in America, Eugene had dedicated himself to the considerable task of helping his mother and his aunt. All his odd jobs and long hours of work had as their eventual goal the day that he would one day become a success and free his mother from the toil of the garment district. The first morning after he opened at the Hollywood, Eugene's mother and Aunt Ruth had waited up for him. It was well after three in the morning when Eugene finally came home and proudly produced the fruit of his labor. He emptied his pockets, full of the tips he had received for playing requests at the tables. His mother was dumbfounded. The bills and coins that tumbled from the stuffed pockets totaled over fifty dollars. For Jennie this was more than a week's wages. "Where did it come from?" she asked.

Eugene told her that the money came from playing table requests at the Hollywood Restaurant, but his answer was met with silence. Eugene was tired from his long day and went to bed. The following morning the scene was repeated again, and this time the tips were almost twice as much as the night before. Again the reaction of his mother was anything but what he expected. She seemed to scowl at him as if she disapproved of his success. On the third morning, as he was about to disgorge his treasure, his mother had had enough and blew up. She knew full well that no one could make so much money in table tips at some restaurant during the midst of the Depression. Eugene had obviously fallen in with bad people. The money had to be either stolen, or ill-gotten from gangsters. Eugene was stunned. He again told his mother that all of the money came from playing requests. He insisted that what he had told her was true. His mother relented to his impassioned defense, but he could tell by her look that she didn't believe him.

The only solution was to prove that what he said was true. Eugene arranged to have his mother and Aunt Ruth come to the Hollywood as his special guests. He even arranged with the headwaiter that they would sit in one of the front-row tables—the very ones usually reserved for important celebrities—to make certain that they could actually see how he earned his extra income. The demonstration was convincing. Each time that Eugene got a few tips he brought them to the table for his mother's inspection, but this added bit of evidence was unnecessary. From the moment they stepped inside the Hollywood, they knew that Eugene was probably telling the truth. The word "restaurant" had implied something quite different than the setting they scanned with awe as they were ushered to their ringside table. This was no simple café. Jennie and Ruth had never been to a "restaurant" that seated over eleven hundred people.

On 30 April 1935, less than two weeks after his opening, Jelesnik and his orchestra were signed by the Columbia Artists Bureau, a booking and publicity arm of CBS Radio. He had worked with the network before, both at their experimental TV station and more recently in broadcasts from the Show Boat Garden in Atlantic City, but being included in the Artists Bureau was an important step. It gave Eugene his first access to nation-wide publicity. It seems likely that Sophie Tucker may have had something to do with the listing since at that time she was touted as one of the bureau's principal artists. It was also quickly arranged that a half-hour segment of Eugene's set would be broadcast live from the Hollywood over New York station WHN and CBS affiliate WABC. In the months to come the broadcasts would gain a sizeable following. The Artist Bureau's primary responsibility was to provide information to affiliate stations and sponsors about the artists aired over the network. Eugene's first press releases from the Bureau indicate the importance that the network gave to the Hollywood booking:

> Eugene Jelesnik, well-known violinist and orchestra leader and currently featured with Sophie Tucker at the Hollywood Restaurant, has just been signed to a long-term contract by the Columbia Artists Bureau. Jelesnik and his all-string ensemble are rated among the foremost interpreters of the continental type of music.
> The clever violinist Eugene Jelesnik and his Continental Orchestra . . . recently opened at the Hollywood Restaurant, regaling patrons with their exotic and different dance rhythms, between the nightly shows of Rudy Vallee and Sophie Tucker.[7]

In the years before gossip columnists turned vicious and the paparazzi began stalking celebrities like wild game, there was a symbiotic relationship between the writer and the star. Each needed the other for survival, and they traded information, perks, and compliments like kids trading baseball cards. Favors were returned with favors, and press releases were often turned into feature stories with the simple addition of some complimentary tickets. Sophie Tucker had brought Jelesnik to the Hollywood Restaurant, but she wasn't finished promoting her young discovery. In the process of introducing Eugene to the elite of New York, she would also teach him some tricks of the trade.

The first thing Eugene learned was that getting to the top tier in the entertainment industry meant absolutely nothing unless everyone knew you had arrived. Sophie was a genius at manipulating the press, and over the next two months she took pains to include Eugene in many of her own publicity releases. In the process she taught her young protégé a good deal about the gentle art of milking the press. On May 2ᵈ, she contrived to have a publicity shot taken of Eugene congratulating her on her election to the presidency of the Actors Federation of America. The photograph appeared in many of New York's newspapers the morning of May 5th. On May 6th, Louis Sobol mentioned Eugene in a longer piece about Sophie Tucker, and on May 8th wrote a brief chatty story about Eugene and his supposed dispute with a musician who was envious of his sudden success. There was a flurry of photo clips, which featured Eugene in various settings, including one where Eugene was dressed in a bandanna as a Gypsy, and another in a tux backstage at the Ziegfeld Follies with its star, Willie Howard. The caption read: "Willie Howard donates $50,000 strad to Eugene Jelesnik, the internationally known Gypsy violinist."[8] In one fanciful story after another, Eugene was provided with a number of contradictory backgrounds and experiences. One had him just returning from a European tour, which included his conducting of the "Petersburg Garden Orchestra" in his native Russia and giving a command performance before "the Queen of Romania." One story said he was a Hungarian and another the sole heir to a huge Russian fortune. The point of the campaign seems to have been the creation of an aura of mystery about the violinist, which, of course, could only be resolved by more stories. Leaving no stone unturned, Sophie Tucker, Eugene, and Joe Moss were featured together on the front page of the June 15th issue of New York City's Hungarian language newspaper.[9] By mid-June,

Eugene was generating considerable press on his own. A June 22^d article credited Eugene for his discovery of Yvonne Bouvier, a sultry French vocalist who was heard on WHN with Jelesnik's orchestra.

By the end of June, the publicity blitz was starting to pay off. Eugene was now heard nightly, not only over WHN radio but WABC—the CBS network's anchor station in New York. The announcer for the radio show was Harry Von Zell, who later became the head announcer for George Burns and Gracie Allen's comedy show on television. Many of the radio broadcasts were recorded on twelve-inch aluminum disks that were then sent on to affiliate stations both for promotional purposes and rebroadcast. Soon other affiliates around the country were signing on. On 30 June 1935, Eugene and his orchestra began broadcasting nationwide from the Hollywood Restaurant over the Columbia Broadcasting System. On Saturday evening, July 6th, eighty-six CBS affiliate stations from New York to Seattle and from Minneapolis to San Antonio began airing Jelesnik's programs. On Saturday July 20th, Eugene was a guest soloist on "The Daily Mirror's WHN Radio Frolic" with Kate Smith, Arthur Boran, and Andy Senella. Over the coming year the radio credits would continue to pile up.

In early July, Eugene was approached by Charles E. Rochester, the manager of New York City's luxurious Hotel Lexington, who asked him if it were possible for Eugene to perform for his afternoon luncheon crowd. If so, a smaller string version of the Continental Orchestra might be perfect for the Hotel Lexington's Silver Grill Restaurant. Eugene didn't get out of the Hollywood until after three in the morning. If he accepted the offer, it would mean that he would have to give up something called sleep. But the Lexington was "uptown"—highbrow and sophisticated—as distant from freewheeling Broadway as the moon. A booking at the Lexington Hotel—which seated over 700 each afternoon—would give him another venue to demonstrate his musical range. Eugene consulted with Joe Moss and then quickly accepted. On Saturday, August 3rd, the *Long Island Daily Star* noted the peculiar hours of the young violinist:

Meet Eugene Jelesnik, one of the busiest of the town's mainstream orchestra leaders. From 12:30 to 2:15 P.M. daily his orchestra pleases guests at the Silver Grill of the Hotel Lexington. Then he goes to the radio studio to send his tuneful melodies across the airwaves, and finally to the Hollywood Restaurant from 9 P.M. to 3 A.M. in the morning.[10]

The leader of the Lexington Hotel's regular evening orchestra soon became acquainted with his afternoon counterpart. Ozzie Nelson and his lead singer Harriet Hilliard would frequently come to the hotel early to take in the afternoon shows. Just as with Eugene's other celebrity acquaintances, Ozzie and Harriet were soon Eugene's fast friends.

The period from July of 1935 to April of 1936 was one of the most hectic of his professional career. Eugene was under added pressure in August when he was put in charge of conducting an overture featuring the combined orchestras of Hale Hamilton and Jelesnik's own. In late August, the orchestra also began rehearsals for the fall spectacular "Hollywood Revels of 1936." As with auto-mobiles, the fall revues were always a little ahead of the calendar year. The production was under the direction of Danny Dare who would later direct many of the production numbers in MGM's musicals. For the fall production at the Hollywood, Dare was promising: "An extravaganza unlike anything that Broadway has ever seen!" The headline orchestra for the new revue was Abe Lyman and his Californians. As had many before him, Lyman had quickly fallen victim to the Hollywood Restaurant's principal dan-ger: he and dancer Eleanore Powell were soon engaged to be mar-ried. Romance seemed to be in the air. Louis Sobol, "The Voice of Broadway" for the *New York Evening Journal,* noted on 16 September 1935 that "Eugene Jelesnik, the Hollywood orchestra leader, and Margot Sneed, the Montgomery, Alabama, gossip columnist, are chanting the oldest tune." When exactly Eugene found time to "chant" with Miss Sneed is unknown. Eugene admitted to having already been smitten by Marion Martin, the lead dancer and choreographer of the Hollywood's showgirls.

The new revue opened on Monday evening 30 September 1935, and the advertising prominently featured Eugene Jelesnik.

"His violin solos and his leading of the orchestra in the symphonic renditions are considerable attractions at the Hollywood." The much-touted revue lived up to all expectations and then some. The newspaper reviews were all raves. Danny Dare not only made good on his promise, but was true to his name. The show was nothing if not daring. The papers not only give a detailed description of the production but reveal a good deal about Broadway of 1935.

Louis Sobol/*The New York Journal*/October 1, 1935

Last night's important opening brought most of the town to the Hollywood Restaurant, where it is safe to say that some of the country's leading dolls are glorified in a spectacular new revue. The production consumes close to two and a half hours, and the only difference between it and the customary revue in the theater is that for a minimum charge you also have your meal provided whether you eat it or not, and if you're early enough you may sit close enough to reach out and touch one of the little lovelies—a dangerous pastime. . . . By way of repetition, some of the town's outstanding and most publicized beauties are featured in the chorus and showgirl lineup. Outstanding is the stately, snooty queen of loveliness, Marion Martin in clothes which cover . . . but leave nothing to the imagination. The Hollywood is the oldest cabaret on Broadway and has really come into its own with this production, the most elaborate of its career. It has to be. The competition is formidable. There is that French casino around the corner, and just across the street, the Paradise, which will present a show fully as elaborate and dangerous to the competitor's opening Thursday night. People just naturally capitulate to a good show, a fine meal, and a pretty girl, and when all three are combined in overflowing measure, who could want anything more?

Ed Sullivan—Broadway—*New York News*/October 1, 1935

From the top of its head to the tip of its toes the new show that barged into the Hollywood Restaurant late Monday night is a four-star special. . . . The greatest show hit of the season, perhaps of many years. The girls are amazingly good-looking, the singers can actually sing. Danny Dare's dance arrangements are his finest creative efforts and the principals are something to write home about. Joe Moss can step up and take a bow. All the slightly maudlin things dear to Broadway's heart added to the plush contours of the evening. "I have only to mention his name and you will know him," said Milton Berle, and Edward G. Robinson stepped out on the floor. . . . For the benefit of the cameraman, Eleanor Powell kissed her fiancé Abe Lyman. The parade of celebs was endless. Marilyn Miller, May Murray, Eddy Duchin, Tony DeMarco, Joe Louis, Phil Harris, Jack Dempsey, each spoke of their enthusiasm on being able to attend his or her pal's opening. Slightly maudlin as all of these things (are) Broadway likes 'em. And Broadway is nicest when it is gawky rather than sophisticated. The things I liked were Milton Berle's striptease parody, The Frazee Sisters, two bundles of tuneful class from the Chicago area, and the "International Dares" best dance arrangements that finish with an adagio that stands your hair on its head. I liked the whole darn thing. You can sympathize with the other clubs that will have to play follow the leader.

Walter Winchell—*Daily Mirror*/October 2, 1935

The Hollywood Revels of 1936 presented by Joe Moss the impresario of the renowned nightclub at 48th and Broadway, was Broadway's most exciting event and likely will be for a long, long time. The big news about this new and welcome first-rate entertainment is that everyone of the fifty or more beautiful girls in the cast is lovely enough to be on the smartest magazine covers.

Ted Friend—*Sunday Mirror*

The 1936 edition of the Hollywood revels is sometimes so fast that it becomes down-right furious. It is a lot of show, a good show, well-balanced and stocked with talent. Among those who shine are Jack Waldren, Ben Dova, The Frazee Sisters, Luba Malina, Jerry Cooper, and Eugene Jelesnik.

Variety/October 2, 1935

The new show at the Hollywood, which formally premiered Monday, September 30th, justifies its past good standing. It is a fast snappy diversion with more than ninety minutes of worthy entertainment. Girls who are lookers, draped and otherwise, talent, dancing, etc. . . . the show holds lots of

class and talent. It blends well and paces smoothly. . . .
Waldren as the MC is as saucy as ever but not too much so.
Ben Dova, an inebriate atop a swaying lamp post, works too
dangerously near the ceiling and that makes him a problem
on the café floor. There is a rostrum at the Hollywood, and if
he could do his stuff on stage the effect would par his usual
signal click in theaters. Withall, a corking floor show explains
why 900 to 1,100 customers jam in on both nightly sessions.

The week following the opening of "The Hollywood Revels of
1936" brought yet another memorable booking. Walter Winchell
hired Eugene and his orchestra to entertain at the wedding reception of movie stars Joan Crawford and Franchot Tone. On Friday,
October 11th, the couple were married in Englewood Cliffs, New
Jersey, by the town's mayor, Herbert W. Jenkins. The marriage
took place at the mayor's official residence, but the reception was
held at the Hollywood Restaurant. It was hosted by Winchell who
was a close friend to both movie stars. Eugene Jelesnik and his
orchestra were the entertainment for the evening. The entire
throng of wedding guests was made up of celebrities. Eugene
played dozens of special requests and serenaded the couple with a
solo violin rendition of "I Love You Truly."[11]

But famous writers, actors, musicians, and sports figures
weren't the only patrons of the Hollywood Restaurant that
October. Shortly following the Tone wedding, a strange man
began appearing nightly at the show. He seemed to be there primarily to listen to Eugene's orchestra. The man was in his late
fifties, about five-foot-seven in height, and had a slight build. He
always showed up in a fresh suit of clothes, but had a haggard and
downcast look. The man spoke with a heavy Brooklyn accent and
seemed a little lost and out of place. Eugene knew immediately
that there was something peculiar about the stranger. He bought
out six tables directly in front of the orchestra stand and wouldn't
let anyone sit in any of the chairs except himself. The first night
that this occurred, Eugene thought, "The guy must have been
stood up by a whole bunch of people." But after the second and
third night, it was clear that he wanted to sit there alone with the
empty tables all around him. This went on for more than a week.

Eugene believed that the man was simply eccentric. He didn't give much thought to the circumstances, and didn't think there might actually be a very serious reason for his odd behavior.

Walter Winchell had made it his personal crusade to alert the country to the rising menace of organized crime. For years he had been telling the country of the mob's growing power, but during Prohibition his warnings had fallen largely on deaf ears. Gangsters had existed long before the ratification of the Eighteenth Amendment, but the Volstead Act, which enabled the Eighteenth Amendment, gave organized crime something it had never enjoyed before: widespread popular support.[12] A large number of citizens who otherwise wouldn't think of supporting organized lawlessness, turned their backs when it came to enforcing Prohibition. During the twenties, New York was awash in speakeasies, and many law enforcement authorities whose job it was to implement the law refused to do so, or were bought off. For organized crime, it was the perfect setup.

Altogether typical of the era's gangs was the Amberg/Shapiro gang run by two sets of Brooklyn brothers.[13] Hymie, Oscar, Joey, and Louis "Pretty" Amberg, and Irving, Meyer, and Willie Shapiro were the principal bad actors. The gang got its start at the very beginning of prohibition when they forced the owners of the long-established Brownsville Brewery to take them in as full partners. The tactic they used to secure the merger was the same one they employed to persuade speakeasy owners to sell their product— brute force. Through the twenties, hired henchman and street thugs posing as salesmen used brass knuckles, black jacks, kid-napping, and torture as ways to convince barkeepers and speakeasy owners that "Amberg-Shapiro Beer" was the finest product ever put in a bottle.[14]

Protected from police interference by indifference or bribes, the speakeasies quickly became dens for other illegal activities: gambling, prostitution, and narcotics. There were inevitable terri-torial clashes between rival mobs with conflicting areas of crimi-nal interest. In the late twenties, Leo Byk, a mobster who ran Brooklyn's bookie joints and slot machines, got in a dispute with the Amberg/Shapiro gang over territorial rights. A bloody war raged in the streets for almost a year until "Little Augie Piasano," then boss of all Brooklyn bosses, forced the two warring factions into a treaty under the protection of the Italian mafia. Like most treaties of the period, it was short-lived. Sensing Byk's vulnerability, the Shapiro faction moved in, killed most of Byk's key operatives, and took over the illegal gambling industry. In gangland terms this was little more than a breach of etiquette. (The take-out was a *fait accompli*, and there was little point in fussing over the spilt blood.) But the Shapiro faction soon became emboldened by their success. Flush with money, they started moving in on the garment racket then under the control of Louie Lepke, a Jewish mobster with close ties to the Italian mafia. Lepke—with the full backing of Augie Piasano and invoking the provisions of the earlier treaty—told the Ambergs that unless the Shapiro faction was eliminated, the entire force of the Italian mafia would be brought against them. The Amberg-Shapiro partnership was dissolved. Amberg's men then systematically wiped out the Shapiros one by one.[15]

When Prohibition ended there was widespread hope that the mobsters' hold on the city would be broken. The profits from bootlegging were the principal source of the gangsters' income. The more unsavory areas of the crime business—narcotics and prostitution—no longer enjoyed the sanctuary of the speakeasy, and gambling—while still a problem—could no longer be conducted in the open. Profits were drying up. Faced with financial collapse, the mob turned increasingly to other enterprises: the policy and protection rackets, the numbers game, and loan sharking.

Walter Winchell saw another disturbing trend. Legitimate businesses were being taken over using the same tactics that the mob had used with the breweries. Fish markets, laundries, clothing stores, and restaurants were being forced to buy insurance policies or take on "silent partners." Many of the small businesses were marginal operations and could not afford to pay protection. Inevitably the silent partners simply stripped the businesses of their assets or otherwise ran them into the ground. Winchell reported that one-third of the business failures in New York City were directly caused by mob involvement.

The end of Prohibition brought about greater consolidation of various crime families and also increased competition for the diminishing revenues. The Amberg brothers formed new alliances of their own, hoping to expand their territory into other criminal enterprises. This brought them into direct conflict with Louie Lepke and his interests. One after another, in a series of murders more brutal than any in the city's history, the Ambergs and all their allies were wiped out.[16]

Eugene Jelesnik was a regular listener to Walter Winchell. As had all America, Eugene had shuddered at the chilling stories of the gangland murders. Winchell's crusade against the mob had made the reporter a national figure, and would eventually bring about Congressional hearings on organized crime. Eugene was well aware that New York was a center of mobster activity, and the killings were in the paper almost every week. But at no time did Jelesnik see how any of it was related to him. He certainly didn't associate the murders with the man who sat seemingly transfixed amid his empty tables at the foot of Eugene's stage during the third week of October 1935: "Sometimes you'll get strange people in the audience, and besides, he absolutely loved my playing."

After a week of sitting alone—not saying anything to anyone—the man called Eugene over to his table and said, "Can you see me when you're through? I want to give you something." Eugene told the man that he didn't get off work until after two-thirty in the morning. The man told Eugene that was fine, but he really did want him to come by because he had a gift for him. The man was almost pleading, but he seemed innocuous enough, and he didn't appear to want anything, so Eugene agreed. The man was staying in the Lincoln Hotel just around the corner. Eugene described the strangest rendezvous of his life:

> I got off work about two-thirty, went up to his room, and knocked at his door. He greeted me and seemed happy that I had come. He told me how much he loved my music and then asked me if I would like to know what his hobby was. I said, "Well, I guess so, yes," and he said: . . . "Come here. I'll show you. . . ." We went into the other room. He opened his dresser drawer, and it was filled to the brim with pennies. There must

have been millions of pennies in there. I didn't know what to say. I looked at the pennies, and he looked at me for some reaction, so I said, "Oh, that's wonderful." Then he said: "I really do have a present for you. What size shoe do you wear?" I told him 8-D. He opened up his closet and there were about two dozen pairs of shoes and boots all lined up in neat rows. He went through them and pulled out a beautiful pair of riding boots and said, "Here, I want you to have these; try 'em on." So I tried on the boots and they fit me perfectly. I thanked him, and we talked for a little, about nothing, really. I told him he had an interesting hobby—that it was different anyway. Then I thanked him again for the boots and left.

A day or two later, as Eugene was walking by a newsstand, he happened to notice a picture of the same man on the front page of the *Daily News.* Eugene bought the paper. The man was none other than Louis "Pretty" Amberg, the last member of the Amberg/Shapiro gang. Sometime in the early morning hours of October 22nd he had been kidnapped, stripped, tied up, shot, doused with gasoline, and burned in his car. The burning car— with Amberg's body in it—had been found near the Brooklyn Navy Yard. The papers reported that police investigators had discovered that Amberg had been living at the Hotel Lincoln under an assumed name for the previous ten months.[17] Over that period, his three brothers and a half-dozen other associates had been murdered in a similarly brutal fashion. Combing through Amberg's room in the Hotel Lincoln, the police found business records, personal papers, receipts, and other items that they said shed light on the recent outbreak of mobster killings. The inventory of the room was printed in the paper. It included 15 suits, 20 pairs of shoes, 49 ties, 12 hats (some still in their original boxes), a tuxedo, several overcoats, and one pair of riding boots.[18] No mention was made of the drawer full of pennies. Eugene was in shock: "I went to the Hollywood and showed the paper to Joe Moss. He said: 'Is that the kind of clientele you're attracting?' I said, 'Hey, it's your place, not mine.' Why I told my mother about it I'll never know. But she was absolutely dumfounded—devastated—she couldn't believe I could associate with such people. We were both very upset. After

"Pretty" Amberg, when I saw another mobster, I could pick 'em out, or at least I thought I could."

Why "Pretty" Amberg ventured out of his hiding place in the Hotel Lincoln to bask in the bright lights of the Hollywood Restaurant is a mystery. The single figure sitting alone among the empty tables would most certainly have drawn attention. He must have known that he would eventually be recognized. Perhaps, after the deaths of his brothers and other associates, he had simply given up. Eugene would keep Pretty Amberg's riding boots as a memento of the encounter. After all, they were given to him as a last behest shortly before Amberg was slain.

Eugene and his orchestra continued their long runs at the Hollywood Restaurant and Lexington Hotel through April of 1936. In addition, his radio broadcasts increased to nine live programs a week over the CBS network. On January 19th, the cabaret opened its next version of the Hollywood Revels with Abe Lyman's orchestra, Estelle Taylor, George Givot, Cass Daley and Phil Nealy. By then the romance between Lyman and Eleanor Powell was on the rocks, and she was on her way to Hollywood, California, soon to become a major film star. The "50 Gorgeous Girls, 50" were as beguiling as ever, but the revue didn't match the energy or garner the critical enthusiasm of the October opening—perhaps it really was unmatchable. But while the revue slumped, Eugene and his orchestra continued to pile up accolades in the press. An article in the February 1936 edition of *Orchestra World* is typical:

> Jelesnik has become a fixture at the Hollywood [cabaret], a favorite of the dancers. His continental society music definitely has found favor with New York's musical world. . . . It was with lightning suddenness that the name Jelesnik appeared in the limelight of the musical profession only a short time ago. Jelesnik is a name that signifies the blending of Gypsy and folk music into the rapturous arrangements of dance. Jelesnik has a unique method of [performance] . . . the melodious interpolations that vividly and mentally portray the haunting melodies of Old Europe in modern dance settings. It is something unusual . . . recalling to the dancers the Steppes of Russia, the swing of Old Vienna, the cafés of Budapest—all creeping into the songs of today.

The *New York Inquirer* of Sunday 1 March 1936 reported:

> Visiting the Lexington Hotel Grill the other noon, we were
> delighted no end by the young Hungarian violinist Eugene
> Jelesnik and his string ensemble. Jelesnik is an artist that will
> cause any audience to sit up and take notice. He is a wizard of
> the violin, and we predict that he will become one of our
> leading concert violin virtuosos in the near future.

On March 2^d, the *New York Evening News* reported that columnist Louis Sobol, then vacationing in Hollywood, California, had
became so lonesome for his beloved Broadway that he wired
Jelesnik at the Silver Grill in the Hotel Lexington, asking him to
play "Melancholy Baby" to him via a long-distance hookup and
reverse the charges. Eugene promptly did just that. He had
learned never to trifle with the whims of the inquiring press.

On Saturday 7 March 1936, the *Daily Mirror* noted that the
spring edition of the Hollywood Restaurant's biggest competitor,
the Paradise, just across the street, featured a hit number titled
"Two Silhouettes on the Moon" composed by none other than
Eugene Jelesnik. For a few weeks, Eugene was featured in programs on both sides of Broadway. But the biggest performance triumph that spring was the selection of Eugene's orchestra to
provide the entertainment for the newspaper publishers' convention at the Waldorf Astoria. Fifteen of the country's finest orchestras had auditioned for the engagement, but the Continentals were
selected.

It could be said that Sophie Tucker was Eugene Jelesnik's first
agent. She had discovered him at the Holland Hotel and had introduced him to Joe Moss. She was responsible not only for the booking at the Hollywood Restaurant but also in guiding his early
publicity and introducing him to influential figures in journalism,
radio and the movies. But in the spring of 1936, Jelesnik was
invited to become a member of the most exclusive musical club in
the world: the artists represented by the Music Corporation of
America. MCA owned large office buildings in New York,
London, Los Angeles, Dallas, Cleveland, and Chicago but represented fewer than 120 artists. Their flyer for the spring of 1936 had

photographs of every one of them and among them—dead center in the advertising spread—was Eugene Jelesnik. This was not simply another breakthrough, this was a *huge* step. The flyer touted its lineup as "The Worlds' Greatest Attractions." Eugene's personal agent at MCA was Willard Alexander who also represented Count Basie. The names that adorned the star-studded flyer were the elite of the musical entertainment industry and included: Benny Goodman, Kay Kayser, Louis Prima, Guy Lombardo, Phil Harris, Tommy Dorsey, Xavier Cugat, Eddie Duchin, and Ozzie Nelson. Of the 118 international artists in the MCA's prestigious lineup, there was only one woman—Sophie Tucker.[19]

CHAPTER FIVE

THE MOB

Following their year-long stint at the Hollywood Restaurant, Eugene Jelesnik and his Continentals were booked by MCA into the Hotel Ten Eyck in Albany, New York. The Ten Eyck was a four-star hotel, and the booking probably owed more to Jelesnik's lunchtime engagement at the Lexington Hotel than his long run at the Hollywood. Dewey D. Ellis, manager of the Ten Eyck, was quoted in Albany's *Times Union* as saying:

> Eugene's music will be familiar to many Albanians, who have stopped at the Hotel Lexington where the band was featured in the Silver Grill. Mr. Jelesnik's music is the kind that wears well with dancers, a blending of Gypsy and folk music into the rapturous rhythms of today's dance.[1]

The orchestra was contracted for an eight-week engagement at the hotel's "Roof Garden Restaurant" to provide nightly dance music for the Ten Eyck's dinner crowd. In addition, the band would present concert-style programs on Sunday evenings. Like the Hollywood Restaurant weekend performances, the Sunday concerts would be broadcast live over the radio—this time over Albany station WOKO. For the Ten Eyck booking, Eugene enlarged the orchestra to a ten-piece dance ensemble adding more brass, as well as popular blues singer Nita Norman. As with his Hollywood Restaurant orchestra, the band prominently featured the young Hungarian cymbalom player, Dick Marta. They opened on 31 May 1936 and were an immediate success. On June 14th, Mary O'Neil, the entertainment writer for Albany's *Knickerbocker Press*, heaped praise on the Ten Eyck's new dance band saying in part:

> This is something I've never said before. I have always

modulated my praise for orchestras . . . but this time I say
without reservation or qualification: Eugene Jelesnik and his
orchestra are the best band to ever play in this town.

The *Albany Evening News* was equally lavish in its praise:

> Albany has had excellent dance music in its leading hotels
> and radio stations, but it has never had one quite so adaptable
> as the Eugene Jelesnik organization that broadcasts live from
> the Ten Eyck Roof Garden. . . . You have heard some of the
> famous musical ensembles at the better New York Restaurants,
> and have come home raving about their concert programs, but
> you have never heard any that are better than what comes over
> WOKO these Sunday nights. Of course a trip to the Ten Eyck
> Roof means hearing a lot more after the broadcast is over.
> Whether you hear the brief radio program or the longer one at
> the hotel, you will hear music that is unusual, thrilling, and
> inspiring.

As New York's capital city, Albany was the center of political
power in the state, and many of the Ten Eyck's patrons were politicians. Just as he had with the entertainment celebrities and movie
stars who passed through the Hollywood Restaurant, Eugene
became quickly acquainted with the most prominent political figures of the day, including New York's Governor Lehman, senators,
representatives, and state legislators. Eugene would find that just
as famous celebrities, the politicians were usually personable and
friendly. "It's a two-way street. If you were nice to them, they were
nice to you." For Eugene and his orchestra, being "nice to you"
meant additional bookings. In Albany this translated into performances at public events and celebrations. Eugene's versatility as a
conductor soon proved to be a big plus. He was often invited to
arrange and conduct programs for public events and special occasions. It was in Albany that Eugene began to conduct the patriotic
programs that would become a hallmark of his later career. The
manager at the Ten Eyck knew a good thing when he saw it, and
extended Eugene's contract from eight weeks to five months.

Eugene's success in Albany was noted in all the local papers.
On July 17th, the *Times Union* wrote: "Eugene Jelesnik is a big hit at

the Ten Eyck Hotel Roof Garden." There were also plenty of photo spreads and publicity stories. The *Knickerbocker Press* for June 14th featured a large photo of Eugene demonstrating the new Crosley radio. The *Albany Evening News* for June 24th featured Eugene flying to New York for a special appearance with Kate Smith on Nick Kenny's radio program over WMCA. The *Times Union* for August 27th featured a large photo of Jelesnik and Ziegfeld star Josephine Huston who had breakfast with Eugene on her way to the races at Saratoga. On August 30th, the same paper had Eugene flying to New York again, this time to appear as a musical judge for Benny Rubin's radio talent show over WOR. The September 4th issue of the *Albany Evening News* had a quarter-page spread of Eugene and a bevy of young beauties at a fund-raiser for Albany's St. Peter's Hospital.

Eugene had apparently mastered the fine art of public relations, but there were a couple of crucial things that he seems to have overlooked: Albany was not New York City, and the *Knickerbocker Press* was not the *New York Times*. It was a lesson that every top performer had to learn for himself. To step out of the spotlight—for even a moment—was to risk that the spotlight might never find you again. The annals of Broadway are replete with stories of up-and-comers who ruled the Great White Way for a season and then seemingly vanished from the face of the earth. Like last year's dance craze, musical styles tended to have temporary appeal, and in the fickle world of entertainment, last season's instant sensation could just as instantly become this year's has-been.

There was another aspect to the limelight that was peculiar to the Great White Way itself. It was a well-known fact that it was easier to get a booking in Albany while playing Broadway than it was to get a booking on Broadway while playing Albany. It was a lesson that Sophie Tucker had learned very early in her career, and it was the principal reason that she and her publicist worked so hard at keeping her name in the limelight. Whenever Sophie Tucker left New York City for an out-of-town booking, she always made certain that she returned via London or Paris. Returning from a "triumphant European tour" always sounded better than returning from a triumphant tour of Ohio.

Staying in the spotlight was the name of the game, and accepting an extended booking outside that glare was to risk banishment to provincial obscurity. It was a cruel lesson that would be learned by many of the greatest performers of the era. Milton Berle was one of several former vaudevillians to vanish for a time only to have his career revived by the coming of television. Jimmy Durante, whose career was also rescued by television, would make the simple act of stepping in and out of the spotlight the closing sequence of his television show. It was not a casual gimmick. Durante's career went through several periods of total darkness.

For Eugene Jelesnik, the extension of the Ten Eyck engagement proved unfortunate. By the time the booking ended, the fall season in New York City was already in full swing, and most of the choice venues had been taken. In addition, MCA only booked their performers in the most prestigious of settings. Eugene and his Continental Orchestra would have to wait until an appropriate booking could be found. Unfortunately, Eugene could not wait. It had taken him several years to build his orchestra and hundreds of hours of rehearsal time to mold it into a tight-knit group. If they did not get work soon, his best musicians would be forced to leave for other bands. The solution he arrived at must have seemed like his only option at the time.

Eugene had learned a great deal about both the restaurant and entertainment business over the previous two years. He had also managed to save much of the money he had received for his appearances on radio programs, as well as some of the money from the tips he got playing tables at the Hollywood. By the fall of 1936 he had over two thousand dollars put away. This was a considerable sum of money at the height of the depression. Eugene decided that he would use his savings to try to open up his own restaurant. If he could just break even, perhaps he could keep his band together until MCA came up with a good booking. If the restaurant was a big success, well then, all the better.

The more he looked into it, the more he realized that two

thousand dollars wasn't nearly enough to start a restaurant in New York City. He would have to find a partner who could operate the food end of the business while he himself took care of the advertising and entertainment aspects of the enterprise. After making a number of inquiries, the partner was found. Even so, Eugene ended up borrowing additional money from his mother, aunts, uncles, and friends to get the business off the ground.

The Savoia Restaurant was located at 300 West 45th Street, opposite the Hotel Lincoln where Eugene had met Louis "Pretty" Amberg. If he thought about his encounter with the infamous mobster at all, he might have looked upon the Hotel Lincoln as a bad omen. But the restaurant was also right next door to the Martin Beck Theater. This was a magnificent location in the very heart of Broadway. Advertisements for the Savoia touted the establishment as "New York's newest and most intimate cabaret offering excellent cuisine, dancing, and impromptu entertainment. Dinner served nightly from 6 to 10 P.M. Never a cover or minimum charge." Eugene invited all his friends to the grand opening. The invitation read:

> May I have the pleasure of personally greeting you to my restaurant. I am opening my own cabaret, The Savoia, 300 West 45th Street, next to the Martin Beck Theater and opposite the Hotel Lincoln. The Savoia is New York's newest, smartest setting for my restaurant where I will appear in person for dinner, supper, and dancing—featuring a most smart impromptu floor show. Here you will share my orchestra's music exactly as you have heard it on so many occasions with the same voice, and the same gestures as you have heard before in other New York night spots.[2]

For the "Grand Premier" at the Savoia, Eugene asked one of his celebrity friends if he would help him open the new establishment. The man agreed immediately and told Eugene he would bring his entire vaudeville group. The Savoia Restaurant opened on 6 November 1936 with "The Three Saw Dust Bums"—Jimmy Durante, Lue Clayton, and Eddie Jackson as the opening act. Eugene had gotten to know Durante at the Hollywood Restaurant where he had met most of his celebrity acquaintances. In 1936

Durante could command a thousand dollars for just a brief personal appearance, but he had once owned a Manhattan restaurant himself, and he knew how hard it was going to be for the Savoia to succeed. Jimmy Durante brought his whole "kit and caboodle" to Eugene's opening and charged nothing. "Durante's Bums" were known for doing anything to make an audience laugh, and on opening night they not only packed the house but "brought it down."

At the time the Savoia opened, Eugene was only twenty-two years old. His rise to prominence was meteoric. He was recognized as one of New York's up-and-coming musicians, he was personally represented by MCA—the most important agency in the music world—and he had his own restaurant at the very center of New York's theater district. His personal charm could attract stars of the first order, such as Sophie Tucker and Rudy Vallee, and he could rely on his personal friendships to showcase sure box office attractions like Jimmy Durante and his "Sawdust Bums." It was almost a dream come true. There was only one flaw in the fairy tale: his partner was a full-time crook.

Eugene himself had taken care of the front end of the operation, but it was his partner who operated the kitchen and ordered all the food and supplies. Over the short run of "New York's newest, smartest setting," Eugene's partner had put all of his effort into skimming off the profits while at the same time leaving stacks of unpaid bills. Eugene never named the man who ran the Savoia into the ground, but he described the tragic turn of events and provided enough detail to make it clear that he understood very well his partner's modus operandi.

"The opening was so great. My own restaurant in the heart of Broadway! We got good press and a steady clientele, but after a few weeks I found that there were no profits, only bills. I later discovered that my partner, who was also the chef, was funneling all the profits to his relatives in a crooked meat-buying scheme. I had trusted him. He was to take care of the kitchen, and I was to take care of everything out front. He took care of things all right. It was not long before he took every cent I had. I knew all about this kind of thing from listening to Walter Winchell's news broadcasts, but I never thought that it could happen to me. My partner was telling me that he was paying a thousand dollars for beef when he only put down two hundred, then he kept the rest, ran up bills, sold the stock he never paid for or gave it to his relatives, and then left me holding the bag. At that time I was naive enough to think it was just my partner, that he was just a stupid crook. But I also knew that there was no point in suing him. As I think back on it now, he had his own mob. It just wasn't worth the trouble, so I walked out on the whole business. I lost everything, well over two thousand dollars, which in those days was a lot of money. And it wasn't just my money I lost, but the money of my friends, my mother, Aunt Ruth, and other relatives. After the Savoia went under, I did everything I could to pay everybody back, but it took a long time."[3]

Less than six weeks after its promising opening, the Savoia closed.

Eugene continued to call MCA but it was clear that nothing was going to develop right away. Some of the band had already left him, and he was desperately trying to hold on to a core group of three or four musicians. He played weddings, church bazaars, and charity socials—anything he could to keep body and soul together. It wasn't long after the Savoia closed that Eugene ran into an acquaintance from the Hollywood. He knew that the man was "connected" but he also firmly believed that "If you are nice to people, they will be nice to you." The man asked Eugene where he was playing, and Eugene told him he was looking for a new booking for his orchestra. The man said: "Hey Eugene! We're opening a new restaurant. Do you want to work for us?"

Eugene knew instinctively who "us" must have been, but he pushed it to the back of his mind. He needed any work he could get, and so he replied, "Sure, when can we start?" The man said, "Right away." And the two shook hands.

Eugene had certainly encountered the type before. There had been "Pretty" Amberg and his riding boots, and more recently, his partner with the crooked meat scheme. But at that time, Eugene did not yet suspect that there might have been mob involvement in the failure of the Savoia. That suspicion would only come much later. Eugene had never so much as stepped foot inside a speakeasy, and he had certainly never had a working relationship with any known gangsters. His outlook on life and his religious upbringing made it difficult for him to see anything but good in other people. His positive disposition may have been an asset, but it was more than offset by his naivete: "I never thought for a moment that it was something I couldn't get out of."

Jelesnik and his orchestra opened at The Café Venezia in late December of 1936. The café was located at 209 West 48th Street between Broadway and Eighth Avenue and across the street from the Hotel President. Many of New York's lesser nightclubs catered to the seedy underside of society, and some even flaunted their mob associations. Advertisements for the Venezia only hinted at its darker side. Eugene opened at the restaurant with a comedy team called "The Three Racketcheers" who were billed as "The most hilarious funsters in America, making their first New York appearance after two years of sensational engagements out of town." Also performing at the Venezia was Bea Saxon of the "Saxon Sisters"; Bobbie Hall, an "Enticing Blues Chanteuse"; Irma Rishka, "The Exotic Russian Oriole"[4]; and a singer named Trent Patterson. If Eugene had paid more attention to the marquee displayed at the Venezia the week he opened he might have thought that the fates were trying to warn him about the nature of his associates. The sign seemed to link him to the rackets. It read:

> Appearing nightly: Eugene Jelesnik and his Orchestra
> The Café Venezia: featuring "The Three Racketcheers"

It wasn't long before Eugene realized that he had made a terrible mistake: "The piano player I had at that time drank too much, and he used to go through money like it was water. Sometime after we had been playing at the Venezia, he borrowed some money from the owners as an advance against his salary. Well, he soon fell behind in his payments and so one night after work they took him outside, beat him to a pulp, and dumped him in the gutter. They didn't care who he was, and he was working for them in my orchestra! He was so banged up he couldn't come to work for weeks. And they didn't care if he worked or not, only that he paid them off. How was he supposed to get them their money if he couldn't work? It was stupid. It was also sheer hell."

Eugene had been working at Venezia for about a month when another turn of events made it clear that the decision to work for "the boys" was the worst decision of his life. Late one night, after performing at the Venezia, Eugene was walking to the subway along Broadway near 47th Street when he happened to glance across the street at a famous dining room and rotisserie called the Brass Rail. All of a sudden he realized that there were life-sized posters of himself all across the front of the building. Eugene thought, *What the heck is that?* and he immediately went closer to investigate. The posters read "Our Next Attraction—Eugene Jelesnik and his Orchestra, Appearing Nightly." At the bottom of each poster was the distinctive MCA logo. His agents had finally come through.

The following morning he called Willard Alexander at MCA to ask about the booking at the Brass Rail. Alexander told Eugene that he was to open at the famous club in two weeks. When Eugene asked why they hadn't told him about the booking before, Alexander implied that he wanted to surprise him. Besides, MCA had a contract to book Eugene and his orchestra wherever they could. Given that, and the fact that Jelesnik had been pestering them for several months, Alexander must have been surprised at Eugene's reaction: "Weren't you going to ask me first?"

Eugene explained that he had taken a job at the Venezia and was worried about his bosses' reaction to the Brass Rail booking. Alexander said: "We have a contract don't we? You'll just have to tell them that you are signed with MCA. That you are under contract to us. Give them their two-week notice and just tell them that you are opening at the Brass Rail."

For Willard Alexander it must have all seemed very simple. No musician in his right mind would give up a chance to play an established nightspot like the Brass Rail for a cheap café like the Venezia. Alexander could not understand Eugene's concern. But then he had no idea the type of people who operated the Venezia. Eugene did.

That afternoon Eugene met with the owners of the Venezia in

their office. He told them that MCA—the Music Corporation of America—had booked him and his band at the famous Brass Rail nightclub. The manager seemed unconcerned. "So what's the problem, Eugene?" Eugene then explained that he was under contract to MCA and that he was giving his notice because he was to open at The Brass Rail in two weeks. The reaction of the Venezia's manager threw Jelesnik off guard. As Eugene later described their meeting, it was clear that the employer and the employee were in two entirely different worlds: "The guy said, 'Ehh, Eugene, don't worry about it, no problem, no problem.' And I'm thinking, *well that wasn't so bad,* and we shook hands and I said, 'alright' and 'thank you,' and we were all smiles. It all seemed very nice and amicable. But as I was leaving the office I heard this guy say, 'We'll take care of it, Eugene.' I didn't know what he meant by that. I'd just given him my notice, or thought I had. What was he going to take care of?"

A week went by and nothing more was said about the Brass Rail. Then one day a new sign went up in front of the Venezia, which again advertised: "Eugene Jelesnik and his Orchestra Playing Nightly." But the posters and publicity in front of the Brass Rail also had Eugene and his orchestra opening there the very next weekend. He was beginning to suspect that something had gone very wrong. His worst fear was that the Venezia wasn't going to let him go after all. He worried so much about it that he was sick to his stomach the rest of the afternoon, and he couldn't sleep that night. The next morning he went back to the manager of the Venezia to make certain that he understood the situation— that his bosses knew he was leaving. The obtuse dialogue between Eugene and the manager was almost a replay of the first interview, but with some of the more important details fleshed out:

I went into the office and the manager said, "Hey, what's up, Eugene?"

So I told him, "I was just wondering, my picture's still out in front here, and I'm supposed to open at the Brass Rail in a week."

And the manager said, "So what are you worried about, Eugene?"

And so I said, "I don't know what's going on here. I have a contract with MCA."

He said, "Do you want your contract back from them or what?"

And I said "No! Why would I want that?"

And he said, "Because we're certainly not going to let you go from here!"

I said, "What do mean?"

And he said, "You're too good for business."

This was a revelation. I was stunned. I said, "Well, what am I supposed to do? I have a contract with MCA?"

And he said, "Don't worry about it, Eugene, we'll take care of it."

I told the guy, "I don't want to jeopardize my position."

And he said, "Don't worry so much, Eugene. We'll talk to MCA and see what we can work out."

When Eugene left the room his head was spinning. There were only 118 MCA headline artists in the world, and he was one of them. Whatever happened, the last thing he wanted was for the Venezia's manager to somehow jeopardize his standing with the most prestigious music booking agency in the world. He hoped and prayed that the man realized what was at stake. But Eugene Jelesnik's prayers were not enough, and once again his own naivete had not helped the situation. The men at the Venezia had no idea what was at stake for Eugene Jelesnik, and more significantly, they didn't care. Over the previous twenty years, men like them had repeatedly demonstrated that they were immune to human emotions such as caring. They cared no more for Eugene's career than they had for his piano player's face. They understood nothing but their own greed. After all, they were gangsters.

The very next day—on his way to the Venezia—he noticed that the photographs and posters in front of the Brass Rail had been taken down. When he arrived at the café, the manager called him into his office. The conversation was brief:

"Hey, Gene, come in here. I got a present for ya."

And I said, "Thank you. What is it?"

Then he took out a sheaf of papers and showed them to me. It was my MCA contract—I hate to think how he got it—and he proceeded to tear it up in front of my face.

When the manager of the Venezia tore up Eugene's contract with MCA, he destroyed more than a piece of paper. Everything that Eugene had carefully built through years of hard work seemed utterly lost. Everything that he had suffered for and worked for and strived to achieve from the time that his family fled Russia was laying in shreds on the floor of the manager's office in Café Venezia. It was the lowest point in his life. At that moment Eugene felt helpless and trapped. He finally came to see that he had "married into the mob" and couldn't get out of it. The realization itself was terrifying.

The episode made a lasting impression, and from that day on he was on the lookout for mobsters. More than twenty years after his ordeal at the Venezia, Eugene would experience a frightening flashback of the whole experience.

"While living in Salt Lake City, I used to go to Las Vegas—not to gamble but to get acts and select musicians for pops concerts and other special performances. I had been good friends with Wilbur Clark who owned the Desert Inn hotel and I usually stayed there during the trips. One day as I walked into the lobby, I ran into this guy who had been a minor figure at the Venezia. His face had been horribly mutilated—cut to pieces in many ways, but I recognized him immediately. He looked at me like he had seen a ghost and he said, 'Eugene?' and I said, 'Pete?' It was automatic. Just like that! After all those years. We didn't have anything else to say to each other. I just stared at his mutilated face, and he turned away. It gave me shivers just bumping into him. I later recalled that his full name was Pete Telurini. He was one of the biggest mobsters that Walter Winchell was after in the thirties. I couldn't believe that I actually knew somebody like that. It scared the heck out of me."

Jelesnick and his orchestra had yet another of their bookings extended indefinitely. They would suffer their impressed service at the Venezia for an additional four months. He later learned that the mob was trying to lure a new partner into the Venezia, "probably to fleece the guy of his investment and then strip the place of its assets." The story had a familiar ring to it. Eugene and his musicians were apparently part of the window dressing. Fortunately, no suckers were found, and the Venezia eventually closed, liberating Eugene from a scary situation.

Eugene was once again a free man, but the whole episode had cost him dearly. He had lost MCA—permanently—as his agent. He had lost his innocence. He had lost a great deal of money. And he had lost some of the momentum from his earlier successes. He had also learned a bitter lesson at a very great price: When you shake hands with the devil, you stand to lose more than your fingers.

Joe Moss and Sophie Tucker must have watched Eugene's travails in horror. In a little less than two years, the promising career they had launched with so much fanfare and adulation seemed headed for the rocks. The long run at the mob-tainted Venezia alone was enough to kill a career, but the sudden dropping of Jelesnik from the ranks of MCA's artists—so quickly after his first appearance—was tantamount to pronouncing his career "dead on arrival." Then there were the matters of the cancellation of the much publicized booking at the Brass Rail and the money he had borrowed to open the ill-fated Savoia. This was the very stuff that was the grist of New York City's gossip columnists and muckrakers. The only reason they didn't eat him alive was that most of the columnists knew Eugene personally and recognized that his fall had been brought on largely by the greed of others. Eugene had been the victim in every case, and the only blame that might be assigned to him could be attributed to his relative inexperience and innocence. Still, there was no question but that other performers had been murdered in the press for lesser mistakes and similar misfortunes.

Although he had lost all of his money, his agent, members of his band, and some of his reputation, Eugene still had a couple of things going for him. His drive to succeed was as strong as ever, and his loyal friends had never given up on him. Principal among those who now came to his aid was Joe Moss. Jelesnik's Continentals had enjoyed the longest run of any orchestra in the history of the Hollywood Restaurant, and Moss had no reservations about booking them again. On Friday, 21 May 1937, Moss announced in advertisements placed in a half-dozen New

York papers "The return engagement of Eugene Jelesnik and his famous European Society Orchestra." This was the same star treatment that Moss usually reserved for Sophie Tucker when she returned from the continent, as she had most recently done in March of 1937. Moss apparently believed that Eugene's return was equally deserving of that level of publicity. Perhaps he was right. Miss Tucker had only returned from Europe. Eugene Jelesnik had seemingly returned from the dead.

Jelesnik opened at the Hollywood for the second time on 31 May 1937 and appeared nightly thereafter with Gertrude Neilson, Yvonne Bouvier, Marion Martin, and the Paxton Sisters in the restaurant's "Summer Revue of 1937." Through the summer, they performed in three shows nightly, at 7:15, 10:15, and 2:00 A.M. By the end of June, he was once again being broadcast live over WABC. It wasn't long before eighty other CBS affiliates had signed on. Eugene had found his way back into the spotlight.

At the recommendation of friends, Eugene was able to get a new agent. The Meyer Davis Agency wasn't as big as MCA, but it was a solid, well-run company with a reputation for honesty. Davis personally managed some of the biggest "society" orchestras in the country, providing musicians for lavish parties thrown by the Vanderbilts and the Guggenheims, as well as exclusive debutante affairs and even presidential receptions. Eugene was lucky to get Davis. It was exactly the type of agency that Eugene would need to reclaim some of the ground lost at the Venezia. Unlike MCA, which relied heavily on its own reputation and the collective power of its star-studded clients to promote bookings, Meyer Davis gave individualized attention to a select handful of artists. The personal touch was his specialty, and he often wrote descriptive, first-person reviews of his clients for direct mailings to potential bookings. During the late summer of 1936, Davis began promoting his newest attraction:

> Can an orchestra take some of the selling burden off your hands? Here is one we think that can. Eugene Jelesnik and his CONTINENTALS . . . not unknown by any means with bookings at the Ten Eyke Hotel in Albany, New York, a year-long stay at the Hollywood Restaurant and Lexington Hotel in

New York City, and a series of radio transcriptions to be aired over 200 stations nationwide.

It is difficult if not impossible to describe Jelesnik's performances. He plays so many styles: smooth, hot, symphonic, and theatrical. Many have said that he belongs on the concert stage, but after the next number you think he just left Red Norvo. Jelesnik knows how to intrigue his audience. He has an uncanny intuition concerning what his audience prefers. His band responds to Eugene's every musical whim as if it were his right arm. Sudden stops and unexpected effects startle you. Various unusual combinations and other things are used to make the audience aware that there is much more than an orchestra on the bandstand.

Meyer Davis's campaign was successful and before the Summer Revue at the Hollywood had closed, he had booked Eugene and his orchestra at The Hotel Taft Grill Room in New Haven, Connecticut. Once again Eugene brought his orchestra up to full strength—ten musicians—and also added singer Dorothy Daniels as vocal soloist. Davis was a tireless promoter and, unlike many agents, didn't stop his promotion with the securing of a booking. In the weeks before the opening, he flooded the New Haven papers with release after release. He took full advantage of Jelesnik's celebrity connections and used them unabashedly in a variety of promotional stunts. A number of Eugene's friends were relieved when he began his climb out of the hole he had dug at the Venezia, and they were more than happy to extend not only their best wishes but their promotional assistance to Meyer Davis. In one clever ploy, Davis had Eugene's celebrity friends send wires of congratulations, not to Eugene, but directly to the hotel's manager, J. A. Voit, who they invariably praised for having the "genius" to book their friend Maestro Jelesnik. The Hotel Taft's manager was flattered (as expected) and took out ads in the paper which used the testimonials to promote the new attraction. On 16 September 1937, the *New Haven Evening Register* carried a full-page ad that reprinted some of the telegrams. The banner across the top of the page read "Broadway Congratulates New Haven." The content of the "telegrams" was transparent but effective:

Abe Lyman (famous conductor)

> Congratulations, Mr. Voit. Jelesnik and his Continentals will thrill New Haven as they have Broadway.

Ozzie Nelson (America's premier bandleader)

> Just heard the news that New Haven at the Taft will dance to Jelesnik and his Continentals. That means one of the tops in modern rhythm.

Harriet Hilliard (radio's sweet songstress)

> Tell all my friends in Connecticut that Jelesnik and his Continentals will be at the Taft. They will love his soft, soothing melodies.

Sophie Tucker (herself)

> So Jelesnik is coming to New Haven! You'll like him immensely. When the town dances to his Continentals they will be crazy about him too. Best of luck.

Joe Moss (owner of Broadway's famous Hollywood Restaurant)

> We are sorry to lose Jelesnik and his Continentals where he has been a feature at the Hollywood this past season. Thousands of our guests have danced to his splendid music. Hearty congratulations.[5]

Other congratulatory wires containing similar or even sillier puffs were sent by Willie and Eugene Howard, Irene Bordoni, Will Osborne, Smith Bellew, Leo Reisman, and Richard Himber. The wire from Rudy Vallee merited several separate photo spreads featuring Rudy and Eugene at the Hollywood Restaurant. The photo captions contained bits of radio hype translated freely into print:

> Hi Ho, everybody in New Haven! Rudy Vallee speaking. Eugene Jelesnik and his Continentals brings to the Taft Grill this season one of America's cleverest dance bands. You'll enjoy dancing all the more with the sophisticated rhythm of Eugene Jelesnik and his famous Continentals.

Eugene's orchestra opened at the Hotel Taft Grill Room on Saturday 18 September 1937. The posters for the evening were headed by the cap line "Meyer Davis Presents." It may have been self-promotion, but it was also true. Davis had made Eugene a hit long before he opened. By the end of the month, Eugene was being broadcast live from the Taft Grill over WBRY, WNBC, WATR, WYMCA, and the New York-based Inter City Network. Over the next month Davis would continue to pour it on. "The Eli of Yale will all meet at the Taft Hotel to dance to the 'divine' Jelesnik and his smart Continentals after the big game." All New Haven was buzzing with Meyer Davis's propaganda and the Jelesnik booking was extended to the end of the year.

In December of 1937, Eugene went to the Meyer Davis office in New York City to see what was next. Davis handed Eugene a letter from Guy Toombes, the general manager of a large hotel in Salt Lake City. Davis said, "How would you like to play the Hotel Utah?" Eugene replied, "Where in the world is that?" Meyer Davis was good at publicity, but was no more proficient at geography than Jelesnik: "I think it's someplace out West," he said. Eugene asked if it was in California. He had always wanted to go to California. Davis promised that he would find out, and Eugene told him he would have to check with the boys in the band.

Though Utah did not turn out to be in California, it was some-place near it—or so Eugene was led to believe. His musicians were not particularly enthusiastic about playing a town that even Eugene admitted was west of Ohio. But after some discussion they agreed to accept the booking, on the strict condition that they would stay no longer than eight weeks.

On 6 January 1938, Eugene, singer Dorothy Daniels, and the Continentals piled into a train car at Grand Central Station to begin their trip to Utah. Dick Marta's bulky cymbalom had been carefully stowed in the baggage car. Eugene's mother and Aunt Ruth came down to see Eugene off at the station, as did the friends and relatives of the other musicians. They were all New York City boys, and the only knowledge they had of the wild West was what they had seen in the movies. Jennie Jelesnik was particularly apprehensive about her son's decision to go West. From her point of view, he might have been taking the train back to Alexandrovsk. But good-byes said, the train slowly pulled out of the station.

This was the golden age of American train travel and Eugene remembers the trip well and fondly. It was his first journey west and his first real view of the American landscape. The scenes that rolled by as the New Yorkers made their way toward the unknown future was different than anything most of them had encountered before. The vast plains and seemingly endless open spaces came as a shock to the musicians more used to the concrete and glass canyons of Manhattan. But for Eugene there was something vaguely familiar about it, as if he had seen it someplace before. As they approached the Continental Divide, the snow-covered hills and distant prospects seemed bleak—there was considerable worry among the musicians that Eugene might be leading them into another disaster. Utah was the site where the golden spike had been driven completing the transcontinental railroad. It was—at least metaphorically—"The end of the line." Perhaps, the musicians feared, it was the end of their line as well. Unlike his jittery companions, Eugene had a feeling that he knew what was coming, and that it was good.

When they arrived in Salt Lake City they were met at the Union Pacific depot by the Hotel Utah's manager, Mr. Toombes. While the others were packing their instruments into the bus that would take them to the hotel, Eugene stood on the train platform and surveyed the surroundings. Salt Lake was not a big city, but it still had an impressive skyline, and its streets were wide and clean. Suddenly Eugene became aware of the huge snow-clad mountains looming above the city to the east. He was astounded by the sheer size and scenic beauty of the Wasatch range. "The minute I got off the train and saw those big wide streets and the mountains, it was love at first sight." He was overcome with emotion. It was as though he had arrived in a new world. Perhaps there was something liberating about the view, or perhaps something about that moment reminded him of some earlier experience. Whatever the explanation, his eyes misted over; he was overwhelmed. "I was enthralled then . . . and I still am. I never got over it." The day that Eugene got his first view of the Salt Lake Valley was indelibly impressed in his memory. His reaction was both spontaneous and exuberant. The view and his emotions completely engulfed him. He could find no explanation for his reaction, but it was one the most beautiful sights he had ever seen.[6]

CHAPTER SIX

THE HOTEL UTAH

The construction of the Hotel Utah was completed in July of 1911. At its opening, the builders—the Los Angeles firm of Parkinson and Bergstrom—declared that "It is the most perfectly arranged hotel in the United States."[1] After touring the completed structure, a visiting architect called it, "The finest building west of the Mississippi River." As grandiose as both claims may have seemed at the time, the reputation of the Hotel would do nothing but grow. Less than a month after its official opening, the hotel played host to President William Howard Taft who further enhanced its reputation by declaring: "Your city is exceedingly fortunate in having a hotel like this one. . . . It ranks with any in the world . . . a great and imposing structure, elegantly and magnificently furnished."[2] Every president of the United States, from Taft through Ronald Reagan, would stay at the Hotel Utah.

The architecture was claimed to be an adaptation of the "Italian renaissance style," but there were strong neoclassical elements, including marble pillars and hallways that would normally be found only in grand governmental buildings. The institutional aspects of the design were heightened by the fact that the exterior of the entire building was a dazzling white, similar to the Capitol Building or the White House in Washington, D.C.

When Guy Toombes took over as manager in 1935, he set out to renovate and modernize the hotel, which was then approaching its silver anniversary. By then, "The Utah" was already known as "The Grand Dame of American Hotels." Toombes, who had previously been the manager of the Davenport Hotel in Spokane, Washington, was expected to bring the hotel's occupancy rate up to pre-Depression levels. To accomplish this task, Toombes undertook extensive renovations that would eventually run to nearly a quarter million dollars. The largest ballroom in the hotel, the Empire Room, was extensively redecorated. Toombes also began a continuous program of restoring and replacing the furnishings. He replaced an old-style cafeteria with a modern coffee shop, installed a florist shop, pharmacy, and soda fountain, and illuminated the beehive dome on the roof with electric light. He also rebuilt the hotel's "Roof Garden," which overlooked Temple Square and downtown Salt Lake City.[3] After extensive work, the old Roof Garden reopened in the spring of 1936, renamed "The Starlight Gardens," which Toombes boasted was second to none in the country. Guy Toombes's innovations and restorations were extraordinarily successful. In 1937 the hotel sold 118,000 room-nights, and served over 485,000 meals. Total occupancy for the year was 142,531—which was more than the population of Salt Lake City at that time.[4]

The Hotel Utah was a classy establishment. In the Empire Room a strict dress code was enforced. Even someone as famous as Will Rogers—who stayed at the hotel shortly before his death in 1935—was refused service in the Empire Room because he was not properly attired.[5] The renowned trick roper, wit, and syndicated humorist had to borrow a coat and tie from the front desk before he could be seated. But even with its slightly stuffy dress code, the Hotel Utah prided itself on its friendly atmosphere and royal service. After Will Rogers had been properly clothed, he was treated to the hotel's most lavish service and later admitted that he could not have been treated better.

Guy Toombes did a good deal more than renovate rooms and furnishings and increase occupancy rates. More than anyone else, he was responsible for seeing to it that the hotel's service was second to none. His greatest contributions were in assembling and training the hotel's large staff. Toombes saw to it that the hotel's kitchen and restaurants had the best chefs in the West, that the employees (particularly the bellhops, desk clerks, and waiters) were the most professional and courteous in the business, and that the hotel's orchestra was the finest available. It was to that end that Eugene Jelesnik and his Continentals were brought from New York to Salt Lake City in January of 1938.

When Eugene and his orchestra first walked into the lobby of the Hotel Utah, they were astounded by its size and opulence.[6] The main lobby was a huge space, eighty-seven by eighty-seven feet square. Above the lobby was an elaborately designed leaded and stained glass ceiling supported by twelve massive gray marble pillars, each measuring four feet in diameter. The walls were of pink marble capped with marble carvings of the Utah state emblem, the beehive. The marble floor was covered in dark emerald green carpeting, "so thick you sank into it up to your knees!" There were velvet and brocade chairs and couches, French tapestries, and gold-leaf trim everywhere. The central area of the hotel housed a variety of small shops in neat little rooms. The whole lobby was brilliantly illuminated by huge crystal chandeliers imported from Czechoslovakia, each richly trimmed in shining brass. There were elaborate European-style plaster casts all around the cornices of the ceiling, and hand-carved Italian woodwork paneling of the richest baronial oak. The hotel had over 375 rooms, each richly furnished. Most of the rooms had brass beds, but the elaborate bridal suites, the presidential quarters, and other premium rooms were equipped with beds of polished mahogany. Each of the rooms came with dressers and glass-topped writing tables. There were decorated china trays, and brass candlesticks, fine china water pitchers, and antique porcelain. Western landscape paintings and other artwork adorned the walls. Each room had an informal seating area with comfortable chairs, or in the larger suites, couches. Lighting in the rooms included clustered lights in the center of the ceiling, and reading lamps by the bedsteads and desks.

The restaurants in the hotel were all gourmet. The downstairs "Hotel Utah Grill" was fitted with a beautiful fountain, which fed an artificial pond stocked with the Grill's specialty, "Rocky Mountain trout." A British publication would one day rate the Hotel Utah with London's "Berkley Hotel" and "The Hotel Sacher" in Vienna, as the world's best.[7] Eugene Jelesnik would stay and perform in many of the world's great hotels. He had recently played New York City's Waldorf Astoria and Lexington Hotels, the Ten Eyck in Albany, N.Y., and the Taft in New Haven,

Connecticut. He was unequivocal in his praise: "The Hotel Utah was the world's finest . . . period."

Eugene Jelesnik and his Continentals opened at the Empire Room of the Hotel Utah on Friday, 14 January 1938.[8] In addition to Eugene and singer Dorothy Daniels, the band included bass player Lindell Seacat; Arthur Weiner at the piano; Sid Mendell on trumpet; Dick Marta and his cymbalom; Milt Fried on the sax; Aaron Mallott playing the accordion; and Rudy Van Gelder on the drums or sometimes the xylophone. The advertising for the opening took its cue from the publicity received when they played Albany's Ten Eyck Hotel: "Eugene Jelesnik and his Continentals are the finest orchestra ever to play a permanent engagement in Salt Lake City." The publicity blitz was similar to that which accompanied the orchestra's opening at the Hotel Taft Grill in New Haven, including telegrams from Rudy Vallee, Abe Lyman, Harriet Hilliard and Sophie Tucker. As at the opening at the Taft, the PR clicked and opening night was packed. The Continentals were once again a smash success.

One week after the opening, Guy Toombes and Jelesnik came up with an idea to expose a broader audience to the orchestra than just the evening dance crowd. Beginning on Sunday, January 22, the hotel began featuring the orchestra in a series of late afternoon concerts in the hotel's lobby. The concerts would feature symphonic and classical music arrangements, solo performances by Eugene on the violin, special arrangements of seasonal favorites, and selected popular numbers. The format was similar to the Sunday programs the band had given at the Ten Eyck and Lexington, but these were free concerts open to the public. The concerts were well-publicized and soon became a major attraction at the hotel, which had to increase its dinner staff to accommodate the audience members who decided to stay for Sunday supper after the performance. Eugene and Toombes were of a like mind when it came to promotions and publicity. Both recognized the need to appeal to as wide an audience as possible, and there was truly something for everyone in each program. It was yet another formula that would serve Eugene well throughout his career.

The hotel was generous—even lavish—in providing complete

musical bills for each of the concerts. These were not simple hand-outs, but were elaborately printed in color on expensive card stock. The programs were eclectic. The first concert included: "The Waltz Triste" by Jean Sibelius; "Serenade" by Franz Schubert; and "The Beautiful Danube" by Johann Strauss. There were also violin, piano, and vibraphone solos, there were excerpts from an Egyptian ballet, as well as a Mexican hat dance and the Irish folksong "Londonderry Air." The formula continued every week in much the same fashion. The same program that featured music from Bizet's "Carmen" and Franz Liszt's Rhapsody #6, also had "Indian Love Call," "Ave Maria," "March of the Toy Soldiers," and an improvised rendition of "Mary Had a Little Lamb." Many of the programs contained patriotic pieces, others featured overtures or arias from the opera. There were usually special melodies for children and ethnic melodies from around the world.[9]

The regular issue of *Variety* for 23 February 1939, contained a feature story of Eugene's triumph in far-off Salt Lake City. For any orchestra, an article in *Variety* was a public relations coup, but this was even more so considering how far "off Broadway" the Continentals had traveled for the booking: *Variety's* headline read: "Remarkable Success at Hotel Utah."

> To cope with the rule against dancing on Sunday in Salt Lake City—Mecca of the Mormon religion—Guy Toombes, hostelry manager, imported Eugene Jelesnik's band of entertainers, who are responsible for a healthy uplift of dinner tariff during the week. The trump card of Toombes plan are free Sunday afternoon concerts by the band in the lobby of the hotel. The orchestra plays for dancing, on Thursday, Friday, and Saturday nights. On other weeknights they play for evening dinners. Jelesnik's outfit composed of eight men and a lush fem warbler, Dorothy Daniels, are also heard in Salt Lake over KSL—the local CBS affiliate—who air the band thrice weekly for half-hour stints.
>
> Jelesnik, whose physical makeup resembles Rubinoff, is an ace salesman with his valuable squeaker. He doubles as the band's arrangement maker too. Miss Daniels pipes are good. Arthur Weiner is socko at the piano, being spotted during intermission for featured solos. Tall, personable Lindell Seacat

has a soft baritone and teams effectively with Miss Daniels. Skin beater, Rudy Van Gelder and Milt Fried (sax) are featured in comedy numbers, while Sid Mendell, trumpeter, and Aaron Mallott, groan box artist, get a chance during rest periods.[10]

Eugene and his orchestra were obviously a big hit in Salt Lake City, and it wasn't long before Guy Toombes approached Eugene and asked if the band would stay on through the summer. Eugene explained that he had promised the boys they would only stay for eight weeks. But Toombes told Eugene that he couldn't possibly leave without playing the Roof Garden. Utah's winters were harsh, and the roof-top restaurant was only open during the summer months. So Eugene called a meeting of the orchestra members and told them about Guy Toombes's offer. One of the musicians said "I thought we were only going to come out here for eight weeks." Eugene told them that if they didn't like it at the Hotel Utah that they didn't have to stay. They would take a vote, and if the band wanted to return to New York, they would go back immediately. The vote was unanimous. Everyone wanted to stay, but they also insisted that they be able to bring out some of their relatives so that they could see for themselves what the Hotel Utah was really like. Toombes agreed. The eight-week booking was eventually extended to ten months.

Not long after they signed their extended contracts with the Hotel Utah, Eugene convinced his musicians to participate in some unusual publicity photos. The entire orchestra was dressed in ill-fitting western Garb, including kerchiefs, ten-gallon hats, and cowboy boots. Eugene, violin in hand, wore a pair of huge woolen chaps. Dorthy Daniels—who would later gain fame for her recording "Chanson d'amore" with her husband Art Todd—waved her cowboy hat in rodeo fashion as if she were riding a bucking bronco. Incongruously, many of the photographs were taken beside the marble columns of the Roof Garden with the city clearly visible behind them in the distance. The PR shot would have looked more natural if they had donned togas, but it was silly enough that it appeared in many newspapers throughout the country. One photo caption was probably written by agent/

publicist Meyer Davis. It was typical of the kind of puff he had produced for other engagements.

> "Oh, we're way out west," sings Maestro Eugene Jelesnik, as he leads his orchestra atop the Hotel Utah. In New York City, Eugene, famed orchestra leader and his band make Gothamites swing a sophisticated light fantastic, but on arrival in Salt Lake City, he went western at the famed Hotel Utah, with a bang, along with his Continentals. Maestro Jelesnik, attired in Stetson and chaps, took his be-hatted gang to the rooftop where he could play his music to the big outdoors, and the 12,000 foot adjacent mountains. Now the boys are swinging and shagging to lonesome cowboy rhythms and Jelesnik, a composer of note who wrote "My Gypsy Melody" and "Two Silhouettes on the Moon" has turned to the western theme for his inspiration and has written a song entitled "Big Ranch Boss."[11]

In addition to "Big Ranch Boss," Eugene composed and performed a western melody titled "When It's Midnight on the Range." Eugene's piano player, Arthur Weiner, was also inspired by his new surroundings and composed several piano pieces while in Salt Lake City, including: "Sunrise on the Wasatch Mountains," which he performed in several of the Sunday concerts. Many of Salt Lake's most prominent citizens dined and danced to the music of the Continentals. Among those to frequent the Hotel Utah during Eugene's 1938 engagement were the families of Salt Lake's banker/mayor John Wallace; financiers: Mariner Eccles and J. E. Cosgriff; broker/mining engineer James Hogle and his wife, Bonnie; Mr. and Mrs. George Hansen; and KDYL Radio station owner, Sid Fox. Mr. and Mrs. Makoff—owners of Salt Lake's premier designer store and dress shop—not only attended the dances but occasionally were sponsors or advertisers for the hotel's Sunday concert series. Among the many prominent people to stay at the hotel during the period was Vicki Baum, author of *Grand Hotel*. A photograph of the famous writer, flanked by Jelesnik and Guy Toombes, was featured on the front page of the hotel's in-house newsletter, "The Utah Register," on 17 February 1938. Publicity shots of Miss Baum and Eugene were also taken for the local papers. Eugene's musicians would one day perform a musical version of *Grand Hotel* at the Capitol Theater in Salt Lake City.

Most of the patrons who attended the dances either at the Empire Room or later the Starlight Roof Gardens were young couples just starting their lives together. For *Deseret News* publisher Wendell Ashton and his wife, and for Bonneville International president Arch Madsen and his wife, the name Eugene Jelesnik always brought back memories of their courtship days. Eugene was surprised and pleased by the number of happily married couples who would later credit him and his musicians for playing a role in furthering their romance. Eugene recalls that "the Empire Room was always packed with people, and some of them came back night after night. For decades after, I heard how this couple or that first courted and danced to my music at the Hotel Utah. It's amazing."

Eugene himself was a dashing young man about town and was not immune to the lures of romance. He was frequently seen at dinner in the company of some of Salt Lake's most attractive beauties. One lady in particular to whom Eugene took a shine in his early months in Salt Lake was Ethyl Langwell Clays, a beautiful young artist, later greatly admired for her portraits of children. Miss Clays and Eugene were great friends who enjoyed and appreciated some of the same subjects in the arts and music. But unsuspected by Eugene himself, his days as a carefree, eligible young bachelor were rapidly drawing to a close, and the suddenness of his fall surprised even him. But Virginia Washburn was no casual dinner date. From the moment Eugene first set eyes on her, he knew that she was something very special, and he instantly set about the task of making her his own.

Virginia Belle Washburn[12] was the third of six children (five daughters and a son) born to Edward D. and Lizada Elmore Washburn. Virginia was born on 18 June 1905, in Mulberry Grove, Illinois, and was nine years Eugene's senior. Her father's family originally hailed from Kentucky, but had moved west during the first great migration to Illinois in the late 1830s. The Washburn family had operated Mulberry Grove's first hotel, as well as its principal livery stable. They were among the community's most prominent citizens and were involved in many civic activities. Their stable often provided transportation to parties and dances at Hudson Park Lake, just north of Mulberry. On public holidays such as the Fourth of July, they charged 5 cents for a horse-and-buggy ride to the lake, where residents could spend the day picnicking, swimming, roller skating, boating, or dancing.

Virginia's father owned the town's first automobile—a 1910 International—and photos of the Washburns on outings in the huge touring car were prominently displayed in the family album. Owning the only car in town necessitated becoming your own mechanic. As others joined the motoring fraternity, it was inevitable that Virginia's father was the one sought out when anything mechanical went wrong. As the area's first mechanic, it was only natural that he would soon convert the family's livery business into Mulberry Grove's first automobile repair shop—the Old National Trail Garage. It was also natural that his daughter, Virgina, would learn to drive at an early age. It was a skill that she would put to much use in the years to come.

In 1919, the Washburn family packed up everything they owned and moved to California, eventually settling in Highland Park, a suburb of Los Angeles. Virginia attended school in that city, and graduated from Lincoln High School. She studied law for a time and also worked as a set dresser and floral arranger for a number of Hollywood movie studios, but eventually she decided to go into business for herself. By the midthirties, she owned and operated several of her own shops in Los Angeles and was active in many community organizations. One of the groups she belonged to was the Altrusa Club of Hollywood, California, and in the spring of 1938, she agreed to drive the officers of the club to a Soroptimist convention in Salt Lake City. Virginia and her companions would stay at the Hotel Utah.

Eugene remembers that it was an evening in early spring. The band was still performing at the Empire Room, and Eugene was relaxing just outside the entrance during an intermission break. He remembered that he was dressed formally, in full tails, that he wasn't really looking for anyone, and wasn't paying much attention to anything. Suddenly a group of ladies came into the hotel from the west, side entrance. One of the women was very striking, and Eugene was drawn to her like a magnet.

He recalls, "I still can't believe I did this, but I saw her come into the hotel, and I immediately went over and asked, 'Pardon me, Miss, but haven't we met someplace before?'

"She looked at me like I was absolutely insane, and said, 'I don't believe so,' and started to walk off.

"I followed after her and I said, 'Excuse me again, but my name is Eugene Jelesnik, and I'm the orchestra leader here, will you be staying at the hotel?'

"She said that she was just on her way to register.

"I said: 'Well, I'm playing this evening in the Empire Room and perhaps after you get settled in . . . well, I would be most honored if you would be my guest for dinner.'

"She looked at me like I was crazy and once again said, 'No, I don't believe so.'

"In those days there was a florist shop in the hotel, and while the women were registering, I went over there and ordered just about every flower arrangement they had. I found out her room number from the desk clerk, and before she had got her luggage out of her car I had filled her room with flowers."[13]

Virginia Washburn accepted Eugene's invitation to dinner. He could not have chosen a better approach. Miss Washburn was a professional florist. One of her shops in fact had provided a major floral spray for Will Rogers's funeral. There were other surprises. Over dinner Virginia told Eugene that though they had not been formally introduced, that they had indeed met before. The previous year she had been to another convention—this one in New York City—and she had seen Eugene's show at the Hollywood Restaurant. He had even played at her table. Eugene admitted to her that when he asked "If they hadn't met before," that he was just giving her a line, but he also assured her that he had never said anything like that to any woman before. He wanted to meet her, and couldn't think of anything else to say. Over dinner, Eugene told Virginia of his background and about some of his career, and Virginia told Eugene of her life in California. Her two florist shops had thrived at first, but she admitted that they had fallen on hard times, that she was heavily in debt, and would probably have to find another line of work very soon.

Eugene's reply was a bombshell: "You go back to L.A. and settle up your affairs. Do what you have to do to get squared away and then come back here as soon as you can and we'll get married."[14]

Virginia stared at Eugene as though he were crazy. She was bewildered by the suddenness of his proposal of marriage. They had only become acquainted an hour or so before, and now he was talking in a most matter-of-fact way about their immediate marriage. He seemed to be in the process of planning their lives together. For Eugene it all seemed as natural as anything in the world, and though his intended was shocked, she agreed to consider the proposal seriously. From that moment, Eugene believed they had an understanding.

After Virginia returned to California, Eugene continued to court her with nightly long-distance telephone calls. Whenever Eugene got a day off after that, which was once every two weeks, he flew down to Los Angeles on Western Airlines to visit her. The whirlwind romance seemed a confirmation of the line from Christopher Marlowe's *Hero and Leander*: "Who ever loved that loved not at first sight."

In May, when the skies cleared and the weather became warmer, the Hotel Utah opened its "Starlight Roof Garden" for the summer. The opening also brought the return of Eugene's long relationship with CBS. Salt Lake affiliate station KSL began broadcasting the Roof Garden dance concerts live from the hotel for the network, with KSL announcer Russell Stewart at the microphone. "The Roof"—as it was popularly known—was one of Salt Lake's most beautiful settings. The dance floor was open air, and under its canopy of stars, perhaps with the moon rising from behind Mount Olympus, dancers swayed to Eugene's music in full view of Main Street and Temple Square. But even on the clearest of nights, downtown Salt Lake City can be buffeted by canyon winds, and the musicians quickly learned that sheets of music that weren't tightly secured to their stands were liable to be blown high into the sky by a sudden gust. Worse were the occasional squalls, which blew in from the West across the Great Salt Lake. Paper cups, napkins, and even tablecloths would frequently be blown off the roof of the building. Eugene remembered one occasion in particular when the floor was packed with dancers. As the evening progressed a gale swooped suddenly in and swept everything off the tables. Dresses were blown over the heads of the women and napkins and sheets of music soared off the roof of the hotel, never to be seen again. But the dancers were having such a good time that it was decided to move the whole affair: dancers, musicians, waiters, music stands, the piano, the cymbolom, the drums and even some of the tables downstairs to continue the soiree in the shelter of the hotel's grand lobby. The CBS broadcast for the evening had to be canceled, but the dancing went on late into the night. It was a memorable occasion.

Eugene continued to court Virgina via phone and airplane and by June she had finally accepted his proposal. Eugene called his mother to break the news. Jennie was shocked and surprised at first, but realized that there was probably nothing she could do about it anyway. She then congratulated her son and told him that she was very happy that he had found someone to love. When Aunt Ruth heard the news, she was beside herself. She had known all along that the trip to Salt Lake had been a mistake, and this was the proof of it.

After settling her business affairs in Los Angeles and paying off all her bills and other obligations, Virginia took the train to Salt Lake. She arrived at the Union Pacific depot with $10 in her pocket. Eugene met her at the station with a bottle of champagne. Eugene and Virginia had hoped to be married on the Fourth of July, but soon found that it was next to impossible to arrange a wedding on the national holiday. The marriage took place on 5 July 1938 at the Ambassador Club in Salt Lake City, with Rabbi Samuel H. Gordon officiating. The best man was Arthur Weiner, the orchestra's piano player. Arthur's wife served as the maid of honor. Following the ceremony, which was attended by all the musicians in the band, the newlyweds were hosted at one reception at Rabbi Gordon's suite at the Ambassador Hotel and at another reception staged in the presidential suite at the Hotel

Utah. Jack Kohler, the hotel's head chef and one of Eugene's good friends, prepared all the food for the affair.

Though Jennie, Aunt Ruth, and Virginia's parents were unable to attend the wedding, they were able to participate vicariously over a special transcontinental phone hookup. The link was arranged by the telephone company so that members of Eugene's family in New York City, and Virginia's parents in Los Angeles, could at least hear the event, even if they couldn't witness it. The peculiar ceremony attracted nationwide attention and news of the "telephone troth" was carried by all of the major wire services. That evening *The Deseret News* afforded the wedding "feature story" status, with a two-column photograph of Eugene and his bride standing behind a table filled with telephones reciting their "I do's" into separate receivers. The story, which described Virginia as "a Hollywood society girl and social worker," was capped with the peculiar headline: "Transcontinental Telephonic-Triangle Tieup Today Ties Trothed Two Together. Parental Participation Pleases Parted Parties." *The Salt Lake Tribune* society page carried a two-column portrait picture of Virginia wearing a stylish satin outfit and matching, broad-brimmed hat. The article went on to describe the bride's wedding dress and the gown of her attendant: "The bride was charming in her wedding suit of rose beige crepe with cornflower blue accessories. She carried a bouquet of gardenias and lilies of the valley. Mrs. Arthur Weiner, the bride's only attendant, was frocked in a French blue afternoon gown with white accessories and wore a corsage of roses and blue cornflowers."

The coast-to-coast telephone marriage seemed more than appropriate. The New Yorker and the Hollywood beauty had conducted much of their whirlwind courtship via long-distance telephone conversations.

Following their marriage, Eugene and his bride took a small flat in the Castle Heights Apartments, on First Avenue not far from the Hotel Utah. The booking at the hotel lasted through the first weeks of September 1938. Guy Toombes was more than pleased with the Continentals. It was not only one of the longest engagements in the hotel's history, but was the most financially successful as well. During the orchestra's last week at the hotel, the management held a series of good-bye parties for Eugene and his musicians. Eugene had fallen in love with Salt Lake City and was sorry to have to leave. He promised himself that if he ever got the chance he would return, and asked KDYL station owner, Sid Fox, to keep him in mind if any openings came up. But at the same time, he had grown homesick for New York. The Utah booking was the longest time he had ever been away from his mother and Aunt Ruth.

Unlike Eugene, Virginia was not particularly crazy about Salt Lake during her first extended stay in the city. The couple had discussed the possibility of living in Los Angeles. Virginia's parents owned several bungalows in L.A., and the Jelesniks would be welcome to live in one of them if they so chose. But unlike his wife, Eugene did not drive, and the thought of taking the bus everywhere or having Virginia chauffeur him around L.A. seemed impractical. Virginia's second choice was San Francisco. Like New York City, it was compact, and Virginia had once worked there as a buyer for a large department store. But in the end, Eugene convinced her that New York City was the only place for a musician. Besides, it was his town, and he felt it was time to go home.

With the Hotel Utah contract over, the Jelesniks purchased a used Buick Roadmaster and a trailer to transport their belongings on the long, cross-country trek to New York City. The couple was accompanied by bass player Lindell Seacat and his wife. The trip was a series of misadventures and near disasters from start to finish. The Buick was a piece of junk and leaked quarts of oil all over the highway. The very first day of the journey, they stopped in a town in Wyoming to buy some additional provisions, and while Virginia was walking from the car to the store she was run over by a reckless bicyclist and badly injured her leg. With the exception of Virginia, all the travelers were New York City natives and not one knew how to drive a car. Virginia would have to continue driving, even with her injury. If things weren't bad enough, the weather was horrible. Years later, Virginia described her impression of the trip in a letter to her husband:

I remember the day we left this city to return to New York. What a trip we had through the rain almost two-thirds of the way to New York. I think it was somewhere in Iowa, we took a wrong road and ran into a snow drift, proving how early it got cold that year. Back on the road in the right direction we ran into a rain that filled all the road dips. We drove into a motel where I had a most difficult encounter with a mud hole six inches deep. I can recall getting the car out and turning the trailer we were dragging all the way to New York. I injured my knee, and I had an X-ray to see if the bone was broken. In spite of the pain, I kept driving and I recall one night we spent in a garage getting the rope tightened and some of the load readjusted. We had a bad tire on the trailer, and had to get that repaired, and I found the lemon Roadmaster was using quarts of oil. I was never so perplexed as I was the two days we started on our "honeymoon" cross-country tour. Our stop to see Earl Von Droska's family in Iowa was my first rest in four days.

I started to wonder if I could get us to New York before having the rings changed. I used heavy truck oil and as we pulled into Mulberry Grove, Ill. we did not stop. The rain was pouring, and I was covered with mud from head to toe, but I kept going. I determined then, and every day since, I would never buy a second-hand car again.

When we arrived in New York City, we parked the Buick in a garage. Every time we went to get the car out, another part was missing. Eventually, it was dismantled. [15]

When Eugene and his bride arrived in New York, they moved in with Eugene's mother and Aunt Ruth. The purchase of the Buick, the repairs, and the expenses of the trip had exhausted what little money they had saved. Ruth and Jennie were living in a tiny, three-room apartment on the fourth floor of a walk-up. The place was hardly big enough for two people, let alone four. Things were uncomfortably cramped, and no one had any privacy. It was supposed to be a temporary arrangement until Eugene and his wife could afford a place of their own. Unfortunately, it was anything but temporary. Eugene quickly found that getting a booking in New York City after playing four months in Albany was infinitely easier than getting one after playing nine months in Salt Lake. Eugene had effectively taken himself out of the spotlight, and out of the loop. All the good band venues were already taken. This time he had no resources to fall back on, and there was no contingency fund to keep the orchestra together. One by one, his hand-picked musicians began to drift away. His piano player, Arthur Weiner, who had also been best man at Eugene's wedding, was one of the first to leave. He would go to work in a Broadway nightclub, then owned by the father of future television personality Barbara Walters.

Worse than giving up some of his best musicians, Eugene couldn't seem to find enough work to support both himself and Virginia. He began taking short, out-of-town bookings with small dance band ensembles. Over the next year he would perform in hotels and clubs all over the East, from Cleveland, Ohio, to Jacksonville, Florida. He and some of his musicians also recorded a large number of transcription disks for the infant novelty called "Muzak," which would eventually evolve into the ubiquitous shopping mall and elevator music of today. But even as his bookings increased and his income became more stable, the domestic situation continued to deteriorate.

As the days dragged into weeks, and the weeks into months, the atmosphere at home became increasingly intolerable. Aunt Ruth and Virginia did not get along at all, and everything that Virginia did seemed to rub Ruth the wrong way. No one was happy with the living arrangement, and Eugene would later describe the scene, shaking his head: "They were like oil and water. The tension in that little apartment was so thick you could cut it with a knife. Virginia and I started leaving on weekends and staying in hotels, but things were no better on Monday when we returned. I realized that I had to get Ruth and Virginia separated or the marriage was over."

Eugene had two serious challenges. One was to find a larger apartment, and the second was to get Virginia and Aunt Ruth out of each other's way. As things worked out, he was able to accomplish both tasks when he found an apartment for Ruth on 56th Street, while he, Jennie, and Virginia moved into a larger apartment on 51st. Eugene also began taking Virginia with him on his tours and resort bookings. In the same epistle that described their trek east, Virginia mused on the newlyweds' first year in New York City. It was not what she expected when she married the dashing young bandleader—so flush with success—who had showered her with flowers, taken her on dinner dates, and repeatedly flown to her side from a city more than seven hundred miles away.

> At 24 you seemed to be in a daze, never knowing the shock I got seeing the other side of the world in New York. Poor you! I felt so sorry. No jobs opened up, so in a month I was working at the Astor Hotel in New York. Then I found a job on 42nd Street—the Laurel Dress Shop. It paid me less, but I could sit down and not stand on my feet all day. I remember one time that the "Beer Barrel Polka" was being played at the greasy spoon where I had my lunch and you were still hoping to find a job . . . audition after audition. I was taking home work to make a few extra dollars and packing my lunches and walking home to save bus fare.
>
> I was keeping warm in a $10 coat we bought at Burnette's and somehow we paid our rent. We both knew the day you pawned your silver cup that we had reached the bottom. Then I got a job on Easter and worked for 48 hours straight on my legs, and I wondered then if my legs would hold up. You got a few nights of work, and, finally, a job and we were off to Ohio, Kentucky, and back to New York after stops in Jacksonville, Florida, and Columbus, Dayton, and Louisville.[16]

While Eugene eventually redeemed his silver bar mitzvah cup, there were other belongings that were never recovered. In her letter to Eugene, Virginia recalled pawning some of her own prized possessions just to make ends meet. The things she lost for good included an ermine jacket that had been used in several Hollywood movies, some of her rings, and her portable Singer sewing machine. Nineteen thirty-nine was not a good year for the Jelesniks or for the rest of the world. The approach of the Second World War cast long shadows over the face of the globe. Few saw anything but more clouds on the horizon.

As dark as the picture may have seemed, there were hints of a silver lining. On 30 April 1939, The New York World's Fair opened and gave the world a futuristic and hopeful glimpse at a better tomorrow. The first two weeks of the fair, Eugene and his orchestra were engaged to provide music for the Turkish pavilion. Eugene, who had previously been promoted as a Hungarian Gypsy, could now add *Turkish* to his adopted nationalities. In fact, Eugene's music could be heard all over the fairgrounds. The "Muzak" transcriptions that he had recorded some months before made their debut at the 1939 World's Fair. Another highlight of the fair was the nation's first broadcast of commercial television. Philo T. Farnsworth's brainchild was finally entering adolescence, and within months, the National Broadcasting Company (NBC) would be airing regularly scheduled weekly programs. It had been just seven years since Eugene had painted his face purple to be transmitted indistinctly through six floors of the CBS Building. Over that time many, but not all, of the technical problems that had plagued the earlier period of television had been solved. More importantly, the country was just pulling out of the Great Depression, and there were more people who could actually afford the improved, if still expensive, television receivers. Considering the success that he had enjoyed at the experimental station W2XAB, it was not surprising that Eugene would be called back, now that TV was becoming something more than a scientific toy— this time for NBC's television station W2XBS.

The National Broadcasting Company's Studio 3-H was located in Rockefeller Center. Compared to the tiny box that Eugene had squeezed into at CBS it must have seemed spacious, but the work was still technically restrictive, and the lights needed for the new cameras were much brighter and much hotter than before. By the spring of 1940, Eugene was seen regularly on the "tube" and by June he was given his own regular time slot over the NBC network. Eugene's program "Gypsy Moods" was similar to his earlier radio broadcasts. But unlike his radio programs, Eugene experimented with various combinations of musicians, instruments, and musical arrangements.[17] One of his earliest programs featured his violin, a guitarist, and a vocalist. *Variety* wrote:

> Television Review: Eugene Jelesnik was outstanding with his violin playing, ably supported by Jean Clair who was good on

the accordion and only fair on the vocals, also Harold Corlin on the guitar.

By July 5ᵗʰ, he had experimented with his show, adding a little more "movement" to the screen by including interludes of dance. As time went on, Eugene would continue to tinker with the program's format—always adding more contrast and variety. The July 10ᵗʰ issue of *Variety* provided this more extensive review of the July 5ᵗʰ edition of "Gypsy Moods," which also happened to be Eugene's second wedding anniversary:

> Television Review: Eugene Jelesnik with Eduard Futran, Charlotte Clair, instrumental, dancing, Friday July 5ᵗʰ, 1940/ NBC RCA New York. This combination of continental entertainment reacted pleasantly on the eye and the ear. Eugene Jelesnik, Gypsy violinist, did a return engagement before the electric eye. But this time he was backed up by a three-piece unit consisting of a piano, a cello, and a marimba. At intervals he was relieved by Eduard Futran, specialist on the accordion, while Charlotte Clair came in with a fast batch of pirouettes. It was a smooth sample of radio photography all around.

Billboard reviewed the show, writing:

> Jelesnik's repertoire ran the gamut of Gypsy melodies, continental waltzes, and excerpts from the opera. Futran, who photographs like Valentino, vocalized a medley of Spanish, French, and Dutch numbers.
>
> Presentation of music either orchestral or vocal has long been a tough problem for the tele [vision] producers. On this program Jelesnik's [orchestra] showed to advantage. The maestro putting dash and personality into his posh violin sequences.

The *New York Daily News* columnist Ben Gross's "Listening In" for 6 July 1940, was equally complimentary:

> NBC's visual station W2XBS telecast a colorful entertainment, "Gypsy Moods," starring Eugene Jelesnik's Orchestra and supporting artists during an hour devoted to "Minstrels" (9 to 10). For those seeking something away from the usual variety routine, this show had the answer in its

haunting Gypsy and Hungarian melodies. Jelesnik is a first-rate violinist and his ensemble an outstanding one.

If Eugene had been performing on any stage but television, these reviews might have brought instant riches, but in all of New York City, there were no more than a few thousand privately owned sets. TVs were in the department stores and many display windows, so more people must have watched "Gypsy Moods" in small clusters standing on the streets than seated in living rooms. Television was still years away from becoming a commercial success. It was only the beginning. An NBC press release of the period gave Eugene special credit for his expertise in the new medium and dubbed him as "Television's Violinist." The release claimed that "Jelesnik was accorded one of the highest ratings to be given an artist for his RCA-NBC television broadcasts during 1940." It also noted that his orchestra and that of Fred Waring were the first two selected by NBC specifically for television broadcasts. But the programming aired by the network was extremely sparse, and on some days sparser than others. The entire network offering for July 5th consisted of a western movie with Rex Bell called *West of Nevada*, a fifteen-minute news broadcast by Lowell Thomas, and "Gypsy Moods," with Eugene Jelesnik's orchestra.

Still, publicity was publicity, and Eugene used the plaudits to advantage. From that time on, it was generally recognized that Jelesnik was the conductor of "television's first orchestra." During his tours through the East, he was billed as "Eugene Jelesnik and his Television Orchestra." Some of the special problems facing television's early artists were described by Eugene in an interview he gave to the Columbus, Ohio *Dispatch:*

> Eugene Jelesnik, leader of television's first regular orchestra, which is now "on leave" in the Ionian Room of the Deshler Wallick Hotel awaiting a call to active duty in NBC's New York studios, thinks the new industry is "hot stuff."
> As a matter of fact, explains the genial, stocky little gentleman, it's so warm inside the average telecasting studios that the orchestra's instruments get out of tune in a matter of minutes, making it necessary to obtain musicians who are able to play in tune when their instruments are out. Although the

general public is not aware of the fact when they witness
television from the receiving end, the barrage of lights and the
resultant heat necessary to perfect reproduction is the greatest
problem of the industry today. Lights used in telecasting, he
explains, are even stronger than those used in motion picture
work, and in order to avoid that "pasty pan" impression on the
part of the listener-looker, members of the orchestra must wear
makeup of the same intensity as that utilized by Hollywood.

"When I played my first show for NBC," said Jelesnik, "the
biggest problem confronting me was the seating of the
musicians. They had to be very close together, so close that
occasionally only half an arm and half an instrument was
visible. The purpose of this procedure was to get a good picture
of the ensemble at a reasonable camera range. Should the
orchestra be far apart and the camera have to take the picture
from long range, the musicians would look like dots in the
screen.

Three cameras are used in television at the present time, one
close-up, one long shot, and one panoramic. For the solo artist,
"Gene" believes there are no difficulties involved in a
performance before the television camera. "Of course," he
emphasizes, "the lights are very strong and unless one is
physically well set up he could hardly finish the broadcast
without a severe headache, dizzy spell, or eye ache."

Returning to the heat problem, the orchestra leader told of
his more recent experiences with NBC in New York. "We were
in Studio 3-H in the R.C.A. building, which is a perfectly air-
cooled room," he explained. "In fact it was very cold outside.
Then we went under the ceiling of lights (a few feet away from
where we were standing in the cold).

"After five minutes under the terrific heat all the instruments
went out of tune. There is nothing which can be done about the
situation at present and the strong lights are necessary to
produce a perfect image.

"It is my opinion, therefore, that only thorough musicians
who know their instruments well enough to play in tune when
the strings are out of tune can perform under the conditions as
required by television today."[18]

While Eugene was increasingly reliant on television and radio
to provide an income, he continued to tour with his new band. He
played the Van Cleve Hotel in Dayton, Ohio; the Brinks' Lookout

House in Covington, Kentucky, near Cincinnati; Monoco's Café in Cleveland; and The Iroquois Gardens in Louisville, Kentucky, a favorite haunt of Kentucky Derby visitors. He put together a small band that performed on a cruise ship taking short jaunts up to Nova Scotia and also played at Newman's Lake House, a famous club at Saratoga Springs, which drew a large celebrity clientele. In the late fall of 1941, Eugene and his orchestra received word of a forthcoming engagement that promised to be as interesting as the Hotel Utah. Meyer Davis had managed to get the band into a mid-winter stint as the house orchestra at a large resort hotel in San Juan, Puerto Rico. New York natives were used to harsh winters, but Virginia was a transplanted Californian, and the winter of 1940–41 had been especially hard on her. She had held up well considering that most of her free time had been spent cooped up with Eugene's mother. The Puerto Rican engagement must have seemed a godsend. Eugene accepted the booking with the stipulation that he would be able to bring Virginia along. As things developed, the hotel agreed to provide full accommodations for the couple. The trip was to be a working vacation to a tropical island after two years of enduring cramped quarters in New York and less than ideal living arrangements on the road. Virginia spent much of the late fall planning for the trip, and they both eagerly anticipated the change of scenery.

The day before they were to sail for Puerto Rico, the orchestra members went to the dock to see that their instruments, steamer trunks, music, and wardrobes were carefully stored on board the ship. The following afternoon at the apartment, while Eugene was packing the final items they would need for the trip, Virginia suddenly came into the room and broke the news to her husband. They weren't going to Puerto Rico or anyplace else. The steamship company had just called to tell them that all travel had been suspended until further notice. "Why?" Eugene asked. "Because," she said, "the Japanese have just bombed Pearl Harbor. The country is at war."

CHAPTER SEVEN

ITALY

The war may have arrived at America's shores on 7 December 1941, but it had been raging in Europe for more than two years. Germany's quick defeat of Poland in 1939, and the astounding "blitzkrieg" of Belgium, the Netherlands, and France in the spring of 1940 shocked the world. America was called upon to become the "arsenal of democracy," and began to gear up for full wartime production. The Great Depression became a bad memory, but few rejoiced at the dramatic upturn in the economy. The grave matters that darkened the headlines a few years before—falling stocks, bank failures, and widespread unemployment—seemed almost trivial compared to the headlines of late 1941 and early 1942. Military disasters in both the European and Pacific theaters over-shadowed everything else, and the future of civilization hung in the balance.

The war in Europe also brought a new wave of immigrants to America. New York City was once again the gateway for thousands seeking safe haven in the New World. These refugees were escaping not only the devastation of the war but the racist horrors of the new Nazi order in Europe. As with the fall of South Vietnam thirty-two years later, the fall of France enriched the fabric of American life—and American cuisine. It was no coincidence that many French restaurants opened in New York in the years following the fall of France. Many chefs from Paris, Marseilles, or France's far-flung colonies found use for their considerable talents in the restaurants of New York. For Eugene Jelesnik, it was time to add one more flavor to his soup of musical nationalities: French.

After the cancellation of the Puerto Rican booking, Meyer Davis got Eugene and his orchestra a booking at a French cabaret restaurant, the Bal Tabarin. The restaurant was located on 45th

Street off Broadway. The café was a modest but attractive basement nightclub that seated 150. It was decorated in the style of a
Parisian café, and it harkened nostalgically to a happier prewar
Paris. Outdoor café awnings and French slogans decorated the
walls. In one corner of the room was a French-style bar. For the
engagement at The Bal Tabarin, Eugene reclaimed some of the
musicians from the earlier "Continentals" including cymbalom
player Dick Marta. The small band also had sax, trumpet, piano,
and accordion. Eduard Futran, the accordion player, doubled as
the band's vocalist and sang both French and Russian ballads.
There were also four young French dancers, "The Montmartre
Girls," who performed the cancan.[1] Eugene played solo selections
from French opera, popular French ballads, love songs, and
wartime favorites such as "The Last Time I Saw Paris."

For a short time in late 1941 and early 1942, Eugene also
appeared over the NBC Television Network from New York City
station WNBT. "The Jelesnik Trio," was featured on "Radio City
Matinee" for fifteen minutes each Monday afternoon following an
early info-mercial, "Search for Beauty," which was sponsored by
the Gold Mark Hosiery Company.[2] Eugene's show was routinely
followed by informative civil defense broadcasts. Jelesnik had
some success in publishing his own musical compositions including: "My Gypsy Melody," "Get the Gang," and "Two Silhouettes
on the Moon." But in early 1942, Jelesnik wrote and published
what was to become his most successful commercial composition:
"The Nodocky Polka," which quickly became a top-ten hit for
dance music in the country. The piece was recorded by Kay
Kayser's band on the Columbia label. The flip side of the 45 RPM
record was one of the biggest hits of the early war years: "The
White Cliffs of Dover." "The Nodocky Polka" was also recorded
by Freddie "Schnikelfritz" Fisher and his orchestra for the Decca
label. Mitchell Ayers and his "Fashions in Music" recorded the
"Nodocky Fox Trot" for Bluebird, an RCA Victor label. Organist
Milt Herth and his trio also recorded Jelesnik's composition. For a
time "The Nodocky" was even a dance craze. Arthur Murray created a "Nodocky" dance step, and *Fashion Magazine* featured Judy
Garland in a "Nodocky" dress. In April, "The Nodocky" was the

centerpiece of what could only be described as a music video.[3] In a program called *Music Hall Varieties,* "The Nodocky" was played over a film made of dancers and performers gyrating and catapulting to the music. MTV was many decades away, and reaction to the novel experiment is unknown.

Jelesnik and his orchestra also continued to tour. They played many cafés and clubs throughout the East including: Monaco's in Cleveland, Ohio; the commissioned officers' Supper Club in Fayetteville, North Carolina; the Dubonnet Café in Newwark, N.J.; and Tony Pastors', an uptown New York City nightclub. The band made several more lengthy transcriptions for MUZAK and also performed occasionally over Dumont Television and the Mutual radio network. But his biggest break in 1942 was securing his own weekly broadcast over NBC Radio. The program, *Eccentric Moods,* was both introduced and at times narrated by Milton J. Cross, the network's dramatic and breathy-voiced announcer, later to gain fame for his weekly programs from the Metropolitan Opera. Eugene was the focus and star of the show, and the NBC's superb radio orchestra was his backup. The program was more eclectic than eccentric, and each number varied wildly in theme, style, and tempo. Selections from European folk and Gypsy music were interspersed with themes from classical music and sometimes pop. The show was described as being "unusual and catchy." Being catchy, it caught on, and aired for the next nine months. But while Eugene fiddled, the world continued to burn, and it was only a matter of time before the flames caught up with him.

In the summer of 1942, Eugene was ordered to report and take his examination for the draft. He had been told that the military was looking for people with language skills. The fact that he was well-versed in both Russian and German was noted, but the military seemed more interested that Jelesnik was a classically trained musician. In 1942, the military was very keen on recruiting musicians, not only for regimental bands and orchestras, but for use in military intelligence. "G2" had discovered that musicians were particularly good at working with codes and at code breaking. Eugene took a battery of tests and qualified for the intelligence service. He was given a letter and instructed that when he was formally called up, he was to present the letter at the induction center. It was an assignment to Fort Richie, Maryland, where many army intelligence officers were then being trained.

Sometime in the early fall of 1942, Eugene was walking down Broadway when he happened to run into a man he had known as a theatrical agent for the William Morris Agency. Bert Wishnew and Eugene had been good friends since the days of the Hollywood Restaurant. Bert asked him what he was doing, and Eugene told him he was "One-A" and was just waiting to be drafted. Wishnew had something better in mind. He told Eugene that he was the program director for the USO and that Eugene could do the country a lot more good with his violin than with a rifle. He made Eugene an offer: "We're sending out shows to military and veterans' hospitals all over the United States to perform for servicemen wounded in the war. Why don't you audition for us? If it works out, I can get you a deferment from the draft." Eugene was intrigued by the offer but told Wishnew that he would only be interested if he could go overseas. Wishnew said that he couldn't promise him anything right away, and also that he would first have to audition before the troops to see how he went over. Wishnew wasn't certain how the boys would respond to a Russian violinist. He told Eugene to put together an act and then go to Fort Hamilton, which was a large embarkation point for troops being shipped out. There Eugene could try out his act on the soldiers; if it was well-received, Wishnew would sign him on as a USO performer. He told him that after some stateside touring, he would see what he could do about sending Eugene overseas. Wishnew then reminded Eugene that all this was contingent on how well he did at Fort Hamilton.

The street negotiations completed, Eugene went home and told Virginia and his mother about the offer. Both were enthusiastic. They were particularly heartened by the prospect of a deferment from the draft. Neither of the women wanted Eugene in the army and they could no more picture him with an M-1 rifle than Wishnew could. Eugene neglected to tell them that he had requested and had all but been promised service overseas. Virginia enthusiastically helped Eugene work up an act for his USO audition.

The teenage rage of 1943 was a skinny Italian crooner from Hoboken, New Jersey, who had swept to the top of the charts with hits such as: "All, or Nothing at All," "Night and Day," "Begin the Beguine" and "Close to You."[4] Only a few weeks before, the Jelesniks had read in the papers of how 5,000 screaming teenaged "bobby soxers" had started a near riot at the Paramount Theater during one of the new idol's performances. It was the kind of reception that would later be bestowed on Elvis and the Beatles, but at that time, no one had ever seen the likes of it. It was said that Francis Albert Sinatra was the biggest sex idol since Valentino. Eugene knew of Sinatra. He had been a singer with Harry James's band and later with Tommy Dorsey's. Eugene may also have encountered him when Sinatra made his debut at the New York World's Fair in the spring of 1939, but nothing he had ever heard about the crooner seemed to justify the crazed adulation that "Frankeeee" now enjoyed.[5]

With Virginia's help, Eugene began rehearsing an unlikely skit in which Eugene would mimic the young Sinatra. Sinatra's trademark in his early years was a bow tie. Cartoons had appeared in the newspapers, which portrayed Sinatra behind a microphone stand. All that could be seen of the skinny kid was the tie. Virginia made Eugene a huge bow tie for the act. The large prop, coupled with Eugene's "Rubinoff" appearance must have been a ludicrously comic sight, but the gag was only complete when Eugene played short clips from Sinatra's hit song "Begin the Beguine" on his violin, mimicking exactly the phrasing and languid tempo of Sinatra's style. He would then pause and emit a long, soulful sigh. The skit could have been a caricature from a Looney Tunes cartoon, but it worked. When Eugene played at the embarkation station at Fort Hamilton, the routine "brought the house down." With the audience warmed up by the comic introduction, Eugene then played a medley of tunes—including other popular Sinatra numbers that demonstrated his own virtuosity. Knowing that the young soldiers hailed from every part of the country, he performed in every possible style including western ballads, swing, and even military marches. Just as he had for his CBS radio program *Eccentric Moods* and his Sunday concert series at the Hotel Utah, Eugene was careful to include something for everyone. The audition was a huge success, and Wishnew signed Eugene up immediately for his first USO tour.

Nothing he had experienced in vaudeville or in his bookings with Meyer Davis prepared him for the grueling schedule of his first USO tour. Over the next six months, Eugene would perform in military and VA hospitals from Maine to Florida and from the Carolinas to California. The show, which traveled by train and local bus, was titled "USO High Jinks." The company was made up of fifteen performers and included singer Caryl Gould who had been featured with Rudy Vallee's orchestra and also Sidney Toler who played the detective "Charlie Chan" in the movies. They usually gave five performances a day in hospital wards, recovery floors, and occasionally at bedside in individual rooms. The unit performed in more than a hundred and fifty different locations. It was not unusual to play three or even four hospitals in the same area in one day. In the early spring of 1944, the troupe performed down the eastern seaboard and then through the southern states to Texas.[6] The schedule covering the last three weeks of May 1944, alone gives some indication of the workload:

May 7–8	Longview, Texas
May 8–9	Dallas Texas and Temple Texas
May 9–10	San Antonio, Texas
May 11	El Paso, Texas
May 12–13	Albuquerque, New Mexico
May 14–15	Los Angeles, California
May 16	Palm Springs, California
May 16–17	Riverside, California
May 18	Long Beach, California
May 19–20	San Diego, California
May 21–22	Santa Barbara, California
May 22–23	Santa Cruz and Watsonville, California
May 23–24	San Francisco, California
May 25	Oakland, California

May 26	Palo Alto, California
May 27–28	Treasure Island, San Francisco
May 29	Stockton, California
May 30	Lathrop, California
May 31	Modesto, California

The *Oakland Post Enquirer* for 30 May 1944, gave Eugene and Miss Gould a large photo spread and described the work of the USO performers in some detail:

VETS LAUD USO SHOW TROUPES

"Keep it coming!"

This was the response from Marine and Navy hospital patients at U. S. naval hospitals in Vallejo, Oakland, and San Francisco when USO-Camp Shows introduced its new hospital circuit entertainment troupe last week to west coast hospital wards and recreation halls. Scheduled once every two weeks from now on, these "hospital circuits" number from 10 to 15 radio, screen, and stage artists in each unit and which formerly only appeared in military camps. Specialties in the first troupe, now traveling on the west coast for a two month period, include singing, dancing, juggling, and comic acts with six musicians participating at four afternoon ward shows and one big evening recreational hall performance in each hospital.

. . . Also included in the new national program are smaller traveling units, performing for both ambulatory and bed patients in military hospitals and featuring stars of screen, stage, and radio.

Bedside performances were not unusual, and Jelesnik was frequently featured in newspaper articles playing his violin at the bed of an appreciative wounded soldier. Over his long career the pose would be repeated hundreds of times. The only variable in the composition being the face of the bedridden patient.

After playing the California, Oregon, and Washington hospitals, the unit headed east, performing in seventeen states from Utah to Massachusetts. On July 31st and August 1st they performed for soldiers in the nation's capital. In just six months, the USO performers had circled the entire country.

One hospital that Eugene remembered most vividly from his

first USO tour was Bushnell General Military Hospital in Brigham City, Utah. The hospital was specifically for amputees just returning from the war. Eugene was overwhelmed by the sight of hundreds of limbless soldiers. He couldn't imagine what it would be like if he were to lose a leg, an arm, or even a finger. He had been to dozens of other centers treating the returning GIs from the war, but nothing was like Bushnell. In spite of the visual horrors that filled every ward, Eugene tried his best to remain cheery and upbeat. He felt it was the least he could do for the boys who had given so much for their country.

The sight of the Wasatch range above Brigham City affected Eugene in much the same way as his first view of the same range above Salt Lake. He was reminded of the promise he made to himself six years before: that he if he ever got the chance he would one day settle in Utah. With that goal in mind he took advantage of the Brigham City engagement to call many of his Utah contacts, including Guy Toombes and Sid Fox. He reminded Fox, the KDYL radio station owner, of his request to keep him in mind if something became available after the war.

Without any break or rest, the USO's "High Jinks" performers were supplied with a few new acts, and immediately sent out on a another six-month tour with a schedule that was even more brutal than the first. Eugene was disheartened by the prospect of another lengthy stateside tour. He contacted Bert Wishnew and reminded him of the promise he made to send him overseas. Eugene's second tour started in the South, pushed on through the Southwest, and then back to California. Between August and the middle of October 1944, his second unit performed in fifty-seven hospitals in forty-five cities in twenty-three states.

On October 19th, Eugene was in a railroad station in Modesto, California, when a telegram from Bert Wishnew caught up with him. He was to return to New York City at once. His wish had finally been granted. He was to be sent overseas. Considering what he had seen in the hospitals, his reaction might be considered crazy, if not suicidal, but Eugene considered himself "the happiest man in the world." He wrote Virginia immediately to tell her the news:

My Darling One:

The enclosed railroad itinerary and government order
returning me to New York is self-explanatory. I must ask you
please not to show it to a soul as it is strictly confidential. I
received these orders early this morning and so I am rushing a
duplicate copy to you enclosed with this letter.

As you can see no doubt by looking at the copy, I will have a
most strenuous and long trip back to New York.

I am looking forward to some kind of a rest when I come
home. I will be perfectly happy and at ease as long as I will be
with you my dearest. I am with the thought and confidence that
you left your place long before my arrival so that any last
minute maneuvers will be unnecessary and unthought of.
Somehow my darling this is a great occasion for me to come
home and I am so impatient to get back, I cannot tell you. Your
idea of paying all bills before my arrival is excellent and so there
will be nothing to talk about except ourselves. Baby dear, do
you know that you are the most loved woman in this whole
world? Well, in case you forget, I will constantly remind you of
it. I wish this were Sunday already.

> All my love,
> Your devoted husband, Eugene

Eugene's wish for some rest was granted, and he was given a
six-week leave from the USO before he was to report for his new
assignment. While in New York he learned that Virginia and Aunt
Ruth had fought bitterly during his long absence, and that they
had severed all contact with each other. There was no hope that
the two would ever reconcile, and although Ruth had long since
moved into her own apartment, the delicate situation added tension to the final weeks at home before he was sent abroad. It was
made no better by the attitude of his mother. While Eugene may
have been delighted with the overseas assignment, his mother was
beside herself with worry. She couldn't imagine why her son
would want to leave the country, perhaps to return to the Europe
they had so much difficulty escaping. While not officially in the
military, USO performers going overseas were required to wear
military uniforms. Otherwise, if they were to be captured, they
were liable to be shot as spies. Eugene was instructed to report for

the uniform fittings, which would be paid for by the USO. The supply depot where Eugene was issued his army garb was Saks Fifth Avenue.

When Eugene finally boarded his train at Pennsylvania Station, Virginia, his mother, and Aunt Ruth were there to see "Little Eugene" off to war. It was an emotional and tearful scene. Eugene was not told of his overseas destination until he arrived at Camp Patrick Henry. It was there he learned that he would be going to Italy. Eugene wasn't supposed to tell anyone where he was being sent. The watchword of the day was: "Loose lips sink ships," but he let it slip to Virginia in a final telephone conversation before embarkation that he would probably be eating a lot of spaghetti. As the soldiers waited to board the ship that would take them to the European theater, comedian Red Skelton, who was already in the army, entertained the soldiers at dockside. Eugene had performed a similar service for soldiers embarking from Fort Hamilton more than a year before. Jelesnik and Skelton had a photo taken of their meeting.[7] It was a memorable send-off.

Eugene remembers that the twelve-day voyage to Italy was awful. The seas were rough and the crowded troop ship rolled heavily in the swells. Eugene was never on a boat when he didn't get seasick. He was never sicker than on the voyage to Europe. Although he was incapacitated much of the time, he played his violin for the troops frequently during the passage. It must have seemed vaguely familiar. Twenty years before he had also been seasick, and yet still managed to play his violin for the immigrants aboard the SS *America*. Eugene made many friends among the young soldiers heading for combat in Europe, including professional golfer Vick Ghezzi.

The USO tour was packaged by Bert Wishnew and was titled: "Three Abroad, A Compact Vaudeville Act." There were only two other performers in the unit. Bob Gilchrist was a guitarist and singer. He specialized in Irish ballads and comedy songs and was particularly adept at leading community singing. Like Eugene he had taken up music at an early age. There were other common threads in his past that linked him to Eugene's own experiences. When Gilchrist finished high school, he joined a vaudeville quartet and had toured through the West and Midwest for several years. He located in Florida for a time, entertaining for private parties, hotels, and conventions. He had played a number of New York City nightspots including the Ambassador and Astor Hotels and the Rainbow Grill. In Florida he had enjoyed lengthy bookings at the Breakers, the Everglades, and the Colony Club. Like Eugene he had extensive radio experience and had performed over both the CBS and NBC radio networks. Unlike Jelesnik, Gilchrist had already been on several overseas tours with the USO. He had made three tours to units in Newfoundland, and in 1944, he made a seven-month tour of combat areas in the South Pacific. For the Italian tour, the USO had presented him with a new guitar to replace the warped one he had brought back from the "jungle circuit." Gilchrist had a son, Patrick, who was serving with the U. S. Navy as a radioman, 2nd class, on a PT boat.[8]

The third member of "Three Abroad" was Jack Ber-Mar, who billed himself as a professional "mentalist." According to the advance publicity issued by the USO, Ber-Mar began his career at age fourteen when he foretold his examination marks in school. Later he told his mother where she would find lost earrings, and that led to friends and family consulting him for psychic advice. When he was sixteen he made his first professional appearance, at the Imperial Theatre in Chicago. Before its demise, he had toured the vaudeville circuit from coast to coast with an act that was one-part stand-up comic, one-part mind reader, and one-part fortune teller. He had entertained in Hollywood nightspots and at the private parties of Rosalind Russell, Bing Crosby, Barbara Hutton (Mrs. Cary Grant), Hedy La Marr, Brenda Marshall, and Jack Oakie. The previous year, Ber-Mar had foretold the exact week that Mussolini would be overthrown and Italy would resign from the war, September—1943.[9]

"The Three Abroad"—accompanied by several thousand other Americans with an act of an entirely different sort—landed in Naples, Italy, on 2 February 1945. The war had destroyed the economy of the entire region, and the city was suffering from severe shortages. The only thing that kept Naples from starvation was the Red Cross packages being distributed by the Allies, supplemented by K-rations and candy bars begged from individual soldiers. The poverty was appalling. While southern Italy starved, the north had to endure suffering of a different kind. Many Americans back home mistakenly believed that the war in Italy had been over for some time. Nothing could have been further from the truth. The German army under General Albert Kesselring had more than twenty divisions defending successive lines in northern Italy.

The fighting there would last until the very final days of the war in Europe. One historian of the campaign called the battle for Italy "a grinding, bloody, inch by inch slog through mountains that seemed to go on forever." While the attention of the world was focused on other events—the D day invasion of France, the Battle of the Bulge, and the Russian drive on Berlin—the fighting in Italy slogged on, week after week and month after month.

In the winter of 1945, the famed playwright, journalist, and columnist, Clare Booth Luce, wife of millionaire *Time* and *Life* magazine publisher Henry R. Luce and at the time Congresswoman from Connecticut, made an inspection tour of Italy. *Life* magazine accompanied the Congresswoman and described in detail the hardships being faced by American fighting men on what Luce called "The Forgotten Front."[10]

For more than twenty months, the Allies kept relentless pressure on the well-entrenched Germans. The Americans and their British allies pushed the Germans out of one defensive line only to face another. While it may not have garnered headlines, it was the longest sustained American drive of the war in Europe. The casualties were at times horrific and morale was generally very low. While it was hard to see what the GIs in Italy were accomplishing by their sacrifice, the troops who fought there kept nearly 200,000 Germans from being used on other fronts. Such were the conditions at the time Eugene Jelesnik and his companions landed in Naples. And some of the heaviest fighting of the entire campaign was yet to come.[11]

Eugene's most vivid memories of this tour are not the places he performed, but the faces of the soldiers in the audience. Many of the young infantrymen seemed to be little more than boys.

Eugene was also surprised at the number of familiar faces and former acquaintances he encountered who were now in the service.
The 10th U. S. Mountain Division was made up of a large number
of troops from Utah and the Intermountain West. They had been
recruited specifically for their mountaineering skills and for their
ability to ski. Many had been recruited by the National Ski Patrol.
The division was described by one journalist as "a mammoth ski
club of downhill and cross-country racers, jumpers, and winter-
sports instructors." There were also amateur and professional
mountain climbers, lumbermen, ranchers, and farmers from the
Cascades, the Wasatch, and the High Sierras. Someplace in north
central Italy, Eugene encountered a man he instantly recognized
as someone he had seen before. The soldier had been the head
desk clerk at the Hotel Utah during Eugene's run there in 1938.

Two weeks after Eugene began his tour in Italy, the 10th
Mountain Division assaulted a German fortress near Bologna on
the heights of a 3,000-foot cliff called Riva Ridge. The attack was
in preparation for the final assault on the German army that
would come in April. The night operation involved more than 800
men using pitons and ropes to scale an ice-glazed cliff face. The
Germans did not believe it was possible to scale the cliff, let alone
mount an attack from that direction. The 10th fell upon the astonished defenders on the summit and overran the German artillery
positions. It was one of the most incredible feats of the war. The
American commander in charge of the front, General Mark Clark,
called the successful assault on Riva Ridge "miraculous." The 10th
didn't stop there. On the night of 19 February, the 85th and 86th
Regiments of the 10th Division pushed on to take other fortified
positions on Monte della Torraccia and Monte Belvedere overlooking the Po Valley.[12]

Over the next eight weeks, both sides realigned and prepared
for the inevitable climactic battle to come when the weather
cleared in the spring. The Germans set up successive lines of
defense. Each were taken by the Allies. The last German line in
Italy was the formidable Venetian Line, which ran from the Alps
near Lake Garda along the Adige River to the Gulf of Venice.
During the lull in the fighting, German and American patrols

clashed in nightly skirmishes, and fierce artillery duels broke out sporadically. During this period of relative quiet, Eugene and his unit performed at the front. While the artillery exchanges were nothing compared to what would come later, Eugene believed that "the firing was almost constant." He and his two companions were the only performers serving in the combat area. This was not a casual thing and involved a great deal of risk. The military publication *Stars and Stripes* was so impressed with the spirit of the performers that they featured Eugene's unit in a story on 7 March 1945.

SHOW GOES ON IN FRONT LINES

The audience had to excuse itself every so often to go "fire a mission," but the USO show went on, right in the artillery battalion's front-line positions, during the battles for Mts. Vedetta, Terminale, and Della Piella last Saturday.

While the boom of big guns, the rumble of tanks, and the coughs of mortars intensified, the applause rolled on. Bob Gilchrist of Astoria, L.I., N.Y., played the guitar and sang Irish songs; Eugene Jelesnik of New York City played the violin; and Jack Ber-Mar, Newark, N.J., magician, told the men what they were thinking.

Ber-Mar gave the date on which he said the European war would end. (It's highly cheerful news, and if his forecast proves correct we'll print it then.) He said the 10th Mountaineers would not see service in the Far East and would be eating Christmas dinner at home this time next year.

He told many artillerymen what he believed was in their minds at the moment. And to one said: "You're thinking about a fellow who you're afraid is after your job. His name begins with a C."

"Whoa, that's enough!" said the artilleryman.

"Well," Ber-Mar replied, "He's not going to get it."

A similar show was given by the same performers the day before to foxhole audiences of the 86th.[13]

One soldier who was very surprised that a USO unit had made it so far forward was General T. E. Lewis who caught one of Eugene's Fox Hole performances near the front. General Lewis wrote Eugene a personal note of thanks:

Hq 88th Inf Div Arty
APO #88, U. S. Army
12 March 1945

Mr. Eugene Jelesnik
USO Unit 428
Special Service Section
Allied Forces Headquarters
APO #512, U. S. Army

Dear Mr. Jelesnik:

   Your show has left us with a fond memory, as we never
before had a performance like yours when we were in the lines.
Needless to say this fact alone meant a lot to all the men of this
command plus the fact that the show was excellent. Your
performance with the violin was especially appreciated.
Especially enjoyed was your rendition of "Holiday for Strings."
The dentist who is quite a violin critic put a big stamp of
approval on your part.
   With best wishes, I am

                                Sincerely yours,
                                T. E. Lewis
                                General, U. S. Army[14]

   Sometime in late March, Eugene's unit came across another
civilian group visiting the front lines in Italy. It was Representative
Clare Booth Luce and her team of congressional fact-finders and
photo journalists. The Congresswoman was astonished to find
USO performers so near the battle. Eugene invited Mrs. Luce to
attend a performance they were giving at a field hospital later that
evening. She promised to attend if she could. While the
Congresswoman did not make it to the concert, she did send
Eugene her regrets in a personal letter that was delivered by the
Red Cross several days later.

26 March 1945
Eugene Jelesnik
USO Camp Shows
C/O P R O, 15th Army Group

Dear Mr. Jelesnik:

I'm sorry I never had the opportunity to see your show. But I was travelling fast and hard on a tight schedule. You know, I think your entertainment groups are doing splendid and much needed work in these areas. Everywhere I went the G.I.s wanted more of it, anyway.

Thank you for your kind offer and my best regards to yourself and Mr. Gilchrist and Mr. Ber-Mar.

Sincerely yours,
Clare Boothe Luce[15]

The "Three Abroad" vaudevillians moved from area to area, often performing four or five times a day. They were not specifically attached to any of the units they entertained, and they moved at their own discretion into many places that would normally be closed to civilians. One of the chief advantages of Eugene's USO unit was its mobility. Other than Eugene's two violins and Gilchrist's guitar, they had no other requirements. They carried no sound equipment or microphones, no sets, lighting, costumes, or staging. The only stages he saw during his first few months in Italy were the ruins of Roman amphitheaters. The unit played field dressing stations, mess halls, tents, assembly areas, and hospital wards—any place there were a few soldiers gathered together. In forward areas, even the most well-camouflaged position on the protected side of the surrounding mountains was subject to random blind artillery fire. The longer a unit remained in an area, the more likely it was that the distant artillery would eventually find a victim. The soldiers learned quickly that the gods of war were especially arbitrary and capricious in the Apennines Mountains of Italy. After a week or two in the same area, each soldier had dug his own deep foxhole and seldom ventured from it. Eugene and his companions would often perform off the back of a flatbed truck to GIs who were well dug in and who didn't budge from their holes. Eugene recalled: "I remember looking off the back of the truck and all I could see were a few helmets and rifles sticking out of the ground."

Eugene asked his driver if the performers weren't dangerously exposed. The driver explained that the Germans were on the other side of the mountain and couldn't actually see them and that

the men in the foxholes stayed there because of their long exposure to random artillery fire. The explanations were not very reas-
suring. Such conditions gave the tour a lasting name in the history
of the USO: "The Foxhole Circuit."

Of the thousands of GIs that Eugene met in Italy, the face of
one stands out in his memory. He was a young lieutenant who had
attended one of the Eugene's impromptu concerts near the front
lines. The following day, Eugene was performing at a field hospital and saw the same man again. In the interim of a few hours, the
lieutenant had lost both his legs in an artillery exchange. It wasn't
until that moment that Eugene realized the importance of his
state-side hospital tour. If he had not already experienced the
tragic suffering of the amputees at Bushnell Hospital in Brigham
City, he would have broken down immediately; but he kept a stiff
upper lip and performed a request the best he could.

While the USO performers were treated as honored guests,
they were sometimes left to fend for themselves. Finding transportation in forward areas was a big problem through much of the
tour, and Eugene had to hitch rides in whatever vehicles were
available—jeeps, half-tracks, trucks, and horse-drawn wagons. On
one occasion, after playing at a field hospital, Eugene got a ride to
the next town with a U. S. Army Graves Registration Unit. The
back of the truck was loaded with the bodies of fallen GIs. It was a
sobering experience that confirmed to Eugene the deadly seriousness of his mission.

One night after a late performance, Eugene and his companions bedded down in an army ambulance. During the night, the
unit they had entertained that afternoon got orders to move out.
But Eugene and his companions were not included in the orders
and so no one bothered to wake them. Nor did anyone give them
any word that they were leaving or where they had gone. When
the three performers awoke the following morning, they found
themselves alone. Worse, the ambulance driver was nowhere to be
seen, and the performers had no idea where they were. In survey-
ing the area, Eugene noticed that there was a large red brick building on a low hill about a half mile away. The building had a red
cross on the roof. Eugene rightly assumed it was a hospital, and

he decided to go there, ask directions, and find out what to do. He instructed Gilchrist and Ber-Mar to wait at the ambulance until he returned.

Eugene began walking toward the distant hospital. As he started out across an open field, several patients started waving to him from the building's balconies—some with handkerchiefs, others more exuberantly with both arms. Then suddenly the waving stopped. As he got closer, more and more people joined the others, and below them a large crowd began to gather in front of the building. Eugene was used to being on stage and was well aware of the increasing size of the audience: "They all seemed to be watching me. I wasn't entertaining. I wasn't doing anything but walking. And they were all staring at me. I thought, What's going on?"

For Jelesnik it was the oddest audience he had ever encountered. As he came closer, he became aware of a low murmur of distant voices, similar to the sound made by a restless theater audience after the lights have dimmed, but before the curtain has gone up. As he came up to the building, a single person, a Catholic priest, came forward to greet him and help him for the final few feet. He was wearing a stole over his shoulders similar in symbolism and function to the prayer shawl worn by rabbis. Eugene was puzzled by the crowd of silent faces that stared at him:

"Is this a hospital?" he asked.

The priest put his arm around Eugene as he led him toward the building. "My son," he said, "We've all been praying for you this last twenty minutes."

"Why?" Eugene asked.

The priest told him, "You just walked through a minefield!"

Eugene suddenly realized how close he had come to exchanging his violin for a harp, and he almost passed out on the spot. Fearful that his companions might set out on their own, he immediately asked that someone who knew the area be sent for Gilchrest and Ber-Mar. He also had the hospital report the incident to headquarters in Naples so that they would know that a USO unit was badly lost and in need of an escort. In the annals of the United Service Organization, Jelesnik's encounter with the minefield became legendary. The close call later became the subject of a UPI feature story and was also mentioned in *Stars and Stripes*.[16]

By the second week of April 1945, the weather had cleared and American and British planes were bombing and strafing German positions in the Po Valley and along the alpine passes with impunity. The Allies dropped more than 175,000 fragmentation bombs on German positions, while low-level fighter-bombers strafed and dropped napalm on suspected strong points. Following the air assault, more than 1,000 artillery pieces fired two million shells on the Germans. The big push had begun.[17]

In addition to the 10th Mountain Division there was another unit that helped spearhead the final attack. This force also had a connection to Utah, albeit an unhappy one. The 442d Regimental Combat Team was led mostly by American officers, but was otherwise made up entirely of Japanese Americans. Many of the soldiers in the 442d had families imprisoned in the desert compound of Topaz, Utah, located 140 miles southwest of Salt Lake City in the middle of the Utah desert. In the panic-filled days following the bombing of Pearl Harbor, the Japanese Americans had been rounded up and taken from their homes in California, Oregon, and Washington. The barracks encampment was surrounded by guard towers and barbed wire fences. The "detainees" were told that they had been relocated for their own protection. But the machine guns on the towers were all aimed inward at the camp, and at least one of the residents was shot dead for getting too near the fence around the camp. The explanation of the shooting issued by the military revealed the camp's true purpose: He had been shot trying to *escape*. In outward appearance, Topaz bore a striking resemblance to a German concentration camp. By 1944 it was fifth largest city in Utah. Many of the "Nisei" had everything they owned confiscated, but in spite of the injustice inflicted upon their fellow countrymen, more than eight thousand Japanese Americans volunteered for service in the American army. Japanese American combat teams served throughout the European theater. The 442d had fought in Italy with the 34th Division in July 1944, then in France in the fall of the same year. Now they had been returned to

Italy to help with the last assault. On 20 April near the village of Aulla, Company E, 2ᵈ Battalion of the 442ᵈ assaulted Colle Musatello, one of the most heavily defended positions of the entire front. Leading the attack was Second Lieutenant Daniel K. Inouye. Though hit by grenades and machine gun fire, Inouye and his decimated company refused to fall back. After taking heavy casualties, they eventually pushed the Germans off the ridge and captured their objective. The Germans were dumbfounded by the fact that they had been captured by Japanese soldiers, and one officer remarked: "Everything I have been told about this war has been a lie!" For his bravery Inouye was awarded the Distinguished Service Cross. In one of the most profound ironies of history, the 442ᵈ would become one of the most decorated units of World War II,[18] and Inouye would eventually represent the State of Hawaii in the United States Senate.[19]

The 10ᵗʰ Mountain Division made a spectacular breakthrough in the final assault. Altogether typical of the action was the experience of the 85ᵗʰ Regiment, which was assigned to take a strategic position called Hill 918. One soldier who participated in the attack was one Robert Dole who, like Inouye, would later become a U. S. Senator, and who was also severely wounded in the battle—losing an arm in the assault. When the position was taken, units of the 85ᵗʰ that had been held in reserve, including the 1ˢᵗ Battalion, stormed through the gap, crossed the Po Valley, and with the help of amphibious units crossed the formidable Po River on barges and small boats. Units of the First Battalion, which contained many Utah boys, moved so fast that they soon found themselves far to the rear of the German lines. GIs in one rapidly advancing unit were startled when they found themselves under attack by truckloads of German soldiers approaching from behind them on the same road. The Germans had abandoned their positions and were trying to escape back to Germany. The First Battalion then wheeled around and took up defensive positions facing the direction they had just come, effectively blocking the German retreat.[20] Complete confusion descended upon the German army. It was much the same all along the front. In less than two days, the 88ᵗʰ Infantry alone captured over 11,000 Germans.

As the Allies poured into the Po Valley, bands of Italian partisans went on the attack in Genoa, Milan, and Turin. They quickly seized German command posts, communication centers, and important road junctions and also surrounded enemy garrisons. When the Allied troops arrived to attack some positions, they found that the German soldiers had already been captured by the partisans. Among the German prisoners, the partisans had noticed a man wearing a German greatcoat and steel helmet. But the man's boots were far from the standard military issue, being made of the finest Italian leather. The quality of his "jack boots" gave him away. It was none other than Benito Mussolini, the deposed Italian dictator, who had led Italy to the brink of ruin. On 28 April 1945, Mussolini, his mistress, Clara Petacci, and a trusted aide were executed by the partisans. The following day, their bodies were taken to Milan and dumped in front of a garage in the Piazzale Loreto. Crowds of people came to mutilate and spit upon the body of "Il Duce." One woman fired five bullets into his body in revenge for the death of her five sons in the war. The bodies were then strung upside down in front of the garage. The bodies remained there through most of the following day. Among the Americans who saw and photographed the grisly scene in the Piazzale Loreto was Eugene Jelesnik.[21]

Eugene was back in Florence on 5 May 1945 when news came that the war in Europe was finally over. It was a relief that the guns had fallen silent, but much of his own work was still ahead of him. "The Three Abroad" would continue to tour hospitals and army posts in Italy well into August. He would also continue to experience the horrible aftermath of the war for months to come.

The Italian civilians suffered enormously during those months. While the American Red Cross and other relief agencies did what they could to supply the population with vital supplies, hunger was widespread. Italians bartered services and possessions to get the GIs' C- and K-ration packets—without them many would have starved. Shortly after the surrender, Eugene learned that Benito Mussolini's personal portrait artist was being held in an Allied prison in the city of Livorno. He got permission from the prison officials to visit with the artist. Guido Alvarez was happy to have a visitor, and Eugene arranged to have the artist paint portraits of Eugene and Virginia from photographs. Mussolini was not a great patron of the visual arts, and once confessed that he "did not understand pictures."[22] The Italian Renaissance had produced some of the greatest artists of all history, but in the 1930s Mussolini openly advocated exporting and selling Italy's art treasures to get the hard currency needed for weapons. He later said that he "would prefer to have fewer statues and pictures in Italian museums and more flags captured from the enemy." While he may not have understood art, he did recognize talent if the artist was adept at realism. Alvarez was such an artist, and the portraits of the Jelesniks he produced in Livorno were vivid and lifelike. The portraits would later hang in an honored spot in Eugene Jelesnik's home in Salt Lake City.

The war had been over for six weeks when two notable performers arrived in Italy. The first was Phil Silvers, later to gain fame as the quintessential GI con man, "Sergeant Bilko." The second was the bobby soxer's idol who Eugene had mimicked at his USO audition fourteen months earlier, Frank Sinatra.[23]

Sinatra had been found physically ineligible for military service because of a punctured eardrum. He wanted to entertain troops overseas, but for security reasons, the FBI had denied him a visa to leave the country. Some said it was because of charges of alleged communist sympathies that had been made in the Hearst newspapers. Others suspected it was because of J. Edgar Hoover's personal suspicions of Sinatra's loyalty. Whatever the reason, he was not permitted to visit America's troops overseas until after VE day.[24] Silvers and Sinatra toured North Africa and Italy performing for the troops in June of 1945.

Since Eugene had been in the military theater for more than five months and also had experience managing the logistics of touring entertainers, Jelesnik was put in charge of both Sinatra's unit and his own. One of his responsibilities was to act as the tour's stage manager telling all the performers, including Sinatra, when and where to report for transportation, rehearsals, and company calls. All of the entertainers were billeted together in standard army housing. The army routinely assigned armed officers to escort visiting dignitaries and celebrities including famous musicians and performers. One escort, a Lieutenant Silver (not to be confused with the comedian), had crossed Sinatra the previous day with a comment that Sinatra took personally. The crooner was notorious for holding grudges and for being difficult if he felt he had been slighted.[25] The following day, Lieutenant Silver told Eugene that the group had to be ready to leave for their performance in forty-five minutes and to inform the other performers. Eugene went upstairs and told Sinatra of Lieutenant Silver's message. Sinatra replied: "Go tell Lieutenant Silver that I will leave when I damn well please!" Jelesnik did not know what to think of this but relayed the information to the lieutenant. Silver told Eugene to tell Mr. Sinatra that he had to be out on the truck in forty-five minutes. Sinatra again ignored the request, and when it was clear that Sinatra wasn't coming down, Lieutenant Silver himself went up to get him. Eugene remembered what happened next: "Sinatra lunged out of the room and started fighting with Lieutenant Silver. It took all of my strength to separate them, but I finally broke them apart. It still took Frank an hour and a half to get ready, leaving 5,000 GIs waiting for the show to start. We opened the show almost two hours late, but Sinatra was at the peak of his singing talent and the show went well."

When Eugene played the "foxhole circuit," he frequently performed for very small groups of soldiers. The Sinatra shows were huge compared to what he was used to: "I played for six people, eight people, twenty people, cripples, amputees, even dead people. But Sinatra brought stages, lighting, crews, sets, costumes, pianos—it was huge!" Phil Silvers and Eugene Jelesnik both later remembered that Sinatra was well-received during their tour of Italy. But some soldiers who were in Italy at the time were not particularly impressed with the crooner. Many GIs didn't attend the concerts, and others left before the performer arrived. The attitude of many GIs in Italy was perhaps best characterized by a cartoon caption that appeared in *Stars and Stripes* that June: "Mice make women scream too!"

In late June, Eugene received a cable from Sid Fox saying that KDYL's orchestra leader, Bob Reese, was retiring to a ranch and the job was Eugene's if he wanted it. Eugene immediately accepted, but worried about telling Virginia that they would be moving back to Salt Lake City.

At the end of his tour of Italy, Eugene and his unit received several letters of commendation from both military and USO officials.

Headquarters 15th Army Group
Office of the Commanding General
A.P.O. No. 777, U. S. Army

Headquarters
Mediterranean Theater of Operations
Special Service Section
APO 512, U. S. Army

8 August 1945

Mr. Eugene Jelesnik
427 West 51st Street
New York City, N.Y.

Dear Mr. Jelesnik:

May I express my greatest thanks for the splendid service you have rendered to the officers and enlisted personnel during your recent 21 week tour of the Mediterranean Theater of Operations.

Records of this headquarters indicate that the show was performed 145 times to an audience of 56,640 troops. This is a record of which you may well be proud.

I can say also that this headquarters has been proud to be your host during the tour.

> Sincerely yours,
> Leon T. David
> Colonel, F.A.
> Chief, Special Service Section[26]

Major General Joseph W. Byson, Director of the Special Services Division of the Army Service Forces, awarded Eugene Jelesnik a special commendation which read:

In recognition and appreciation
of your part in the recreational program for
THE ARMED FORCES OF THE UNITED STATES
for The Mediterranean Theater of Operations from
4 February 1945 to 2 August 1945

For his service in Italy, Eugene was awarded by the War Department the highest award given by the military for civilian service: The Civilian Service Ribbon. The distinction was presented to Eugene by Abe Lastfogel, the head of the William Morris Agency and director of the United Service Organization.

Eugene Jelesnik returned to the United States the third week of August 1945. The voyage, while not as rough as his passage to Europe, was on an overcrowded troop ship, and he was once again sick the entire time. During the voyage, Eugene and the returning GIs learned of Japan's surrender. There was a great deal of celebrating by the men who had feared they might be shipped to the Pacific. All Eugene wanted was to get his feet on dry land.

When the ship entered New York Harbor, there was a huge commotion of cheering soldiers, and the ship docked to a tumultuous welcome. But Eugene Jelesnik—who was apt to cry at the sight of the Wasatch Mountains or the playing of "The Stars and Stripes Forever"—was dry-eyed. He felt so distanced by the unreality of the scene, that he felt nothing. Not even the sight of the Statue of Liberty moved him. It was as if he were watching someone else returning from the war. It was not until several days later that the reality of being home sunk in. Eugene and Virginia were at the Palace Theater watching *The Valley of Decision*, a movie about an extended family set in Pittsburgh, Pennsylvania. Greer Garson played the part of a maid who falls in love and marries the master's son, played by Gregory Peck. It was all so normal, so ordinary, and so removed from what Eugene had been through and seen over the previous seven months that he finally realized he was home. In the darkened theater—above the sound track of the movie—could be heard uncontrolled sobbing. An usher came and asked the Jelesniks to leave.[27]

CHAPTER EIGHT

KDYL SALT LAKE

Eugene Jelesnik returned to Salt Lake City on Wednesday morning, 22 August 1945.[1] He took up residence in the Hotel Utah and began looking for a permanent place to live. Virginia would not arrive until October. Eugene got acquainted with his employer Sid Fox, the owner of KDYL, and he began familiarizing himself with his new duties. As Eugene traveled through the city by cab he noted that a lot had happened over the seven short years since he had left. The war had brought many changes and additions to the state of Utah including large military installations, new industry, and expanded markets for the state's natural resources. Transportation, mining, and manufacturing sectors had all experienced unprecedented growth. The war had brought about the construction of Hill Field, the army's training center at Kearns, and the Naval Supply Depot near Ogden. The war effort was responsible for the construction of the Geneva Steel plant in Orem and dozens of other government-funded plants involved in producing war materiel. Kennecott Copper on the west side of the Salt Lake Valley had supplied more than half of all the copper used by the Allies during the conflict. Utah's economy had gone through a period of rapid expansion and prosperity. But though industrial and commercial construction had obviously taken place, there was a serious shortage of housing. Though Utah was temporarily in a postwar slump, as was much of the country, "the place" seemed to be booming. Eugene noticed immediately that Salt Lake had grown since his stay in the city during the depression year of 1938. But something else was different. Throughout America there was a profound sense of renewal and optimism after the end of the Second World War, but nowhere was that feeling more pronounced than on the then crowded sidewalks of downtown Salt Lake City.

Eugene's first order of business was to get to know his new orchestra. The KDYL orchestra had been assembled and conducted by longtime KDYL musical director Bob Reese. Reese had seemingly had enough of either the public spotlight or KDYL and was retiring to live in a more bucolic setting. The *Deseret News* for 15 September 1945 quipped that "Jelesnik had replaced tenor Bob Reese—aspiring cattleman—who resigned to devote full time to his ranch." Though this may have been true, there was something in his departure from the station that at least hinted he may have preferred the company of cows to human beings. In any event it is probable that Reese and KDYL owner Sid Fox had a falling out. Jelesnik never thought to inquire if there were any special circumstances surrounding the departure of the former director. But even if he had learned some of the less pleasant details of the position he was about to fill, it is doubtful he would have turned it down. For the better part of a decade he had been all but begging to return to the Valley, and now he was finally back.

The orchestra had been recruited mostly from local talent, but Eugene quickly found that Reese's boys were all excellent musicians. The KDYL orchestra of 1945 included piano player Larry Pryor, Theron Reynolds on bass, Willard Shingleton on the drums, John Reed, Milt Rawlings, and Carl Sandberg on sax, and Miles Epperson on the trumpet. For their first public performance, Eugene arranged to have the orchestra open at the Empire Room of the Hotel Utah, the same venue he had played with his own band eight years before and the site of his impetuous courtship of Virginia. The return of Eugene Jelesnik to Salt Lake City was duly noted in the papers. While the musicians were all local, they were promoted by the Hotel Utah as "Eugene Jelesnik and His Continental Ensemble," a title that clearly alluded to the multinational group Eugene had brought with him from New York seven years earlier. The latest version of the "Continentals" opened on 14 September 1945 and appeared for several weeks, playing dinner music nightly from 7 to 9 P.M. and for luncheons on Saturdays.[2] Whether the advertising was deceptive or not, the run at the Hotel was a huge success. Many of Eugene's friends from the earlier engagement came to the Hotel to welcome him back. Though his previous stay had been only nine months, Jelesnik felt like he had finally come home.

The KDYL orchestra had a long history of giving public performances. The station had once been owned by the *Salt Lake Telegram* and the newspaper had frequently brought KDYL's musicians to public events, celebrations, and holidays.[3] Even after the sale of the station to Sid Fox, The *Telegram,* or its morning counterpart *The Salt Lake Tribune,* would often sponsor the KDYL orchestra for special events, appearances, or community concerts. These included seasonal performances at all the local hospitals. Through December, Jelesnik must have felt he was still on tour with the USO. Many of the KDYL publicity photos showed Eugene performing at bedside with his violin as he had during his stateside military tours. One particularly touching article described the scene at Saint Ann's Orphanage, where Eugene and the KDYL musicians provided music for the orphaned children's annual Christmas party thrown by the Kearns family.[4]

Another event was the annual lighting of the community Christmas tree in front of *The Salt Lake Tribune* Building. The lighting of the tree and the caroling that accompanied it had been a local tradition, but the Christmas of 1945 was special. It was the first peacetime holiday season in more than four years. By that December, most of the soldiers who would return had finally come back from military service. It was little wonder that the event was turned into a large, multi-dimensional community function— one part Christmas, one part victory celebration, one part thanksgiving for those who had returned, and one part memorial service for those who had not. As the director of the KDYL orchestra, Eugene Jelesnik was put in charge of the entire program. For the Christmas show, Eugene arranged to have the choirs of the local high schools participate. The rehearsals for the Christmas program took several weeks with many sessions lasting late into the night. On the day before the event, Main Street was blocked, and a huge bandstand and stage were constructed in front of the *Tribune* Building.[5] The choir area stretched nearly to the entrance of

Lamb's Café—a half block away. The setup took many hours working in the cold. KDYL announcer Emerson Smith acted as the emcee for the program, which was also broadcast live to those who could not attend in person. The temperature was just above freezing, but the streets were packed with people who braved the weather to enjoy the festivities. The community sing-along may have been a long-standing tradition, but the program had never been as large or more festive than it was that Sunday evening 23 December 1945. Much of the success of the event was due to the energy and organization of the new music director at KDYL. *The Salt Lake Tribune* described the event:

S. L. THRONGS ATTEND STREET CAROLS

Old, familiar strains, invested with a fuller meaning by the war's end, again rang through downtown streets Sunday evening for the city's first postwar caroling program, climaxing a week-long program of Christmas carols, sponsored by the *Salt Lake Tribune-Telegram*, KDYL, and the Junior Chamber of Commerce.

The military note was present throughout the ceremony, opened by Col. James L. Blakely, Ninth Service Command Chaplain, who threw the switch lighting the big tree. Another uniformed participant was Sgt. Kenneth Knapp, Chicago radio and stage tenor, who sang "We Three Kings of Orient Are" and "Jesus Bambino." The crowd was liberally sprinkled with men in khaki and navy blue.

Mrs. Thomas A. Clawson Jr., Salt Lake soprano, sang "Come unto Him" and "Oh, I Love a Christmas Day," written by the late Irving Jenkins of Salt Lake City, and Eugene Jelesnik, KDYL orchestra leader, presented a violin solo of "Ave Maria."

For the Russian immigrant Jew, whose earliest memories were of Christmas lights and caroling in the public square in Alexandrovsk, Russia, the program had a nostalgic ring to it.

In the years between the First and Second World Wars, the American Federation of Musicians (AFM) and the American Society of Composers, Authors, and Publishers (ASCAP) were two of the most powerful forces in the cultural life of the country. ASCAP had been founded in 1914 to protect the copyrights and performance rights of creative artists. Its first president was the composer Victor Herbert. The AFM—founded in 1895—was a trade union representing the interests of performing musicians. As both a published composer and a performing artist, Eugene Jelesnik was a member in good standing of both organizations. To no small degree it was because of their existence that Jelesnik had found it possible to return to Utah in 1945. Both organizations had long feared that the rise of mechanical and electronic recording devices threatened the livelihood of performing artists and even the continued existence of live music. Under the strong leadership of men such as AFM's president James C. Petrillo and ASCAP chief Otto Harbach, labor and copyright use agreements were signed with radio networks that required each affiliate station to employ a specified number of professional musicians for live weekly broadcasts. Network affiliate stations in Utah were not then immune from the requirement, and each of the local affiliates had their own orchestras. It was this requirement that was ultimately responsible for Sid Fox hiring Eugene Jelesnik at KDYL.[6]

Local station owners often paid more attention to the bottom line than the bottom note, and they were not particularly overjoyed by the networks' labor contract requirements. While they themselves ultimately made most of their money from the talents of musicians, performers, and other artists, that did not necessarily mean that they believed in actually paying them. Some viewed the musicians as little more than "superfluous employees." Others saw the benefit of carrying the orchestras for their PR value, and a rare few hired musicians because they actually liked their music. What Sid Fox liked was getting full value for his money. For Eugene Jelesnik that meant performing many duties largely extraneous to those that might normally be expected of a radio station's musical director. During his employment at KDYL, Eugene would act as music arranger, conductor, talk show host, publicist, promotion director, booking agent, stage manager, contract specialist, and as Sid Fox's personal gofer.[7] Much of the time Eugene felt like a musician of Imperial Russia as described by Mischa Elman's father in his memoirs. Though a musician in the old country might have been applauded for his talent and his music, he was otherwise treated as an indentured servant. Such was the relationship between Sid Fox and Eugene Jelesnik.

As music director for the station, it was one of Eugene's responsibilities to arrange for guest appearances by musicians, musical personalities, and other celebrities who might be visiting or performing in the Salt Lake area. One of the first notables to visit Eugene in his new position was Rudy Vallee. Vallee had been a close friend of Jelesnik since the early days at the Hollywood Restaurant. In the spring of 1946, Vallee and his wife were passing through Salt Lake City on their way to California. When he learned that Jelesnik was living in Salt Lake and employed at KDYL, he brought his old friend a box of caramel popcorn, which he knew to be Eugene's favorite. What then happened established a pattern that would last through Eugene's tenure at the station. Whenever one of Eugene's celebrity friends came to town, Mr. Fox would invariably push himself into the relationship. Fox would take pains to make it clear to the visitor that he was the station's big shot and that Eugene was only an employee.[8] A photograph of the meeting with the Vallees shows Fox sitting on a couch with one arm around Mrs. Vallee, holding a large imperious cigar in his other hand. Rudy and Eugene are smiling stiffly. Vallee recognized the awkward position that Eugene had got himself into at KDYL, but whenever he came through Salt Lake, he always made it a point to have a personal visit with Jelesnik. The two remained fast friends. On one occasion, Vallee sent tickets to Jelesnik for his Broadway hit *How to Succeed in Business without Really Trying*.

While Mr. Fox may have been a little overbearing, and always got his money's worth from his employees, he was also open to suggestions and good ideas. As musical director, Eugene was free to decide what sorts of programs and promotional activities might be undertaken. In the summer of 1946, Eugene inaugurated a series of band concerts to be held in the old band shell in Salt Lake's Liberty Park. The concerts featured the KDYL orchestra and were presented as part of the station's general promotions for the summer. But the musical content of the concerts was similar to the programs that Eugene had presented with his "society orchestra" on Sunday afternoons at the Hotel Utah. Each concert offered a wide mix of light classical instrumentals, Broadway and Hollywood show tunes, and contemporary favorites. It was a formula that had never failed to please, and it was the basis of what was soon to develop into Eugene Jelesnik's crowd-drawing "Pops Concerts." More importantly, the Liberty Park programs came closest to what Eugene Jelesnik really wanted most: to foster an appreciation of music and disseminate that appreciation to the widest possible audience. Jelesnik never forgot the concerts that "Uncle" Robert Spiro had put on in Central Park in New York City to promote "Parents Day." He remembered specifically that Spiro's free park concerts drew more than 20,000 people. As he prepared his Liberty Park concert for KDYL, his mind was drawn back to that other park. If he were to accomplish what he had in mind, he would need a large orchestra of his own.

The Salt Lake Philharmonic Orchestra was first organized under Royal W. Daynes and Clarence J. Hawkins in 1913.[9] For several years it had thrived as one of the area's premiere musical aggregations, but it had gradually fallen into inactivity. Though it still remained an active Utah corporation on paper in 1946, it had actually ceased to exist after its last public performance in 1925. Ethyl Langwell Clays, the attractive portrait artist who had befriended Eugene when he first came to Salt Lake in 1938, had married the son of Royal Daynes, Gerald R. Daynes. With the blessing and active assistance of the Daynes family and the encouragement and financial support of *The Salt Lake Tribune* and the American Federation of Musicians, Eugene began auditioning local talent for the purpose of resurrecting the Salt Lake Philharmonic Orchestra. The process of building a viable orchestra from scratch would take years, but by August the Philharmonic was in rehearsal for its first concert, which was given in Liberty Park on 1 September 1946.[10]

From the very beginning, Eugene had intended that the orchestra would be primarily used for presenting free public performances, and over its long history the Philharmonic would succeed in never charging admission to its concerts. All of its performance costs were underwritten by a variety of local sponsors, including *The Salt Lake Tribune;* the *Desert News;* the Junior

Chamber of Commerce; the Salt Lake City Parks Department; the Days of '47, Inc.; the Salt Lake Exchange Club; the Easter Seal Society of Utah; KSL; and the Antelope Island Chapter of the International Footprint Association, an organization of law enforcement officers. Though many individuals, organizations, and companies helped sponsor the free concerts, most of the funding came from the Music Performance Trust Fund of the American Federation of Musicians. The fund came from the union's share of recording royalties, and they yearly supplied Local 104 with matching grants to promote the appreciation of live music. Through the Salt Lake Philharmonic Orchestra, Jelesnik would use the grants to "introduce the uninitiated to classical music, to demystify operatic music, and to expose Salt Lake audiences to the finest concert soloists." These were the goals of the grants as stated in concert programs, but their actual function was to mount exciting, crowd-pleasing shows.

While the basic format for the Philharmonic's concerts rarely varied, the venues changed frequently from year to year. The earliest performances were at Liberty Park, and later concerts were staged at Kingsbury Hall on the University of Utah campus. The historic Assembly Hall on Temple Square was used for the Pops Concert in 1950 and for several seasons afterward. Other early performance sites included the old Terrace Ballroom and the Utah State Fairground's grandstands. But hotel ballrooms, high school auditoriums, and public parks were frequently used for the pops concerts as well. Most of the performances were given on or around public holidays such as the "Holiday Pops Concert" on the evening following Thanksgiving, and the annual Labor Day Pops Concert, sponsored by *The Salt Lake Tribune*. From time to time, pops concerts were given for special occasions or commemorations. After a little experimentation, Jelesnik and the Philharmonic settled into a routine that his large and faithful audiences grew to love. Sponsors, occasions, venues, and performers would be changed many times, but there was one constant: from 1946 on, Eugene Jelesnik remained the principal conductor of the Salt Lake Philharmonic Orchestra.

Though the Salt Lake Philharmonic's "Pops Concerts" would

highlight many a local celebration, it was the orchestra's link to the Days of '47 that would be remembered by most Utahns. Nineteen forty-seven was the 100th anniversary of the entry of the Mormon pioneers into the Salt Lake Valley. Jelesnik recognized the unique significance of the occasion and convinced organizers that it was important to honor the observance with a special musical program for the entire community. Eugene also promoted a contest for the composition of lyrics that would pay tribute to the original Mormon settlers. Eugene himself would compose the music for the centennial salute. The winner of the contest was an eleven-year-old sixth grader from Sandy, Utah, Kay Smith, whose lyrics "The Mormon Trail," were selected by Eugene from more than seventy-five entries. "The Mormon Trail" would become Utah's centennial song of 1947. At a special ceremony in the governor's office, copies of the "The Mormon Trail" were autographed by Kay Smith and Jelesnik, and presented as a gift to Governor Herbert B. Maw.[11] Smith later became a professor at Brigham Young University, and the song would become the official theme song for The Days of '47. Eugene would arrange through friends at George F. Briegel, Inc., in New York, to have the composition published.

From 1947 on, Eugene Jelesnik was deeply involved with the Days of '47 celebration, volunteering and working on countless committees and in various capacities. One day he would become vice president of the Days of '47 committee. The Philharmonic "Pops Concert" was quickly adopted as one of the principal events of the annual celebration, often kicking off the week-long festivities. The Days of '47 productions became the Philharmonic's most elaborate affairs and always attracted large audiences. Big-name celebrities were usually brought in to perform with the orchestra, including Las Vegas headliners, Hollywood stars, and television personalities.

In 1949, TV's Roy Rogers and Dale Evans were the headline stars for the annual Days of '47 Rodeo. Evans was a star in her own right before she teamed up permanently with Rogers. She had been an accomplished songwriter and country western artist before turning to acting. Her most well-known songs included "The Bible Tells Me So" and "San Antone." She had sung on the radio in Memphis, Dallas, Louisville, and Chicago. In 1943 she went to Hollywood where she frequently appeared in Western films with Roy Rogers. Evans and Rogers were married in 1947 and shortly afterward began starring in the television series that became a staple of early juvenile programming. It was Evans who wrote "Happy Trails," the song which the couple adopted as their theme song. In 1946, when Jelesnik's "Nodocky Polka " was first published in sheet music form, Dale Evans was selected by the publishing company to appear on the cover. Jelesnik and Evans didn't meet until her appearance at the rodeo in 1949. By that year, Jelesnik was musical director for the rodeo as well as the Philharmonic. Eugene and Dale Evans traded autographed copies of the "Nodocky Polka" sheet music at the Utah State Fairgrounds, and publicity photos of the double signing were featured in the newspapers. The shots may have helped spark renewed interest in the polka. The following spring "The Nadocky" was featured as part of singer Ella Logan's floor show at the Thunderbird Hotel in Las Vegas.

Jelesnik also continued to compose music, and by October of 1951, he had published and recorded enough music to be elected as a member of the ASCAP (the American Society of Composers, Artists, and Publishers). By that October his list of compositions included: "My Gypsy Melody," "Two Silhouettes on the Moon," "The Mormon Trail," "Memory of You," "Why Should I Wait?" "I Heard," "A Gypsy Dream," "The Peanut Vendor's Sister," and "Well, Butter My Beans." In addition he published a violin arrangement of "The Orange Blossom Special," which became a steady royalty producer. He collaborated with other artists on several pieces including: "Rain across the Moon," which he composed with Utah lyricist Maryhale Woolsey who also wrote "When It's Springtime in the Rockies."[12]

Through the late forties and early fifties, Eugene continued to develop close friendships with celebrities. His KDYL radio program afforded him the opportunity of interviewing many of the most popular and influential figures of the day. Among those to sit before Eugene's microphone in those years was Claire Booth Luce. When they met in Italy during Eugene's "Fox Hole Tour,"

Jelesnik had told the Representative that he was going to have a radio program in Salt Lake City, and he invited her then and there to be on his show after the war was over. Mrs. Luce agreed to appear, and more than a year and a half later she kept her promise. The veteran news announcer and world traveler Lowell Thomas also visited Salt Lake and broadcast the NBC News from KDYL. Thomas was also a guest on Eugene's program. There were many other notables that Eugene would encounter during his stay at KDYL, including comedians Jack Benny and Bob Hope, singer and TV personality Bob Crosby, actors Keenan Wynn and William Demerest, actress Polly Bergen, and Metropolitan Opera star James Melton. Jelesnik even managed to have his photograph taken with President Harry S. Truman in the lobby of the Hotel Utah.

But of all the important figures that Eugene met in those years, there was one who excited him the most. The man was a completely bald, Russian violinist who bore a slight resemblance to Nikita Khrushchev and who was even shorter than Eugene Jelesnik. From the time when Eugene was a young student, he had marveled at the man's talent and his passion and had always considered him the greatest of all the great violinists. The man was Mischa Elman. He had come to Salt Lake City to perform a concert at the University of Utah. Eugene found out where Elman was staying and called him on the telephone. He told Elman that he was also a violinist and that he had admired Elman since he was a boy. He related how he used to save his money to buy a fifty cent seat at the back of Carnegie Hall so he could hear Elman play. He told him how he still remembered what pieces Elman had performed the first time he heard him: Mendelssohn's "Violin Concerto" and "The Meditation" from *Thais* by Jules Massenet. He then asked Mischa Elman if he would be so kind as to appear on Jelesnik's show. After such a lead-in, Elman could not possibly have refused. Eugene was "thrilled to death."

On 19 April 1948, KDYL began broadcasting with its new transmitter and by so doing became the only television station between St. Louis and Los Angeles. The invention by Utahn Philo T. Farnsworth had finally come home. With the flip of a switch,

KDYL-TV was on the air, and just as instantly Eugene's workload doubled. Jelesnik's experience in television back in New York had made him a key man in the new operation. But Eugene was still expected to continue his duties on the radio while at the same time helping to develop programming for the new medium. Many years later in an interview with *Deseret News* staff writer Howard Pearson, Danny Rainger, who was the first station manager of KDYL-TV, recalled an incident involving Jelesnik: When the station first went on the air Eugene had a number of duties and among them was the task of operating the station's movie projector. Jelesnik had run projectors before, but on his first day he forgot to secure the film securely on the take-up reel. The movie had been running for some time when Rainger stepped into the booth to see how everything was going.

There sat Eugene as contented as he could be—and completely oblivious to the fact that the floor was filling up with film: "He was so entranced with the movie that he hadn't seen that film was not winding on the take-up reel."[13] It took hours for Eugene and Rainger to get the film back on the spool.

Eugene's first programming contribution to the art of television was an innovative set piece called *Café Continental*. Loosely based on Eugene's experiences in the nightclubs and cabarets of New York City, the program was a fifteen-minute interlude built around a fictitious nightclub. Eugene played the part of the café's master of ceremonies who would introduce acts as well as interview visiting notables who just happened to be in the audience. *Café Continental* was vaguely reminiscent of newspaper accounts of one of Sophie Tucker's "Celebrity Nights" featured at the Hollywood Restaurant. The set consisted of a painted backdrop with simple tables and chairs set up café-style. Entertainers and celebrities would move among the pretend diners informally, while the master of ceremonies would introduce acts while standing on a crepe paper-covered stand or sometimes seated at a table with a hand-held mike. Eugene would frequently perform at the tables, wearing a Gypsy bandanna, invoking the flavor of Yorkville. For those not familiar with the true milieu of New York's nightclub scene, the whole setup might have seemed contrived and tawdry, but in fact the setting bore a good resemblance to photographs of New York's Bal Tabarin night spot. The program was an early vehicle for displaying local talent, but many visiting celebrities were induced to participate in the charade, including such notables as Broadway actress Carol Omart and big band leader Stan Kenton. *Café Continental* aired only once a week, but Eugene also had an afternoon program called *Video Frolics* which was broadcast live every Monday, Wednesday, and Friday.

Rocky Mountain Magazine described KDYL's bold experiment in a Denver newspaper supplement. It was clear that commercial TV in Salt Lake City was still very experimental:[14]

> From Aunt Jennie and her pickle display at the state fair to the sprightly dancers of the local Swedish club, everything is fair game for KDYL-TV Channel 2 Salt Lake City, America's "guinea pig" small market television station. Lacking Hollywood stars and top-notch sports, KDYL's operations give every promise that television in the smaller cities is going back to the people. Vaudeville, once mourned as dead, is showing every sign of a new and lusty rebirth.
>
> "Sometimes we know where we're going, sometimes we can only cross our fingers and hope," said volatile Danny Rainger, KDYL-TV's program manager. "And sometimes," he winced, "the darndest things happen."
>
> KDYL, Utah's only NBC station, and a highly successful independent, started life as a pioneer in 1922, the thirteenth commercial radio station in America. Interestingly enough, KDYL-TV brought to Salt Lake whatever honor can be attached to becoming the thirteenth city in America to have commercial television. KDYL's radio wave length is 1320.
>
> Perhaps those are the reasons the number thirteen holds no terrors for Sid S. Fox, dapper, rotund president of KDYL. When 45,000 persons jammed a three-day demonstration in a Salt Lake department store the summer of 1939, Fox waxed enthusiastic. "Brother, television's the thing," he told intimates, and shortly afterward applied for a license.
>
> An experimental license was granted in 1941, but it was not until July of 1946, using "90 percent tailor-made equipment" constructed in its own studios that the station finally pioneered by becoming the first independent studio in the nation to

televise a test pattern. That is, it televised geometric designs to test both telecasting and receiving equipment.

Approximately 60 percent of current program time, which runs a minimum of 12 hours a week on a five-day schedule, is made up of films, ranging from an occasional old western to smart NBC shorts. The remaining time is about equally divided between telecasting local events with mobile equipment, and studio productions.

Through its own talent department, headed by Eugene Jelesnik, KDYL-TV is willing to audition anyone for live shows. Out of this contest search has come the Utah girls, university student actors, music and dramatic school singers, dancers, comedians, and [other] hopefuls that help fill the insatiable demands of television. A weekly feature at KDYL-TV is "Café Continental." A studio show, it requires several couples in evening clothes, representing the audience in a night club. Only half the problem of the show is getting talent for the acts. The other half is obtaining the persons for the café audience.

Eventually, Fox says, Salt Lake City should be able to support two or three local non-network television stations. Pointing to the high investment, heavy overhead, space and talent problems of non-network television, Fox believes stations will not be feasible in communities under 100,000 population.

More than 700 television sets have been installed in the Salt Lake area, including those in taverns. Admittedly, sale of sets has been somewhat slow, but they are expected to climb during the winter, and within two years Fox is optimistic enough to believe 10,000 will be in use in the metropolitan area, an area which now has 44,000 radio homes.

Occasionally, KDYL television programs were broadcast from local movie theaters in much the same way that variety acts appeared in theaters in the dying days of vaudeville. TV was still enough of a novelty that promotional stunts were often necessary just to keep people aware of the fact that it was around. For this reason one of Eugene's afternoon programs, *Video Frolics*, was often broadcast live from a variety of remote theater locations. The show would even be billed at Salt Lake's Holladay Theater as a "vaudeville program."[15] The notion was very close to the truth. Many of vaudeville's greatest stars were beginning to make comebacks on television. Milton Berle was already well on his way to becoming "Mr. Television," and others, including Jack Benny and George Burns and Gracie Allen, were starting to make the transition from radio. All of these former vaudevillians would visit Salt Lake in the early days of KDYL. Ten days after KDYL-TV went on the air, one of vaudeville's most endearing and enduring characters arrived in Salt Lake to climax a fund-raising drive for the American Cancer Society. In fact, Jimmy Durante had come at the request of an old friend. The newspapers—while focusing on the comedy of the "old schnozzle"—made much of the relationship:

DURANTE WILL CLOWN AND JELESNIK WILL PLAY

It will be a version of hands-across-the-sea for two old chums when Jimmy Durante and Eugene Jelesnik get busy in their roles Friday night at the fairgrounds Coliseum's big program—climax of the fund-raising drive of the Utah division of the American Cancer Society.

Mr. Jelesnik will be wielding the orchestral baton in the good cause while Mr. Durante, comedian star, will be bringing down the house in his own inimitable fashion.

Durante probably will be singing his famous "Inka-Dinka-Do" that he did in New York when in the old days he and Jelesnik worked together in that city. The twain concocted rib-tickling episodes for hilarious audiences. This time their object is more serious but they are going at it just as intensely. The Salt Lake conductor has made his own arrangement of an overture in honor of Durante from Hollywood. It is written around a rollicking song, "There's No Biz Like the Show Biz." Last minute touches are being given the scintillating program by Ferrell H. Adams, state chairman of the special committee for the Friday night event. Mr. Durante is furnishing his services without charge.

The vaudevillian's generous gesture did not go unnoticed. On the day before the performance, Durante was escorted from the Hotel Utah by Salt Lake Mayor Earl J. Glade and Utah's Governor Herbert B. Maw for an old-fashioned hero's parade down Main Street. The party was lead by a troop of mounted riders, "The Ute Rangers," and was followed by a brass band. *The Salt Lake Telegram* sent a reporter to cover the unusual parade. He caught up with the procession as it returned to the Hotel Utah.

JIMMY DURANTE

Making a round of the city, the parade returned to Hotel Utah,[16] where crowds affectionately surrounded the gent with the prolonged proboscis. Spectators, fearful of missing some of the comedian's famous quips, followed him into the hotel. Side-splitting guffaws punctuated the hum of the crowds. The veteran of vaudeville commented on Salt Lake's wide and clean streets: "They're just the way I remember them as being 20 years ago. Brigham Young showed great foresight, only he shoulda gone to 'Philly,'" he wisecracked.

Durante will appear at the Coliseum in a vaudeville act he started in 1923 in the New York circuit, with Eddie Jackson, original member of the act, and Jack Roth, a drummer. "I'm really going to break things up," he threatened, explaining that the act features a musical number which ends in confusion and smashing of instruments.

A. Wally Sandak will be master of ceremonies. Music will be furnished by Eugene Jelesnik and his 12-piece orchestra. Jimmy spent the late morning and early afternoon in rehearsals for the show.

Other celebrity-vaudevillians made charity appearances in Salt Lake City. Jack Benny performed with Eugene Jelesnik at the V. A. Hospital's Little Theater in a duo violin act that was long-remembered by some of the staff. Jelesnik would play long complicated passages, which would only occasionally be punctuated by Benny playing a single note on his violin. The effect was hilarious.[17]

As NBC's only affiliate in Utah, KDYL was a frequent stop for many NBC artists and performers who were regularly sent on national publicity and marketing tours by the network. Jelesnik would often be expected to act as the local host for the visiting celebrity. Not infrequently this involved solving unexpected problems. William Warfield was one of the principal baritones of the New York City Opera. He had studied at the Eastman School of Music and had performed with the Metropolitan Opera and the Opera of Vienna.[18] In 1949 he had been the principal baritone in Blitzstein's *Regina* on Broadway, and the following year Warfield sang the title role of "Porgy" in *Porgy and Bess*, a role he would play for several years worldwide. When Warfield came to Salt Lake City for a concert, the sponsors had got him reservations at the Hotel Utah, but when he arrived at the desk the hotel refused to register him. Warfield was black, and at that time the only blacks allowed in the hotel were bellhops and elevator operators. Utah educator A. Ray Olpin was involved in sponsoring Warfield's concert. When he learned what had happened, he was horrified and immediately called Eugene Jelesnik and explained the situation. Knowing that Eugene had a good relationship with the hotel, he asked if Eugene would intervene. Jelesnik was furious. He and Olpin went to the manager and demanded that their guest be registered at once. They gave in and Warfield stayed at the hotel. Unlike other black performers who would complain of having to take freight elevators and back stairs to their rooms, Warfield entered and left by the front door and was given access to the main elevators. The following afternoon he appeared on *Video Frolics* with Jelesnik.[19]

Another of Eugene's guests was Otto Harbach, one of America's greatest lyricists and librettists. Harbach had studied composition at Knox College and Columbia University. In 1908 he collaborated with the composer Karl Hoschna on the successful musical *Three Twins* and subsequently wrote more than forty works for Broadway. He had collaborated with the greatest theatrical composers of the day, including Oscar Hammerstein II, Rudolf Friml, Vincent Youmans, Jerome Kern, and Sigmund Romberg. His most popular lyrics included "Rose Marie" and "Indian Love Call" from Friml's *Rose Marie,* which he wrote with Hammerstein; "The Night Was Made for Love," which he wrote with Jerome Kern for *The Cat and the Fiddle;* and "Smoke Gets in Your Eyes" from Kern's *Roberta.*[20] Unlike most of Jelesnik's guests, Harbach did not have to be shown around town. He was a native son, having been born in Salt Lake City on 18 August 1873. At the time of his visit Harbach was serving as the president of ASCAP—the American Society of Composers, Authors, and Publishers. Harbach knew of Eugene's experience in composing, and during his appearance on *Video Frolics* he suddenly asked Jelesnik if he might be interested in collaborating on a composition. Jelesnik was so stunned that he later said he could have been knocked over with a feather, "I almost died!" he said. But he immediately accepted the offer. The process of writing went on for a number of weeks. Habach would send Eugene a lyric and Eugene would compose a line of music for it. The result of their collaboration was a song titled "The Perfect Symphony." It was a pleasant ditty in the style of the popular music of the day. Others who appeared on *Video Frolics* included blues singer Peggy Lee and musical madman Spike Jones. Eugene was surprised to find that the irreverent Mr. Jones was an excellent musician.

One guest on *Video Frolics* was a man who the casual observer might suspect would have been featured often, but in fact he made only one appearance. That man was Maurice Abravanel who in 1947 was named conductor of the Utah Symphony Orchestra.[21]Abravanel was eleven years older than Eugene, having been born in Salonika, Germany, in 1903. He had studied music in Lausanne from 1919–21, and at the University of Zurich from 1921–22, and then in Berlin with Kurt Weill (also 1922). When Maurice made his debut in Berlin in 1924, Jelesnik was living in the refugee compound in Bremen. As a young man, Maurice had conducted at Zwickau, Germany, and in opera houses in Berlin, Rome, and Australia. From 1936 through 1938, Abravanel conducted the orchestra at the New York Metropolitan Opera—debuting with *Samson et Dalila*. He had spent time conducting on Broadway, and Eugene remembered many of the places that Abravanel worked. They were not necessarily the finest bookings on the street. Before coming to Utah, Abravanel had conducted the Chicago Opera Company. The TV interview with Eugene Jelesnik was unremarkable and mostly dealt with upcoming programs of the Utah Symphony. There was no indication of what was about to happen.

It was not too long after Abravanel's appearance on the program that Eugene encountered Maurice again, this time on Main Street in front of Arthur Franks clothing store: "I will never forget it," Eugene recalled. "I was walking down Main, and I saw Maurice Abravanel coming toward me, and he gestures to me and says, 'I want to talk to you!'"

"Well, I stop, and he begins talking and at the same time he is pointing his finger at me, and then he's tapping me on the chest, and, finally, he's backed me up against the Arthur Franks window. And what he's saying is:

"'Listen, Eugene, Salt Lake City is not a big town. There's only room here for one orchestra, and that's the Utah Symphony!'

"I said, 'What are you talking about? I don't compete with you. You play the serious symphonic works, and I play the lighter pops concert materials like the Boston Pops. How do I compete with you?'

"And he says, 'That's not the point. You take people away from our concerts, people who should be attending the symphony, and you should close up!'"[22]

For Jelesnik, Abravanel's comments were threatening and echoed the old western oater line: "This town ain't big enough for both of us!" Eugene was not about to get out of town by sundown, and the confrontation escalated as both men hurled epithets and threats at the other, attracting no little attention in that public setting. In the end, "The shout-out on Main Street" ended with both conductors going their opposite ways. The two men would not speak again for decades, and the feud would cause many problems for musicians in the Valley.

Yet another Jelesnik program, seen during the early 1950s on KDYL, was *Spotlight Revue,* co-starring singer Marlene Kinghorn, pianist Larry Pryor, and dancer Marlene Melroy. On 4 April 1951, *Variety Magazine,* an internationally distributed entertainment industry trade paper, published an eight-and-one-half inch review of the show. The *Variety* critic described the program as "a variety show sparked by station music director Eugene Jelesnik. It is a far-west imitation of Broadway Open House, tightened up to run a fast-paced 30 minutes. The highlight of the show, which premiered on May 30, was Jelesnik's rendition of 'Ave Maria' played against a choral group, which added to the number's effectiveness and [featured] the violinist against a stained glass background. The technicians did a smart bit of lighting that snapped up the video aspects of the offering."

While programs like *Broadway Open House* and *Spotlight*

Review were short-lived, *Video Frolics* would become one of the
most successful programs ever mounted by KDYL-TV, and it garnered considerable praise in the press. Most reviewers were
enchanted by the simple, straightforward approach that Eugene
brought to his interviews, but at the same time some were put off
by the sometimes "show-biz" contrivances that often surrounded
them:[23]

> Slotted alongside such big city names as Kate Smith and
> Miss Susan, Eugene Jelesnik's afternoon vaudeville series
> stands up well with afternoon audiences, with additional
> interest provided by well-known, hometown talent, plus an
> occasional sprinkling of visiting names.
> The show centers largely around the emcee and his fiddle
> and Larry Pryor on the piano, with acts generally brought on
> camera with chatter between emcee and pianist, or through a
> camera switch to one of two alternate backgrounds.
> Experienced showman Jelesnik, now in charge of all talent,
> and music director for the National Broadcasting Company
> outlet here in Salt Lake City, takes the brunt of the camera time,
> and his experience stands up.
> His feature offering of [yesterday] afternoon was a tuneful
> rendition of the perennial favorite, "Stardust." A strong video
> assist in camera work brought on a pleasant effect when the
> maestro's fiddle was superimposed over clusters of painted
> stars. The fiddler garnishes his musical sequences with the kind
> of schmaltz and pash that comes with long experience on miles
> of circuits.

Another reviewer focused on some of the same elements:

> The show is highly seasoned with extreme informality.
> Guests who wander into camera range do so with a refreshing
> change from the "I just happen to have it with me" routine.
> The show is well-adapted to participating spots, and it
> compares well with other fine varieties which come into this
> territory. Camera work is neat and precise, offering effects and
> composition and adding substantially to the wrappings.

On St. Patrick's Day of 1952, Eugene presented a special Irish
music program featuring singers and dancers from the local
Catholic schools. It was one of a series of ethnic and holiday

specials that Eugene presented from time to time. The program established yet another format, which Eugene would further develop in the years to come—the amateur talent competition. That same afternoon, Eugene announced that *Video Frolics* would be honored by the network and *The Salt Lake Tribune* reported:

> Immediately following his television program on Thursday, March 27, Eugene Jelesnik boards a plane for New York City to appear as guest artist on the *Kate Smith Coast to Coast Live Television Program* over the National Broadcasting Network. The Honor was announced yesterday by S.S. Fox, president and general manager of the Intermountain Broadcasting and Television Corporation.
>
> On Monday, March 31, at 4 P.M. EST (2 P.M. Salt Lake time), national recognition will be accorded Mr. Jelesnik by Kate Smith personally in a special interview, during which time Mis Smith will request Mr. Jelesnik to perform on his violin. Fifteen minutes of the hour-long Kate Smith television program will be devoted to Mr. Jelesnik and Salt Lake City.

The recognition was not restricted to coverage in the Salt Lake newspapers. Eugene's old friend Nick Kenny at the *New York Sunday Mirror* also picked up on the story:

> New York's loss was Salt Lake City's gain when Sidney Fox grabbed our violin playing maestro, Eugene Jelesnik, back in 1945 to be musical and talent director for Sid's radio and television station KDYL and KDYL-TV in Salt Lake City. Sid cabled Jelesnik in Rome in 1945, where the famous violinist was entertaining our soldiers on a USO tour. The contract was signed immediately for the Jelesniks to move to Salt Lake City. Jelesnik used to be a member of our *Daily Mirror* "Radio Gang" and his fiddle was heard at hundreds of our benefits each year. Today he is the pride of Salt Lake City, and his four pops concerts annually are attended by thousands. Governor J. Bracken Lee of Utah even sent a congratulatory wire to a big program in New York on which Gene recently made a guest appearance. It was his first visit to the old home town in six and a half years. It was like old home week when he hit Tin Pan Alley. All the music boys remembered him and he has often remembered them with his six shows a week on KDYL-TV.

Very early in his employment at KDYL, Eugene was asked by Sid Fox to accompany him to Las Vegas, Nevada, ostensibly to attend a booking exposition and to review new talent for upcoming station programming. Though Las Vegas was indeed a place where celebrities, agents, and producers gathered to hammer out performance contracts, the city had other attractions. As time went on, Eugene realized that the talent scouting and contract negotiations were secondary to the real reason Sid Fox took Eugene to Las Vegas.[24] Everyone knew that Sid was a gambler. What they could not have known in the late 1940s was that he was an *addicted* gambler who in later times might have benefited from the professional counselors of "Gamblers Anonymous." Fox may not have realized it, but he was suffering from an addictive disease. The more he lost at the tables, the more he wanted to play. The alternating emotions of elation and disappointment, fear and guilt can produce powerfully addictive chemicals including endorphins, enkephalins, and adrenalin. The pathology of the "gambling disease" is now well-recognized, but in the late 1940s it was unknown.

The flights to Las Vegas were sporadic at first, but gradually increased in frequency until they became part of the regular weekend routine. During these sojourns it was Eugene's thankless job to see to it that his employer didn't lose too much money. It was a task that was doomed to fail from the start. The gambler's "natural high" is driven by extremes of emotion, and without losing, the chemical cocktail would be incomplete.

Virginia was infuriated by the weekly trips to Vegas and naturally suspected that a good deal more was going on than watching Sid Fox gamble. Finally after months of arguing she insisted that from then on she would accompany the duo to Vegas to see for herself what was going on. While Mr. Fox could be flamboyant, and even extravagant when he wanted to impress a visiting celebrity, he was usually more frugal when it came to his employees. While Fox luxuriated in one of the swankiest rooms in their hotel, he set Eugene and Virginia up in the cheapest room he could get. Virginia was soon satisfied that her husband's accounts of the frequent trips were on the up and up. It also didn't take her long to realize that Sid Fox was an "inveterate gambler," but she also saw how he treated Eugene, and this infuriated her to the point that she blew up and told Fox exactly what she thought of him. She did not go to Vegas again, and the episode did nothing to improve the working relationship between Jelesnik and Fox, but Virginia was satisfied that it was worth it.[25]

It was inevitable that Sid Fox's gambling debts would eventually catch up with him. Whether they specifically had anything to do with his decision to sell KDYL is unknown, but on 31 March 1953, Fox sold the station to TFL Broadcasting, a division of *Time* magazine for 2.1 million dollars.[26] The announcement of the sale was made in Salt Lake City on April Fool's Day. Fox provided for many of the station's employees, seeing to it that some would be retained by the new owners or that those near retirement would be otherwise taken care of. But Eugene and Virginia were left out in the cold with no provisions made for them whatsoever. Perhaps Fox blamed Eugene for not taking better care of him in Vegas, or perhaps the row with Virginia had made him bitter toward the couple.

When G. Alvin Pack took over as artistic director of the station on 10 July 1953, Eugene Jelesnik was once again out of a job. Worse, he had no prospect for local employment in his chosen work as a professional musician. As a firm believer in the union, he was not about to accept substandard wage. Even if he were, none was being offered. For months Eugene did what he could to stay alive, playing weddings and banquets and doing all the scrambling that he had done in the first ten years of his career, but it was increasingly clear that the new state of affairs in Utah was hopeless. While his reputation was as good as ever, much of his work had been donated to the community. The Philharmonic's Pops concerts, the Days of '47 musical programs, and the hospital and charity appearances were only partially compensated for by the Musician's Union Trust Funds. Most of the organizational and executive duties that Eugene had provided were on a volunteer basis. Eugene wrote his former agent and a number of his friends back East, but he had been out of circulation there for so long that it would be difficult if not impossible for him to break in, particularly with so many young musicians scrambling for work as well.

Finally—out of desperation—he wrote his old friend Bert Wishnew with the United Service Organization to ask if they might have any use for him. The reply was almost immediate. Of course the USO would hire Eugene. There was only one catch: he would have to go to Korea.

CHAPTER NINE

KOREA, THE CINEGRILL, AND LIBERACE

On Saturday 7 November 1953, Salt Lake City newspapers reported that Eugene Jelesnik was unable to play his violin.[1] Jelesnik had received a "full battery" of immunization shots in preparation for his upcoming USO tour to Asia. The papers reported that the injections had made his arm so sore that he couldn't even lift it. But papers are sometimes known to exaggerate. Eugene had to lift a good deal more that day than his violin. That same afternoon he would board a plane for New York City. With him went the luggage, music, and personal belongings that he would need for the next five months. Shortly before Eugene left for the airport, he received a call from Utah's governor, J. Bracken Lee, who had read in the paper about the tour. The Governor asked Eugene if he would deliver a message to his son who was serving with the U. S. Army in Korea. Eugene, of course, was happy to oblige Utah's most colorful—and at times most difficult—politician. Virginia would not accompany Eugene on the tour. She would remain in Salt Lake and take care of their home on Coatsville Avenue. It was always hard on Virginia when her husband was away, and particularly hard when she was left alone for holidays like Thanksgiving and Christmas. This time, as he had in 1944, he would be gone for both. She had gotten used to staying behind, but "keeping the home fires burning" was forlorn duty. Unfortunately, through their long marriage, the couple would endure many such separations, and sadly enough, they would spend relatively few holidays together.

The Asian tour was the creation of Bert Wishnew, and though Jelesnik was the "leader of the band," he had nothing to do with the selection of any of the acts or the itinerary. The tour was billed as "Magic and Melody," and rehearsals for the show began on Monday evening November 9th in a rented hall on 45th Street in downtown Manhattan.[2] The company consisted of Jelesnik and nine other entertainers. Headlining this unit was former Radio City Music Hall Rockette and one-time Bill Monroe performer Lynne Jackson, who would appear as a leggy novelty act and tap dancer. There was also a Swedish tenor named Jon Otness who was the company's only vocalist. The Jerry Allen Trio (accordion, drums and saxophone) provided the music for both dancer and singer. Two husband-wife teams—magicians Herbert and Lotte Novelli, and black comedians Strawberry and Julia Russell—were also signed on.[3] Jelesnik, as usual, would perform multiple tasks during the tour, acting as the troupe's manager, spokesman, and master of ceremonies. He would also perform with his violin in the shows.

The company spent less than a week in rehearsal in New York before the ten performers flew to San Francisco. On November 16th they took off from Travis Air Force Base for the first leg of their tour of the Far East. The trip would include stopovers and performances in Hawaii and Japan.[4] Jelesnik was shocked at the widespread destruction that was evident in every Japanese city they visited. It had been more than seven years since the end of the Second World War. He thought there would have been more effort given to cleaning up the rubble. What he did not realize at the time was that shortly before his arrival, Japan had been struck by a series of strong earthquakes.[5] Some of the damage he saw was less than a week old. After spending several weeks in Japan, "Magic and Melody" arrived in Pusan, Korea, on 22 December 1953, for the most extensive and arduous part of the tour. Nothing he had seen in Italy, or more recently in Japan, prepared him for the utter devastation that now met his eyes.

The war in Korea had been a bloody, seesaw affair from beginning to end, with each side gaining advantage at various stages of the conflict. The initial North Korean attack on 25 June 1950 was devastating. North Korean tanks and infantry poured across the 38th parallel, which marked the boundary between communist North Korea and the Republic of Korea to the south. United Nations intervention in the form of the U. S. 24th Infantry Division was too late in arriving to prevent the fall of Seoul, South Korea's capital city. By the beginning of September, all of South Korea had been overrun with the exception of an area in the extreme southeast part of the country known as the Pusan Defense Perimeter—an area encompassed by the port cities of Pusan and P'ohang and the town of Taegu, to the northeast. On 15 September 1950, U. N. forces under General Douglas MacArthur made a daring amphibious landing at Inchon, a coastal town far up the western side of the Korean Peninsula. The North Koreans were taken completely by surprise. Their supply lines were quickly cut and their armies to the south were forced to retreat from the Pusan Perimeter under strong attacks from South Korean and U. N. forces. By October 2nd United Nations units had retaken Seoul and were pushing across the 38th parallel. By October 19th, the U. S. First Cavalry Division had taken Pyongyang, the North Korean capital.[6]

But the fortunes of war reversed again. As U. N. forces approached the Yalu River and the Manchurian border, they found that they were no longer facing only North Korean troops, but Red Chinese forces. On November 26th the full force of four Chinese armies crashed into the U. N.'s forward positions. By December 5th, Pyongyang had been retaken by the Communists, and by the first week of January, Seoul was also in their possession. The seesaw battle continued through the early months of 1951, with Seoul again in U. N. hands on March 15th. Attack and counterattack would mark the next two years of fighting. A series of offenses and retreats became known as "The Battle of the Hills" with places such as "White Horse Mountain," and "Heartbreak Ridge" being scenes of the bloodiest prolonged battles. Truce talks began as early as June of 1951, but the situation on the battlefield seemed to influence the willingness of the negotiators to make concessions. While talks were underway at Panmunjom, "The Battle of the Hills" went on. It was not until 27 July 1953 that an armistice was finally signed bringing the Korean War to an end.[7]

By the time Jelesnik arrived in Pusan, the shooting war in Korea had been over for almost five months. While the armistice had brought about a cease-fire, there had been cease-fires before. Tensions were still very high, and there was no guarantee that war would not break out again at any moment. Everyone recognized that the agreements had not brought an end to the conflict, only an end to the immediate shooting. Few doubted that the American military would have to remain in Korea for many decades to come.

The fighting had lasted thirty-seven months and had been costly. U. S. Armed Forces alone had suffered 103,259 casualties, including over 33,647 killed.[8] More than one million Korean civilians had died in the conflict, and two and a half million more had been made homeless. What Jelesnik saw during his tour of Korea was unbelievable suffering. The roads were filled with Koreans who had lost everything during the war. Most of the cities had been flattened. Many of the buildings that were left standing were little more than gutted shells. The country's economy had been ruined, and the population was dependent upon foreign aid for survival—most of it from the United States. Near Pusan, there were many thousands of homeless, and thousands more were living in tent cities. Nearly four thousand refugees in Pusan were crowded into warehouses and wharfs along the city's docks, the victims of a more recent Pusan fire. Appalling as the situation would have been under any circumstances, the tragedy was made infinitely worse by the weather. Korea was freezing. Photographs of Eugene's arrival at the U. S. Air Force base in Pusan give vivid testimony to the bitter cold of that December. The group resembled a party of antarctic explorers more than they did entertainers.[9] Much the same conditions would prevail during their entire stay in the country.

Like his previous USO tours, the schedule was grueling, and the unit often gave eight or nine shows a week. Performances were given at air force bases, army bivouac areas, and hospitals. Sometimes mess halls were used. On other occasions shows were performed on makeshift stages on airfield runways and tarmacs, as well as in hangers. Sometimes there were performances given off the back of trucks, reminiscent of Eugene's days on "The Fox-hole Circuit" with the 10th Mountain Division. But there was no mistaking Korea for Italy. Most of the unit's big shows were given outdoors, and Eugene remembered times when his hands were so cold, he couldn't finger the violin. Audiences ranged in size from twenty lonely soldiers at isolated posts and radar stations to 8,000 freezing GIs sitting on the snow-covered ground in open-air amphitheaters.

This was a demanding tour, and the accommodations were generally uncomfortable. The performers were lodged in bombed-out hotels and hovels. Many of these buildings were without electrical power. At most locations they were quartered in uninsulated tents or corrugated metal Quonset huts where the only heat was provided by potbellied stoves. Like Eugene Jelesnik the stoves were multipurpose. They not only provided heat for the tents, but hot water for cooking, washing and shaving, as well as other uses. Personal laundry was done with the aid of the potbellied stoves as well. Large cauldrons of water would be heated on the stoves and then taken outside to a big table where everything was washed by hand. Then the laundry was rinsed and brought back inside to be dried—over the potbellied stove.

While in Italy, Eugene had acquired a taste for local Italian cooking. The mess hall fare in Korea was only passable, and so he attempted to eat as much of the local Korean cuisine as was possible. One dish that he remembered particularly was a pickled vegetable called kimchi. In good times, when vegetables were plentiful, only the best went into the kimchi; in bad times, only the worst. Nineteen fifty-three and 1954 were the worst years for kimchi that the country had ever known. Jelesnik would later shudder at the memory of it. Toilet facilities usually consisted of a four-inch diameter pipe sticking out of the ground about two feet. But the pipe latrine provided no shelter from the biting wind or anything else. There was just the pipe, which was connected to a hundred-gallon drum buried underground. Each "facility" served two or three huts. The conditions were horrible, and the only thing that Korea had over Italy in Eugene's estimation was that he heard no shelling.[10]

Korea also provided Eugene with new material for his press releases. As if the war's aftermath, the cold, the general starvation, and the deplorable living conditions were not enough, a good PR sense could always come up with something worse. The following was such a potential calamity that it earned a feature spot in *Stars and Stripes:*

> A mishap in the "Magic and Melody" USO show that recently toured the 45th Div., almost cost show manager Eugene Jelesnik $10,300. His Stradivarius and another violin valued at over $300.00 were dropped into the path of a truck descending an icy hill. The driver tried to stop, but the truck kept right on moving with locked wheels. At the last moment PFC Marvin Shnayer, New Haven, Conn., who had dropped violinist Jelesnik's double violin case from another vehicle, dashed in front of the sliding truck and snatched $10,300 worth of violins out of harm's way.[11]

Although the troupe performed under many circumstances and in extremely cold conditions, they were universally lauded in every place they appeared. The December 24th issue of *Stars and Stripes* (Pacific edition, Tokyo-Yokohama) carried a short review of Eugene's opening in Korea. The headline read: "USO Troupe Scores Hit with 19th Regt." The review lauded the troupe and gave special praise to Jelesnik, Lynne Jackson, Jon Otness and the comedy team of "Strawberry and Julia." While those singled out for special mention changed frequently in the stories, the players were routinely given rave reviews every time they performed.

The Korean "police action," as it was then commonly known, left many soldiers with a sour taste in their mouths. Their valor had been proven in battle, and their sacrifices had been great, but after all the suffering and death, the final positions of the two warring sides were only a few hundred yards from where they had been at the beginning of the war. Many Americans questioned whether that kind of "substitute victory" was worth the enormous cost in life and material that had been expended to obtain it. Soldiers at the front were uncertain of what Americans back home thought of their efforts. USO tours like Jelesnik's were extremely important to the boys who fought in Korea. The shows helped reassure them that they had not been forgotten and that their sacrifices were indeed appreciated. The soldiers were particularly aware of the effort that the performers made just to get to the military areas. The entertainers then shared many of the same hardships as the soldiers. It was little wonder that mutual admiration developed between performer and audience member. It was a special relationship that could happen in no other venue. It was not surprising that Eugene considered the GIs stationed overseas as the best audience a performer could ever have. Capt. Thomas A. Eagan, a special service officer in Taegu, Korea, wrote a letter to the *Deseret News* and *The Salt Lake Telegram* to inform the folks back home that Jelesnik and his fellow troupers "are one of the finest [performing groups] we have received here in Korea, and it has been a pleasure to know them personally as well as professionally." During the last week of December 1953, somewhere in Korea, Jelesnik met a young lieutenant from Utah. His name was James Lee, and his father just happened to be the governor of the State of Utah. Eugene delivered the message he had been given the day he left for the tour and arranged to have photographs taken of him and Lieutenant Lee shaking hands. These he had sent to the newspapers back home. The Governor would have no doubt that Eugene had kept his promise to see his son.

On 3 January 1954, Eugene Jelesnik was made an honorary member of "The Fighting Seventh Division" in a ceremony following his troupe's performance before 4,000 GIs of the 17th Infantry Regiment. The man who pinned the division's patch on Jelesnik's left shoulder was Major General Lionel McGarr, the commander of the division.[12] In a letter written later, the General expressed his appreciation:

> Dear Eugene Jelesnik:
>
>   On behalf of the officers and men of the 7th Infantry "Bayonet" Division, I desire to express my sincere appreciation for the outstanding entertainment provided by your act in "Magic and Melody" for members of the Division on 3 and 4 January 1954.
>   Your show was highly entertaining and indicated professional skill in the finest traditions of show business. The

energetic manner in which you presented your act is a credit to
you and will long be remembered by the personnel of the
"Bayonet" Division.

You are performing an important public and patriotic
service.

Sincerely,
Lionel C. McGarr
Major General, USA
Commanding

Over the years Eugene would receive scores of such letters
and patches, as well as certificates, plaques, awards, and citations
from U. S. military units in every corner of the globe. But in Korea,
Eugene would also receive thanks, praise, and honors from soldiers in armies not his own. The Korean War was officially a U. N.
fight, and other troops beside U. S. forces fought alongside South
Korean forces. The response from the international units that saw
"Magic and Melody" was even more appreciative, if possible, than
that of the American troops. Eugene found their reactions to be
almost "incredible." The troops from India and Turkey were particularly exuberant and vocal in their expressions of appreciation.
Perhaps he should not have been surprised. After all, he had been
selected to perform at the Turkish Pavilion during the 1939
World's Fair. And then, too, Jelesnik had spent much of his life
billing himself as an international artist. It was about time that the
rest of the world got to hear him.

"Magic and Melody" was not the only USO unit touring
Korea at that time. A few days ahead of Eugene's group was a
USO show that included Marilyn Monroe. Eugene did not see
Marilyn's performance, but he could testify to the fact that she was
a very hard act to follow. In addition to the "Blond Bombshell"
herself, the show apparently featured a number of other beauties.
At many of the places that Eugene performed he could tell that
the soldiers were disappointed that his troupe did not have an
equivalent number of nubile dolls to entertain them. Even though
"Magic and Melody" was well-received and even deeply appreciated, Eugene knew that what the boys wanted most from
home wasn't necessarily magicians, mind readers, tap dancers,

comedians, or even violinists. What they wanted to see were girls. Eugene resolved that if he were ever to go on another USO tour he would do the casting, and there would be plenty of girls—gorgeous girls. Fifty seemed like a good number.

Through the first weeks of February, "The Magic and Melody Tour" continued its arduous trek through Korea. They played to frontline troops still dug in along the 38th parallel, they performed before South Korean units, and occasionally for special groups that included high-ranking officers and South Korean government officials. After the bulk of the Asian tour was completed, the performers were flown to Tokyo for four days of "R and R." During their stay in Tokyo, Jelesnik was awarded the Silver Medal Citation, the highest award given by the military for Americans not in uniform. The troupe then flew to Okinawa for performances at Lackland Air Force Base and received a four-star review from the base newspaper, the *Ryukyuan Review* on 18 February 1954:

USO SHOW GETS GREAT OVATION AT LACKLAND

"Magic and Melody," USO show 1158 currently touring the Far East, stopped in the Lackland Theater on Kadens Tuesday night, and a full house of critics raised the roof with their applause.

From two strenuous months of touring Korea, the Jerry Allen Trio, Eugene Jelesnik, Herbert and Lotte Nivelli, Jon Otness, and Strawberry and Julia Russell bought themselves a return trip ticket to the island and will always be honored by show-goers here.

The trio, featuring a piano, drum, and sax blended in with each act, and when the three mainstay instruments weren't enough, someone would come up with an accordian or other fit-the-mood device.

Jelesnik, manager of the troupe that originated in New York City, displayed modern violin art that was a real treat to the ears considering that top-notch violin talent is seldom heard locally.

Herbert and Lotte Novelli presented magical entertainment that had everyone amazed, jovial, and wanting more.

Prior to each of his numbers, tenor Jon Otness would ask, "May I sing for you . . ." and then proceed to name the tune. Audience reaction indicated that you can sing for us any time Jon! To tie up a neat bundle of entertainment into one of the best

USO shows seen locally in quite a while, Strawberry and Julia
Russell, with a combination of comedy and song had the theater
roaring with laughter and rocking with jazz . . . encore after
encore. This weekend, "Magic and Melody" will leave Okinawa
for the Philippines. With them go the thanks of well-entertained
island audiences, and sincere wishes to come back again. Robert
E. Pinkus / *Ryukyuan Review*

After the show on Okinawa, the troupe gave performances in
the Philippines, Guam, and Hawaii. On the island of Oahu they
performed at various military installations, hospitals, and rehabil-
itation centers. The last official performance of "Magic and
Melody" took place at Tripler Army Hospital in Honolulu on 12
March 1954, when they appeared before a large and appreciative
audience of patients, staff, and military personnel. Ten days later
Eugene would be back home in Salt Lake City. He had traveled
more than 35,000 miles and had been gone for exactly one hundred and forty-two days.

Eugene's USO tour received a good deal of notice in the local
Utah press. He was invited to speak before several service clubs
and community organizations. Eugene told one group about the
importance of the USO to the morale of the troops and to another
he said that the Korean tour had taught him a great deal about the
world and also himself and that he had been humbled by the
experience. Virginia was happy to have him home again, and
everyone else he met on the street seemed pleased that he was
back. Unfortunately, Jelesnik was in exactly the same position as
he was when he desperately wrote Bert Wishnew back in August.
He was out of work and had no solid prospects for employment.
His solution to the problem was surprising, particularly considering that he had tried it once before under similar circumstances
and with disastrous results. At least when he started the Savoia
Restaurant back in 1936, he had some money stashed away to
work with. This time he had nothing. But Jelesnik was certain
that the time was right for Salt Lake City to have a cabaret-style
restaurant.

The Cinegrill had been in operation before Jelesnik decided
that it was the perfect locale for a nightspot. The owner, Ed Allem,

48. Eugene Jelesnik and President Harry S. Truman at Hotel Utah.

49. KDYL Television goes on the air with Eugene Jelesnik, April 1948.

50. Eugene Jelesnik performs with the Nat King Cole Trio on KDYL Television.

51. The only known photograph of Maurice Abravanel and Eugene Jelesnik together. *Video Frolics*.

52. Eugene's marquee in front of the Cinegrill Restaurant, April 1954.

53. Ed Allem describes Cinegrill menu to Ted Mack, host of *The Original Amateur Hour*, summer 1954.

54. Liberace, Jelesnik, and "My Brother George" after Liberace's
first concert in Salt Lake at the State Fairgrounds, 1955.

55. Eugene and Count Basie—one of several jazz artists Jelesnik
brought to Salt Lake as part of his *Celebrity Concert Series*.

56. Celebrities: Jelesnik and Danny Thomas.

57. Senator John F. Kennedy on *Talent Showcase* with Jelesnik, 30 January 1960.
Kennedy's appearance would inspire Jelesnik's composition the "JFK March."

58. Bob Hope and Eugene exchange a book and promotional materials at Deseret Book, September 1963.

59. Jose Iturbi, Mischa Elman, and Eugene at *Celebrity Series* concert, 3 January 1963.

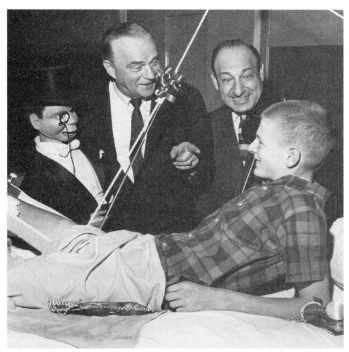

60. Edgar Bergen (Candice Bergen's father) and Charlie McCarthy
with Eugene at Primary Children's Hospital.

61. Minnie Pearl and Eugene at the Utah State Fair.

62. Heavy-weight boxing champion Jack Dempsey with Eugene at Dempsey's restaurant in New York City.

63. Funnyman Don Rickles with Eugene at KSL.

64. Jelesnik showing off his "hometown" to one group of lucky winners of *Talent Showcase*.
Jelesnik always escorted his Utah performers to the finals on *The Original Amateur Hour*, held in New York City.

65. Jelesnik and comedienne Martha Raye during a USO tour of Vietnam, 23 January 1968.

66. *Talent Showcase* finalists, 24 August 1975.

67. Eugene Jelesnik finally catches the circus train.

68. Jelesnik and George Burns in Las Vegas.

69. Movie star Betty Grable and Eugene Jelesnik.

70. Jelesnik makes one of his many Christmas hospital appearances.

71. Virginia in the early years of her marriage to Eugene Jelesnik.

72. Eugene listens to tribute paid him by Bill Powell, managing director and
publicist for Ringling Brothers Barnum and Bailey Circus.

73. Jelesnik, President Joseph Fielding Smith, and wife, Jessie Evans, after Pops Concert.

75. Good friends Virginia Belle Washburn Jelesnik and Carleen Hall Jelesnik

74. Eugene and President Spencer W. Kimball.

76. President Thomas S. Monson and Eugene at reception at KSL.

77. President Thomas S. Monson, Eugene, and Mrs. (Janet) Rex Lee, at BYU, 22 April 1993.

78. Carleen Hall Jelesnik.

79. Eugene and Carleen with friends and family members on their wedding day, 24 October 1994.
From left to right: Judge Ray Uno, Rabbi Fred Wenger, Eugene, Jeff Brown, Susan Ogzewalla, Larry Brown, Marla Walton, Melanie Layton, Barbara Madsen. Seated: Carleen and Jessica Brown.

80. The last concert at the Salt Palace. Left to right: Jack Imel, Dolores Park, Cliff Cole, Eugene, Jerry Floor, Jim Tsoufakis, Carleen, Chris Kaniakas, Billie Loukas, Frank Layden, Commissioner James Bradley.

81. Eugene, his violin, and some of his USO memorabilia.

was a member of a large Catholic Lebanese family that would contribute substantially to the cuisine of Salt Lake City. Ed was a year younger than Eugene and had served in the Pacific with the Marine Corps during World War II. He was a self-trained chef, and he had perfected many of his recipes while preparing large spaghetti dinners as fund-raisers for his parish, Divine Savior's Church (later Sacred Heart) near downtown. He had previously operated another restaurant, and at least one of the partners from that venture, Gus Floor, had an interest in the Cinegrill. The name of the establishment came from the restaurant's location at 230 East First South in part of the block then known as "Film Row" or "Cinema Row." All of the major motion picture studios had their film distribution offices on the block. The "grill on cinema row" was one of the few restaurants to have an open kitchen where customers could watch the food being prepared. It was also one of the first restaurants in Utah to offer "Pizza Pie," "Pasta e Fagioli" and special spumoni ice cream dishes.

The recipes at the Cinegrill were unique. The green salads were topped with gorgonzola and provolone cheese, pepperoni, and olives. The distinctive salad dressing of herbs, capers, imported olive oil, and Burgundy wine vinegar was a family recipe that Ed Allem had learned from his parents.[13] Most of the dishes had been developed by Ed with the help of his wife, Melba. The Allems had a special knack for inventing sauces, and they were famous for their spaghetti and baked lasagna. Though most of the food was Italian, they also offered other Mediterranean dishes, such as shish kebab, as well as American favorites like corned beef on rye, cold cut meat plates, and steak specials, such as chateaubriand. The spumoni and other ice creams on the menu were also Ed's creations and were served, "with nuts and fruits nestled in a mellowed rum-cointreau sauce and topped with macaroon bits." In 1954 a full plate of spaghetti, complete with tossed green salad, toasted garlic bread, and coffee was priced at one dollar and fifty cents.[14]

Jelesnik fell in love with the Allems's cooking and was a regular customer at the restaurant. He and Allem were also close friends, and Allem often prepared kosher meals for Jelesnik.

Shortly after he returned from Korea, Jelesnik approached Allem and told him that he needed a job. Ed Allem informed Eugene that he would like to help but that the Cinegrill was failing. He could not seem to attract enough customers to justify its continued operation. Eugene was shocked that the Cinegrill was on the verge of closing up. He couldn't believe that one of the city's finest eateries could possibly fail. He was certain that the problem was simply one of promotion—that if more people were induced to sample the Cinegrill's menu, they would be hooked. Eugene told Allem about his idea that the Cinegrill would make a perfect cabaret restaurant, and he made Allem an offer. Jelesnik would run the front end of the operation, acting as host, promoter, and nightly entertainer. This would leave Allem free to run the kitchen and the restaurant end of the operation. Jelesnik promised to bring his celebrity friends and entertainers to the Cinegrill when they were in town, and he would otherwise encourage his friends and acquaintances to eat there. He promised that he would be a tireless promoter and that before long the restaurant would become the "in" place to be. Allem was skeptical, but he felt as if he had nothing to lose, and so he agreed to let Eugene try out his ideas.

Ed Allem and Eugene Jelesnik had sharply contrasting personalities. While Eugene was outgoing and gregarious, Ed tended to be more reserved and a little introverted. But he loved his family and did everything he could for them. The Cinegrill was a family business in the most extended sense of the word *family.* In addition to his wife, Melba, Allem would employ many relatives over the years, including his sister, nieces, nephews, and cousins. During one period, three generations of Allems—a grandmother, her daughter, and granddaughter—would all be working at the Cinegrill at the same time.[15]

Salt Lake City had a well-deserved reputation as a very staid and conservative town. Prior to Eugene Jelesnik, no musician had ever strolled like a Gypsy among the tables in a local restaurant without being either ejected or arrested. It took awhile for the locals to warm up to Eugene's notion of continental dining. But Eugene had made good money in New York playing tables for tips. He was certain that he could do the same thing at the

Cinegrill. Having a Gypsy violinist play beside your table was expected in the cafés of Yorkville, but to many Salt Lakers in 1954, such a sight was as exotic as watching the new neighbors roasting a pony on the parking strip. Not a few customers were put off by the little man trying to poke his violin bow in their ear while they were eating. But even those who might have felt uncomfortable by the scene contributed by word of mouth to the promotion of the Cinegrill. The few brave souls who timidly ventured into the restaurant in the spring of 1954 told others of the unique dining experience. They in turn tried it out, and it wasn't long before the whole town was talking. Gradually, Allem's restaurant started to show a profit.

As Eugene hoped, much of the talk wasn't just about his violin playing, but also Allem's cooking. The Cinegrill's bill of fare was soon the stuff of urban legend. The Cinegrill's provisioners included Frank Granato's Import Market and Landures Produce Company. The story got around that Ed Allem used more fresh garlic in a week than all the other restaurants in the Valley combined. Ed's sister, Jennie Boyer, who worked for many years at the Cinegrill, also remembered the place's reputation for garlic: "I remember I was riding the bus one day, and this man got on and sat down by a woman directly across from me. Well, as soon as he sat down, this woman turned to the man and said, 'Boy, I know where you had lunch! You ate at the Cinegrill, didn't ya! I can smell the garlic.' Then she got up and moved to another seat."[16]

Eugene Jelesnik would serve as host, promoter, and strolling musician at the Cinegrill for the next seven years—usually alternating with accordion player Norma Zonay as the evening entertainment. Over that time he would continuously promote the establishment, and true to his word, he would bring in dozens of the most important entertainers and celebrities of the day. In 1956, the Cinegrill played host to The Kingston Trio. For the two days that the Trio stayed in Salt Lake, the Cinegrill was their hangout, and crowds of fans waited in line to have their 45 RPM records of "Tom Dooley" signed by the artists. Over the years the entrance hall of the Cinegrill turned into a picture gallery of the famous people who had eaten there. Signed photographs and menus dedicated to Eugene or Ed became attractions themselves. Eugene had kept his promise, and the Cinegrill became *the* place to be. For many, the restaurant's ambiance was the quintessence of Salt Lake City in the 1950s. The red-painted, cinder-block walls, the burgundy leather booths, the red-and-white checkered tablecloths, and the candles on the tables are all fondly remembered by Cinegrill customers. But mostly, they remember the food. Over the long run of the restaurant, Ed never changed his recipes. Jennie Boyer, who gave a good deal of credit to Jelesnik for bringing in a lot of customers, recalled: "It was unusual, and people remembered it. They might have come in when they were younger or in high school, and maybe they had moved or gone away to school, and then years later they'd return to Salt Lake—perhaps for a visit—and they would make a point of coming to the Cinegrill, and they'd be amazed that it never changed. They'd remember Eugene playing the 'Flight of the Bumble Bee' or 'Hot Canary' and then they would taste the food and say, 'That's exactly the way I remember it!' And sometimes it was quite an emotional experience for them, and their eyes would water."[17]

But then garlic has been known to produce tears as well.

While a substantial portion of Eugene's income came from performing at the Cinegrill, he continued to develop and nurture his other pet projects, including the Salt Lake Philharmonic Orchestra and his annual concerts for the Days of '47 Rodeo. It was in the midfifties that Eugene hit upon the formula of combining both local talent and established headline stars.

For a concert in the spring of 1953, staged at Kingsbury Hall on the University of Utah campus, the Philharmonic's soloists included baritone Howard Ruff, then a student at Brigham Young University. The same Howard Ruff would later gain fame as a conservative commentator and international investment genius. The same concert featured Salt Lake-born soprano Ann Cardall, who had just been acclaimed by New York critics as "the new singing sensation." Also on the program was Jelesnik's KDYL pianist Larry Pryor. The program for the 11th Pops Concert, of 27 April 1956, at Kingsbury Hall included "The Beachcombers," a prominent California trio comprised of Carl, Geri, and Bob Engemann.

Bob was one of the original "Lettermen." In the years to follow, the concerts continued to draw heavily on local talent, but also promoted "celebrity" artists brought in for the Days of '47 concerts. Guest soloists such as Broadway tenor Robert Peterson or Lawrence Welk star soprano Billie Loukas would often highlight the program. Loukas, who began performing with the pops concerts in the midfifties, would be a mainstay of Philharmonic for the next thirty-seven years. Sometimes local soloists such as vocalists Cliff Cole or Margo Watson would be featured, but whoever the soloist, behind them were always Eugene Jelesnik and the musicians of the Philharmonic.

On occasion Eugene would present special concerts to honor specific artists. On 23 October 1957, he produced a concert paying tribute to librettist Otto A. Harbach. The concert was presented in the Assembly Hall on Temple Square. All twenty selections in the 1957 concert were Harbach's, whom Jelesnik had interviewed on KDYL several years before. Guest artists for the Harbach tribute included the sixty-five-voice Brigham Young University a capella choir, directed by Norman Gulbrandsen. Another Utah native honored in the Philharmonic's Pops concert was Harold Orlob. This concert was given 26 September 1961 and was also in the Temple Square Assembly Hall. Orlob had composed music for twenty-six plays and operettas between 1909 and 1931. He had composed music for Paramount Pictures, the University of Utah, and the Days of '47. Orlob also wrote the theme song for Ted Mack's Original Amateur Hour, "The Show's On," but perhaps his most famous composition was "I Wonder Who's Kissing Her Now," one of the great popular numbers of the time. Guest artists for the Orlob tribute included violinist Aladdin and tenor Joe Feeney, both major stars from the Lawrence Welk Show. Pops concerts frequently featured university student performers. While the BYU choir performed for the Harbach tribute, the University of Utah men's chorus, directed by John Marlowe along with U of U tenor Ronald Christensen, performed for the Orlob Tribute. The program also featured Canadian singer Dolores O'Connell and Billie Loukas. Other soloists of the period included a young trumpet player by the name of Newell Dayley who would go on to become a major force in Utah's musical community, and Salt Lake native and Broadway star Art Lund, whose career had included singing with Benny Goodman's orchestra and starring in the Broadway hit, *The Most Happy Fella.*

Nineteen fifty-five was the pivotal year in the long career of Eugene Jelesnik. Many of his most enduring and memorable enterprises got their start in the period when he was struggling to be able to stay in Salt Lake City. It was hard at the time to tell where anything was leading. But some of Eugene's most stable and lasting enterprises came out of the most improbable and tenuous starts.

By 1955 Ted Mack had taken over *The Original Amateur Hour* from Major Edward Bowes. Mack, like Jelesnik, had been a New York City bandleader, and the two men were well-acquainted. Mack was visiting Utah and told Eugene that there was a need to develop local talent to feed the national program, which Ted Mack hosted over the CBS network. He encouraged Eugene to start his own talent show in Salt Lake City. The very first version of Eugene Jelesnik's *Talent Showcase* was sponsored by the Midvale City Harvest Days Festival—a very temporary sponsor for what was to become one of the longest-running programs in the history of television.[18] Among the first winning contestants were two young girls from St. George, Utah: Carla and Rebecca Terry who had won a talent contest at the local Kiwanis Club. The Terry Sisters advanced through numerous competitions to eventually win on Ted Mack's *Original Amateur Hour* in New York, and went on to become professional performers. They credited Jelesnik with changing their lives,[19] and both of them fondly remembered Eugene and his wife, Virginia. They particularly remembered that Virginia had a talking parakeet named "Sandy" that she had taught to say all sorts of phrases, including, "Liberace is a pretty boy," and "Here comes Eugene."[20]

Everyone who knew the Jelesniks remembered Virginia's bird. One visitor who came to the Jelesnik's home was Zolly Walchek, owner of the Seattle Supersonics. He was impressed by the bird, but not enough not to challenge Virginia by saying, "If you can get that bird to say 'Zolly Walchek,' I'll buy him a golden cage." A few months later, Eugene invited Walchek over to the house. As the guest entered the living room the bird started screeching, "Here's Zolly Walchek! Here's Zolly Walchek!" The man was astounded and several weeks later returned with the promised cage. It was gold-colored.

In 1956 Ted Mack came to Salt Lake to witness the finals of *Talent Showcase,* an honor he would extend to the Utah program through the next decade. The Terry Sisters were among the finalists. The competition was especially keen, and to soften the blow Mrs. Terry promised her daughters that she would take them to Disneyland if they lost. But the Terry Sisters won. Ted Mack congratulated the young girls and asked, "Well, young ladies, you're off to New York City. What do you think of that?" Rebecca Terry burst into tears and told the startled *Amateur Hour* host, "We wanted to go to Disneyland!"[21]

But the Terry Sisters went to New York and won there as well. During their stay in the metropolis they met Eugene's mother and Aunt Ruth and toured the sights of the city. Rebecca Terry, the little girl who had been the reluctant winner of *Talent Showcase,* went on to have a long career as a professional entertainer and became one of Utah's most successful homegrown celebrities as "Uvula" of the always outrageous singing trio, "The Saliva Sisters."

Jelesnik's *Talent Showcase* turned out to be Eugene's most successful endeavor. From 1955 to 1958 it appeared on Channel 2 (KUTV). From 1959 to 1965 it was on Channel 4 (at that time, KCPX), and from 1965 to 1986 it aired on Channel 5 (KSL). It was *Talent Showcase* that put Eugene Jelesnik on the map regionally and made him a household word in the Intermountain West. The performers for the weekly *Talent Showcase* productions were selected through auditions conducted by both Eugene Jelesnik and his wife, Virginia. When Eugene was out of town, Virginia would supervise the auditions herself. Unlike *The Original Amateur Hour,* poor performers were not simply dismissed with a hoot and a whistle. Neither Eugene nor Virginia were in the business of destroying other people's egos. Rather they would generally let the performer down easily by encouraging them to practice more and inviting them to try again the following year. Winners on the show received a variety of prizes, including all-expense-paid trips to Las Vegas, cash, and locally donated merchandise. The grand prize winner in the annual finals received a trip to New York City to appear on Ted Mack's nationally broadcast program. Jelesnik would eventually take promising acts to New York three or four times a year, and Ted Mack would come to Salt Lake each year to co-host the talent search grand finales.

Viewers of *Talent Showcase* were treated to an incredible range of acts over the years: barbershop quartets, tap dancers, baton twirlers and drill teams, jugglers and magicians, a man who performed musical numbers with his arm pits (he lost), and precision marching tuba bands. Performers would range in age from a 3-year-old girl who sang "Wouldn't it Be Loverly?" to an 86-year-old woman who played both guitar and harmonica simultaneously. The show would make many important discoveries including the Osmonds, country star Tanya Tucker, and award-winning accordion player Evan Dahl. Dahl, the daughter of Midvale's mayor, would later become a star on *The Fred Waring Show.* Strangely, the big discoveries seldom won top honors in the weekly talent competitions. Tanya Tucker lost out to a tap dancer, and the Osmonds were beaten out by a ragtime piano player. Since winners were determined by a phone-in balloting system, it was possible to stuff the ballot box if the performer had a large family or a lot of friends. There was also nothing to prevent supporters from calling in more than once.

Just as with Eugene's pops concerts, the program would occasionally highlight professional and celebrity guests. Both Robert Peterson and Billie Loukas made *Talent Showcase* appearances. Early programs were broadcast live, and just as with all live TV, the format presented unique problems. The dropped baton, the missed cue, the forgotten lyric, and stage fright made the early programs exciting to watch and nerve-racking to produce. A dancer in a group from Brigham Young University passed out under the hot studio lights, and the show had to be stopped while attendants and technicians revived her. Occasionally, a performer would be announced, but at the last minute would get stage fright and disappear. By the time the program had moved to KSL, it was recorded on tape for transmission later in the week. The name was also changed to *Utah Showtime*. This program was an upgraded version of *Talent Showcase* and included professional talent as well as celebrity interviews with visiting stars such as Jerry Lewis, Don Rickles, and Glen Campbell.

There was little indication in 1955 that *Talent Showcase* was destined to be a record breaker. But for longevity, nothing would match it. The program's long run would surpass even the famous enduring network programs such as *M*A*S*H* and *Gunsmoke*. All told, *Talent Showcase* and its successor *Utah Showtime* would rack up an endurance record of more than thirty-one years, and over that time more than 10,000 performers would appear on the show.

In the summer of 1955, Eugene received a call from a man named Seymour Heller in Los Angeles. Heller was the agent of the ever grinning pianist sensation Liberace who had just finished a big, sell-out show at the Hollywood Bowl. Heller was in the process of booking the pianist's first nationwide tour and was looking for a promoter who would be willing to bring the dressy, perfumed tinkler of the ivories—complete with candelabra and "My brother George"—to Salt Lake City. Liberace was at the height of his fame. His weekly, nationwide television show had the highest possible ratings. The agent assured Jelesnik that the performance was certain to be a sellout. There was only one problem. Heller insisted that the local promoter had to come up with a $15,000 guarantee to secure the contract.

In 1954 that was an almost unbelievable sum of money. Jelesnik had been booking local talent for years. He had arranged for performers at KDYL Radio and Television, for the Days of '47, for the Pops Concerts, for celebrity appearances at charity fundraisers, for the Ted Mack show, for conventions—as well as talent for the Utah State Fair. But he had never taken personal responsibility for anything even remotely as big as this. Eugene talked it over with Virginia. There were huge problems. The only place that Eugene could get at a reasonable price that was big enough to hold a concert and could return a profit was the grandstand at the Utah State Fairgrounds. But the grandstand was outdoors, and if it rained and the concert was canceled he would still have to come up with the guarantee.

After several days of soul searching, Eugene mortgaged his house. Years later he would shake his head at the enormity of the risk: "It was a very brazen thing to do. I can't believe the risk I took. If it had rained, I would have lost everything. Probably gone to prison. Or at least bankruptcy court. It was the biggest undertaking of my life to that time. It was a project that I'll never forget, and it made me a nervous wreck."

Jelesnik had a forty-by-sixty foot stage built in front of the grandstand at the Utah State Fairgrounds. He hustled through the myriad details: tickets, staging, lighting, sound system, ushers, concessions, and accommodations. He borrowed an additional $5,000 to promote the event and spent it all on advertising. He worked all his waking hours, beating publicity drums for the event. The $15,000 guarantee hung over his head like the Sword of Damocles.

The show was scheduled for a Tuesday evening. Sunday morning Eugene awoke to the sickening sound of a heavy rainstorm beating against his window. He knew that the rain was drenching his stage and the equipment at the fairgrounds and washing away any public enthusiasm for an outdoor event. Jelesnik thought he was ruined, and he felt like crawling back into his bed and staying there forever. Monday morning was cloudy and miserable, and as he stared at the puddles on the stage, he prepared to take the biggest financial bath of his life. But Tuesday dawned bright and clear, and before nightfall the crowded parking lot told him that he could relax. It turned out to be a beautiful night. When Liberace played "The Moonlight Sonata," the moon rose above Mount Olympus and shone brightly in the sky above the city. The show ended up being a smash hit, and drew an audience in excess of 7,000. It was one of the largest grosses for such an event in Salt Lake history.

The pianist was delighted with the turnout and overwhelmed by the enthusiasm of the Salt Lake crowd. Liberace stayed until 3 A.M. signing autographs, then took Eugene and all his concert staff out to eat at Harry Louie's King Joy Café, a Chinese restaurant on Main Street. The owner and his family had stayed up to cater the party, which included the large orchestra Liberace brought with him from Hollywood.

With the success of the Liberace concert, Eugene Jelesnik became a big-time promoter and founded "The Celebrity Artist Series" as a vehicle for his concert promotions. It wasn't long before articles began appearing in trade journals applauding the Salt Lake staging and promotion of Liberace. Eugene was soon inundated with offers from booking agencies and representatives of top stars from Hollywood and New York. The exhilaration of the success was overwhelming. He realized that he had taken an enormous gamble and had won. He also understood for the first time the appeal of Sid Fox's addiction: "In some ways, it's the worst thing that could have happened to me. If I had lost on that one, I'd have turned to something easier on the blood pressure, something that would let me sleep nights."

Flushed with success, the budding impresario arranged an appearance by Jan Peerce, the Metropolitan Opera tenor, who was said to have "the most beautiful voice in the world." The concert was well-promoted and the papers were enthusiastic, but Eugene's timing was faulty. He had scheduled Peerce for Halloween night and Salt Lakers stayed away in droves. They were either spooked by the highbrow nature of the concert, remained home to pass out goodies to goblins, or had trouble getting baby-sitters. Whatever the reason, Eugene lost his shirt.

But it was too late to turn back now. Jelesnik was hooked. He brought in a succession of jazz and popular artists: Count Basie, Sarah Vaughn, Billy Eckstine, and Fats Domino. He lost varying amounts on every one of them, and his big-time booking adventure was now $7,000 in the hole. He brought in Victor Borge, who was riding national acclaim and who looked to Jelesnik like money in the bank. Borge drew laughs, but not enough audience to cover his fee and also meet expenses. Jelesnik now spent most of his nights pacing the floor wondering how he could ever recoup his losses. He even thought about going into a safer business. But just as he was about to take up gunrunning, Liberace's agent called him again and asked if Eugene would be interested in bringing Liberace to Salt Lake for a return engagement. Jelesnik took the plunge, and once again the powdered, perfumed pianist came through. The party after the concert—held this time at the Cinegrill—was even more exuberant than it had been the year before. Liberace and Brother George signed autographs until the wee hours of the morning.

The following year, Liberace's itinerary was too tight to perform in Salt Lake, but Eugene learned that the performer and his orchestra would have a short layover in the city before making connections for Chicago. Jelesnik, Allem, and the Cinegrill staff prepared a huge feast for the performers and brought it to the train station. Liberace's manager, Seymour Heller, remembered the occasion: "It was completely unexpected, and Liberace and George never forgot the gesture. All during that tour, whenever a sponsor forgot to make room for eating or some other thing was forgotten, Liberace would say: 'In Salt Lake they provided a three course meal for us and we didn't even perform there!' After that, even years later, if things weren't going just right, he'd say, 'Next year we're playing Salt Lake.'"[22]

Jelesnik became the sole presenter of Liberace in Salt Lake City, and the artist appeared three more times. Jelesnik believed that he had finally learned how the game was played. He would no longer take any gambles on uncertain performers. He would only book sure things—acts that couldn't possibly lose money. He called Frank Sinatra's agent and arranged to bring his old USO co-performer to Salt Lake. The guarantee was huge, but after all, it was Frank Sinatra, and there was no risk on a sure thing—or so Eugene thought. Sinatra brought his son Frank Jr. to Salt Lake for the concert, as well as the actress Lauren Bacall and the famous agent Irving Lazar.

There was good press and there seemed to be a lot of interest in the Sinatra concert, but the skinny kid from Hoboken drew an even skinnier crowd. Jelesnik was embarrassed. Fewer than 2,200 showed up at Fairgrounds Coliseum, a building that regularly drew 5,000 for professional wrestling. Sinatra knew that Jelesnik had taken a bath, and gave him a thousand dollars from his wallet as personal gift after the show. Jelesnik next booked Leonard Bernstein's *Candide*, then the National Ballet of Canada, and then

British conductor Mantovani and his orchestra. All of the shows were artistic and critical successes, but every one of them was a financial flop. Lawrence Welk took his own gamble on an outdoor show at Derks Field. The weather was perfect, and Eugene was back in the money. But one month later, a concert by Martin Denny and his orchestra barely broke even.

Through the mid-1960s Eugene Jelesnik continued to bring top entertainment to Salt Lake City. These shows included the Broadway touring productions of *Mary, Mary; The Music Man;* and *Carnival* at the Capitol Theatre. Headliners included such celebrities as Fred Waring and his Pennsylvanians, pianist Roger Williams, French chanteuse Genevieve, flamenco dancer Jose Greco, piano duo Ferrante & Teicher, country comedienne Judy Canova, and a European musical revue, *Vienna on Parade.*

In 1960–61, Jelesnik presented Roger Williams, then at the apex of his career, in concert at the Terrace Ballroom in downtown Salt Lake. Other attractions that season included Hal Holbrook's acclaimed one-man performance of *Mark Twain Tonight,* the New York Opera Festival Troupe, Flamenco dancer Jose Greco and Company, and a revue featuring stars of the *Lawrence Welk Show.* Jelesnik utilized both the Terrace and the 2,000-seat Capitol Theatre. The only show to make money was Welk's. Jelesnik also sold seasons of *Celebrity Artists* packages, offering choice seating to season subscribers.

In 1961–62, Jelesnik's *Celebrity Artists Series* opened with stand-up comedian Mort Sahl in the Terrace Ballroom on Main Street. "He was one of the hottest comedians of the day." He then brought funnyman Shelley Berman to Salt Lake. Jelesnik recalled Virginia's reaction: "When I told her I was bringing in Berman, she went into orbit. Her response was: 'Are you out of your mind? Are you telling me that you're bringing a SMOKING comedian to perform in Salt Lake City on LDS Church conference weekend?'

"I had never thought about his smoking, just his political humor. Virginia was convinced that people would not show up, but the contract was already signed, and I had the gut feeling that he would do well, even at Highland High School auditorium. It was amazing. The hall was packed to the rafters and we even had to add eight rows of additional folding chairs just to accommodate the overflow. He was very funny and not the least bit offensive. It was one of the best shows I ever did."[23]

For a concert on 3 January 1963, Jelesnik booked both Mischa Elman and Jose Iturbi together for one big concert. Their only request was they needed a full-sized symphony orchestra. The Utah Symphony was just beginning to get a reputation beyond the Mountain West. Iturbi's agent felt that the appearance of the two internationally famous artists with the symphony would be good for the prestige of the orchestra and also good for the local gate. Eugene approached the Utah Symphony, but was turned down flat. The feud with Maurice Abravanel was still on. He asked the Musicians' Union to see if the symphony's musicians could perform unofficially without using the Utah Symphony's name, but there was no help there, either. Jelesnik recalled the flap with mixed feelings of sadness and anger: "The rebuff from the Utah Symphony was an insult and affront to both Elman and Iturbi, not just to me. Elman was outraged. He called the National Musicians' Union office in New York, and the answer from there was, 'If Maurice Abravanel doesn't want to farm out his orchestra, there is nothing that anyone can do about it.'"

While Jelesnik was pondering the consequences of canceling the contract, Elman was more intent than ever on giving a concert in Salt Lake, no matter who the orchestra ended up being. Eugene was able to arrange to have the seventy-one piece Utah Valley Symphony Orchestra perform, and the concert went on as scheduled. Jose Iturbi conducted the orchestra, and Elman was featured in three major violin concertos: by Brahms, Bach, and Mendelssohn. The venue for the performance was the auditorium of Highland High School. Although the Utah Valley Symphony had been together for only a few months, the concert received excellent reviews in the papers. Harold Lundstrom wrote in the *Deseret News*:

> In the musical world, in ideal circumstances, one plus one equals one. Thursday evening, as an example, Mischa Elman, violinist, and Jose Iturbi, conductor, each a distinguished artist in his own right, joined forces with the Utah Valley Community Orchestra to form a satisfying performing unit.

> They appeared Thursday evening in Highland High
> auditorium, playing three violin concertos by Bach, Brahms,
> and Mendelssohn. The concert, which attracted an appreciative
> audience of 1,400 persons, was sponsored by Eugene Jelesnik as
> part of his current "Celebrity Series."
>
> This is the fifth performance of this same program that Mr.
> Elman and Mr. Iturbi have presented recently, and it is safe to
> say, I'm sure, they could not have played more congenially.
> They saw eye-to-eye regarding elements of style.
>
> Both approached the music with a kind of aristocratic
> romanticism, which was modified one way or another to suit
> the demands of the music. And Mr. Elman's elegant and rich
> violin tone was a perfect match for the restrained warmth of Mr.
> Iturbi's interpretations.[24]

But while the concert was well-received, the gate was barely enough to cover expenses.

Still, Jelesnik considered the concert one of his finest achievements, particularly considering the difficulties involved. But even as Eugene gained more experience, he still continued to lose money on concerts he expected to be moneymakers. In 1963 Jelesnik booked and sold out a performance of Johnny Mathis for a concert at the Utah State Fairgrounds Coliseum. The morning of the performance, Mathis's agent called Eugene to inform him that Mathis was ill and wasn't coming. The ticket prices would all have to be refunded. Jelesnik had spent a good deal of the anticipated gate on promotion, lighting, technical support, and hall rental. Now he was expected to come up with more than thirty thousand dollars in small bills on a Saturday afternoon with the banks closed. Jelesnik did the only thing he could think of. He went from grocery store to grocery store borrowing the money from store managers and owners. He went to Z.C.M.I. and the Hotel Utah and to the Safeway store on South Temple. The managers at each handed Eugene a sum of cash. It seemed that everyone knew Eugene Jelesnik, and they trusted that he was good for the emergency loan. By evening he had enough cash in hand to refund the price of every ticket presented by a disappointed concert-goer— money that he pulled from grocery bags. In a way, it was Eugene's finest hour.

Jelesnik was learning the hard way about the concert business and also about the local audience. He said, "Attendance may be disappointing on an artist's first appearance here, but if he pleases the crowd the word will spread and a return engagement is likely to fill the hall." Jelesnik also learned that attendance is something you have to build up for each show. He also came to appreciate that booking concerts was a lot like shooting dice. As in roulette, there was more luck than art in the high-stakes game of concert booking, and it was next to impossible to gauge an artist's appeal in Salt Lake by how he had done in other towns. Every venture was a dangerous gamble and an iffy proposition at best. Success depended on not only the caprices of public taste but also the weather and a dozen other unpredictable factors. Eugene often came up empty, but an occasional winner kept him trying for the jackpot. If he had given any thought to the real risks he was facing, he probably would have canceled the entire celebrity series. Most of the time he didn't seem to be promoting concerts as much as he was betting on the weather. His old employer, Sid Fox, might drop two or three thousand dollars over a weekend at the tables in Las Vegas, but Jelesnik was risking three or four times as much with each new show.

Jelesnik made a lot of money on some concerts, lost a great deal on others, and broke even on the rest. But whether Jelesnik won or lost, there was always one big winner: the citizens of Salt Lake City. Before Jelesnik began his *Celebrity Concert Series*, big-time entertainers rarely came to Utah; after Jelesnik, Salt Lake became a regular stop on the concert circuit. The risk was always Jelesnik's, and that gamble was heightened by the prices he charged for his concerts. While audiences in other areas were used to shelling out large sums for tickets to a big-star show, Jelesnik knew that most Salt Lakers were not inclined to do so, and he kept his prices within means. The subscription prices to see *The Music Man* were only $4.50 for the best seats in the house and $2.50 for a seat on the sides of the Highland High auditorium's mezzanine. Tickets for Roger Williams's concert topped out at just $3.00, and student seating was only $1.00. But perhaps more incredible than the prices he charged was his constant willingness to risk it all, again and again, and to bounce back undaunted after taking a beating.

While Jelesnik's *Celebrity Concert Series* occupied his sleepless nights, his television program *Talent Showcase* continued to run along smoothly week after week and year after year. One "celebrity" who appeared on the show was in fact auditioning for an unusual role far more important than any he had ever taken on before. The celeb was a young U. S. Senator from Massachusetts named John Fitzgerald Kennedy, and he was running for President. The brief interview that Jelesnik conducted at the beginning of his regular talent show on 30 January 1960, was one of the only live TV appearances that Kennedy made in Utah during his campaign. Utah was Nixon country, and the Senator had little hope of garnering many of the state's votes. That Kennedy's one-day, whirlwind tour of the state would include an appearance with Jelesnik was an indication of the stature that Jelesnik's program had achieved. Jelesnik's studio audience was packed, not only with the day's regular slate of contestants, but also with Democratic Party politicos who were eager to see their presidential hopeful up close. The interview was of necessity brief, but Jelesnik succeeded in asking questions about family and the campaign that would be of most interest to a Utah audience:[25]

> Jelesnik: In what way does your family play a part in your political career?
>
> Kennedy: Well, of course, my wife has been a great help to me. And then I have eight brothers and sisters. One of my brothers was a council of the McClelland's select committee and he is now working for me, helping me out in this campaign. And my brother Teddy, who just got out of law school, is also working in the field in this campaign. So, both of my brothers, and I'm going to get my sisters to help out too.

After mentioning that Kennedy had a very famous in-law (actor, Peter Lawford), who probably was better known at that time than the Senator, Jelesnik proceeded to interview the Senator as if he were a contestant on the program. Perhaps hoping that

Kennedy would perform a soft-shoe routine for his audience, Jelesnik asked: "Have you ever been asked to participate in any phase of show business? Do you sing or dance or play a musical instrument?"

The unmusical Kennedy was frank: "No, I don't have any of the necessary talent. In fact I saw him, Peter Lawford, only yesterday. They're making a movie in Nevada, and I happened to see him and my sister over there yesterday when I was in Nevada. When I travel around, frequently these young ladies say to me, 'where's your brother-in-law?' They don't show any interest in my political views."

> Jelesnik: Can you give these young people some advice on what they should look for and how they should work to become what they want to be?
>
> Kennedy: Well, I'm not an expert in that field. I just think that anything you do is worth doing well. And I would say that a chance to entertain people and to amuse them in a very difficult time in the life of our country, occupies an honored place.

Jelesnik was most impressed with the young Senator, particularly with his bearing and the way he walked. The back brace that Kennedy always wore made him walk in a somewhat rigid and striking mode, similar to a soldier on parade. The image stuck in Jelesnik's mind, and after Kennedy was elected President, Jelesnik composed a piece of music in his honor: "The JFK March." The work was premiered on 17 July 1962 at the annual Days of '47 Pops Concert, which that year was given at the Highland High School auditorium. The dedication read: "The JFK March by Eugene Jelesnik. In honor of President Kennedy's recent trip to Mexico and to the solidarity of the United States and the Republic of Mexico."

Nineteen sixty-three was a year that Eugene Jelesnik would remember as the most sorrowful in his life. On Tuesday morning, April 30th, while preparing for a concert that approaching weekend, Eugene received word from Aunt Ruth that his mother had died. She had suffered from heart trouble for several years but had not told her son of the seriousness of the ailment. She had died at

6 A.M. that morning at St. Clare's Hospital in New York City. Of the eight children of Rabbi Aaron Rothaus and Riva Fedler, only two remained: Aunt Ruth and Eugene's Uncle Abe Rothaus who lived in Cleveland, Ohio. Eugene immediately flew back East to attend the funeral, which was held at Riverside Chapel in New York City. Jennie Rothaus Zheleznykov had been a fighter. She had survived countless pogroms, the Russian Revolution, the Russian Civil War, and the great famine of 1921–22. She had made sacrifices of every kind to protect and instruct her son. The lessons Eugene learned at her apron strings he would live by his entire life. Jennie had the satisfaction of seeing her son grow to maturity and prosper. She would share his disappointments and exalt in his many successes. At the time of her death she was seventy-six years old. She was buried at Beth Cemetery, New Jersey.

After the death of his mother, Eugene threw himself into his work with feverish activity. In addition to *Talent Showcase,* the Days of '47, the *Celebrity Concert Series,* and the Cinegrill, Eugene continued to appear at special promotions and benefits. In early September he helped Bob Hope promote his new book *I Owe Russia $1,200 Dollars* at a book signing outside Deseret Book. On Friday September 20th, he conducted the Philharmonic for the dedication of the amphitheater at Zion National Park in southern Utah. The *Utah County Herald* wrote a long story about the event and focused on Eugene's accomplishments as well as his many hats:

> On Friday, Jelesnik will reach another pinnacle of success. He will wave his baton in the dedicatory concert for the 5,000 seat amphitheater near Zion National Park in southern Utah. The facility, known as the James H. Wardle Zion Park Bowl, is located a mile from the park entrance at the foot of Watchman Mountain, in one of the most unique and picturesque areas of the world.
>
> "It is a fascinating place," says Jelesnik. "The towering majesty of the mountains and cliffs created a wonderful atmosphere in which a musician can perform at his greatest."
>
> Jelesnik and his 35 musicians perform "not for the financial reward but because we love music. We are subsidized to some degree by the city and the music performance trust fund, but all of us have other full-time jobs."

Jelesnik notes that the Philharmonic was organized to participate in all types of events. He is the orchestra's permanent conductor, but his livelihood stems from his restaurant, shows, celebrity presentations, and a television amateur hour, plus recordings and compositions.

"I have no partners, donors, or angels," he says. "All of the risks are mine completely."

The performers for the opening of the amphitheater included many who would continue to make appearances with Eugene in the years to come, including Billie Loukas and Bob Davis. Also appearing on the program were two of Eugene's *Talent Showcase* winners "The Terry Sisters" who would perform with Jelesnik in a number of capacities in the coming years.

September 1963 was a busy month even for Eugene Jelesnik. It was during that month that President Kennedy made a triumphal visit to Salt Lake City, and Eugene's "JFK March" was performed for the President at his arrival at the Salt Lake airport by the Tooele High School marching band. On October 23rd Kennedy acknowledged the tribute in a personal letter to Jelesnik:

THE WHITE HOUSE
Washington

October 23, 1963

Dear Mr. Jelesnik:

I am delighted to learn through Senator Moss that you composed "The JFK March," which the Tooele High School Band played upon my arrival at L.C. Romney Field in Salt Lake City. I appreciate this thoughtful expression of your great musical talent. I thoroughly enjoyed my visit to Salt Lake City and hope to return again.

Sincerely,
John Kennedy

Eugene Jelesnik was having his hair cut in the old barbershop under the Walker Bank Building at Second South and Main Street when he first heard the news that Kennedy had been shot. Like all of America, he was stunned. It had been less than a month since

Kennedy had written Jelesnik the note of thanks. When he heard a short time later that Kennedy was dead, Eugene cried as he never had in his life. The "JFK March" would be performed numerous times in tribute to the President. Robert F. Kennedy accepted the composition for the family and made it a part of the Kennedy Presidential Archive in the Kennedy Library in Boston, Massachusetts. The President's brother also wrote to Eugene to thank him for the tribute. In June of the following year, the "JFK March" and Eugene were both praised by Utah's Senator Frank Moss from the floor of the U. S. Senate:

Congressional Record
Washington, Tuesday, June 16, 1964

The "JFK March" by Eugene Jelesnik, Utah composer

   Mr. Moss: Mr. President, it was my pleasure yesterday morning to be present at a Pentagon ceremony in which Eugene Jelesnik, distinguished Utah composer, presented the score of his "JFK March" to representatives of the U. S. military service bands to be played at times when it is appropriate.
   The score was accepted by Col. John J. Christy, Director for Community Relations, Office of the Assistant Secretary of Defense for Public Affairs, and by representatives of two of the bands: Lt. Col. Hugh Curry, Director of the U. S. Army Band, and Capt. James B. King, Jr., Assistant Director of the U. S. Marine Band. The score will also be made available to the U. S. Navy Band and the U. S. Air Force Band.
   Composer Jelesnik wrote the "JFK March" during the late president Kennedy's lifetime and dedicated it to him. It was played for the President during his visit to Salt Lake City in September 1963, just about two months before his assassination. In a letter dated October 23 of last year, President Kennedy acknowledged the composition in his honor and commended Mr. Jelesnik on his "great musical talent."
   Mr. Jelesnik is a Russian-born professional musician who received his training in Hungary, Germany, and the United States, coming to this country in 1925. For the past two decades he has made his home in Salt Lake City.
   Eugene Jelesnik typifies very well the spirit of the famous admonition in President Kennedy's inaugural address. He has not asked what his adopted country and community can do for

him, but he has shown his willingness to do whatever he can for them.

Senator Frank E. Moss.

Several days later, Eugene received a personal note of thanks from Attorney General Robert F. Kennedy for the "JFK March." The note read:

> Senator Moss has presented to me the manuscripts, printed music, and tape recordings of "the JFK March," which you wrote in honor of President Kennedy. It was very generous and thoughtful of you to do this, and I just wanted you to know how much my family and I appreciate having this fine musical tribute to my brother for the Library.

A film tribute to President John F. Kennedy's "Thousand Days in Office," commissioned by the Kennedy family, did not end in Dallas, Texas, but in Salt Lake City, Utah. For it was in Salt Lake that the Kennedy administration felt they had achieved one of their greatest successes. The huge crowds and warm reception in the heart of Nixon country was more than a political triumph, it was a very personal one that would be remembered as the high-water mark of "Camelot." Eugene Jelesnik was proud to have been a small part of it.

In January of 1964, Jelesnik again brought Mischa Elman to Salt Lake City as part of his *Celebrity Concert Series.* This was a recital with just Elman's personal pianist. No orchestra was needed, and no confrontation with Maurice Abravanel would be forthcoming. The concert was a huge success financially and artistically. Several weeks later Elman called Jelesnik and said he had a proposition for him. Eugene recalled what happened in amazement: "Elman called me from his home in New York and requested that I fly there to discuss some business matters with him. This is the same man who, when I was a boy and going to school in the Bronx, I would save my pennies to see from the back balcony of Carnegie Hall. He was my idol. To present him later in Salt Lake City was one of the proudest achievements of my life."

When Eugene flew out to New York to visit with Mischa and

his wife, the internationally renowned violinist told Jelesnik that he was disappointed in the way impresario Sol Hurok was handling his career. Hurok managed both Elman and Jascha Heifetz, and Mischa felt that Heifetz was getting better exposure. Jelesnik knew that there was a lot of rivalry between the two musicians, but until that moment he didn't realize that Elman felt that he was getting the short end of the stick from Sol Hurok. Then he laid the bombshell on Jelesnik: "Elman explained the situation to me and then said: 'and that's why I want you to become my personal manager and agent. I'll pay you whatever you want.' I was in shock when I heard that. I could hardly speak. I said something like 'Why me?' Mischa said he had never been treated as well anywhere else than he had been in Salt Lake City . . . that the way I handled things was exactly the way he wanted to be promoted. He felt strongly that I was the one person who should manage his career. I was so awestruck by the proposal and the praise that I said very little. I told him I wondered if I was really that capable. I also said I would have to talk it over with Virginia."

Virginia was hugely enthusiastic about Elman's offer. She called it "The chance of a lifetime." Eugene was surprised at her reaction, but Virginia believed that it would be the crown jewel in Eugene's career. She also saw that it would be their ticket off the financial roller coaster they had been riding in Salt Lake. Jelesnik realized that as well, but he also knew that he would have to give up everything he had been building in Utah for more than twenty years: the Philharmonic, the pops concerts, *Talent Showcase,* the *Celebrity Concert Series,* and the rest. After several days of soul-searching, Eugene reluctantly explained to Elman that he could not give up his home and career in Salt Lake City. Mischa Elman would remain with Sol Hurok. While Elman was disappointed, he understood Jelesnik's reasons for wanting to stay in Utah. Virginia could not. Although Jelesnik had turned him down, the Elmans and the Jelesniks remained close friends. Eugene recalls, "Mischa loved Virginia. When I was overseas with USO tours, he would call just to check up on her to see how she was doing. We became dear friends. He was normally very terse, but as our friendship grew, he became just like family."

FROM SOUP TO PEANUTS AND THE USO

To the casual observer in 1964, the life of Eugene Jelesnik must have looked like everything was going along well. The *Celebrity Concert Series* was drawing large audiences, the weekly televison program had a steady and devoted following, the Pops Concerts continued to grow in reputation and popularity, and he seemed to be involved in every annual and seasonal event in the Salt Lake Valley, from Labor Day and Christmas concerts to Fourth of July celebrations and the Days of '47 Rodeo. But making a living as a full-time professional musician in Salt Lake City was not as easy as it looked. Jelesnik's most public endeavors often brought in only enough to cover the program. Then too, a large portion of his time was devoted to charity causes and fund-raising events. In order to make a living and keep his name before the public, Jelesnik continued to scramble. As in the past, he gave bedside performances at the Primary Children's Hospital, at the Veteran's Administration Hospital and at the Shriners Hospital for Crippled Children. He donated countless hours to the Days of '47 and other community events, and all the while he continued to play tables in the evenings. In 1964 his table playing had moved to the Restaurant Teogra where he recorded one of his better-known singles, "Music by Candlelight." Henry Mancini appeared in Salt Lake City in 1964, and the orchestra leader/composer led the Salt Lake Philharmonic Orchestra at a performance at the Tabernacle, one of the few times the ensemble was led by anyone other than Jelesnik. Eugene also frequently accepted invitations to play his violin for friends or community leaders on special occasions. He played yearly for Mormon Church President David O. McKay and his wife, Emma, at their birthdays and anniversaries in their apartment on the top floor of the Hotel Utah. He would also perform for J. Bracken Lee who was by then serving a stint as Salt Lake City's mayor, and for Utah's governor, George Dewey Clyde. In short, he never passed up any opportunity to perform for anyone, anywhere, and he continued to actively seek new engagements, even when he was completely booked.

Before he ever set foot in America, Eugene had been instilled with a strong work ethic. His mother had told him repeatedly that work was the key to success. Under her strict instruction, and her own example, Jennie had made Eugene into an exceptionally hard worker. Now that Jennie was gone, Eugene seemed to intensify his efforts, perhaps in tribute to her memory. But over the years, Eugene had learned other lessons that had not come at his mother's knee. There were hard knocks and bitter experiences that pushed him to the point of exhaustion. Unlike the salaried employee, the tenured professor, or the hourly wage worker, the professional performing artist cannot rely on the certainty of a paycheck. Mortgage payments and utility bills arrived like clockwork, and the occasional medical bill or unexpected expense might bring him to the brink of ruin. To be out of an income for even a short time invited disaster.

Driven by such anxieties and inspired by ambition, Jelesnik became a severe workaholic. The newspapers of the time noted the impossible schedule that Jelesnik was keeping. It was not the first time that his work load had drawn the attention of the press. Back in August of 1936, the *Long Island Daily Star* had run an article about the seldom sleeping Eugene Jelesnik when he was working at both the Hollywood Restaurant at night, the Lexington Hotel during the day, and performing on network radio in the afternoons. Thirty years later, little had changed: *The Salt Lake Tribune* for 12 July 1964 wrote a similar article with the same theme. The only things that had changed in thirty years were the place names.

JELESNIK—PERPETUAL MOTION MACHINE

Mr. Jelesnik, who has been associated with a huge number of musical enterprises since he first came to Salt Lake City with his own orchestra at the Hotel Utah in 1938, is currently knee-deep in preparations for the Days of '47 concerts, which will be presented Tuesday and Wednesday at Highland High School auditorium. The concerts are entirely produced by Mr. Jelesnik who engages the hall, the talent, directs the rehearsals, and finally conducts the Salt Lake Philharmonic at the shows.

Mr. Jelesnik, who is proud to say he is "subsidized by no one," has been giving of his time and talents for more than 30 years in such enterprises as the Days of '47 concerts. Each year during the Christmas holiday, he assembles a group of musicians and entertainers to go to children's wards and hospitals in the state. These are but a few of the enterprises which Mr. Jelesnik and his wife, the former Virginia Belle Washburn engage in during the year in Salt Lake City.

Why does he do it? Mr. Jelesnik says, "I did it when I was a little boy. I did it in New York. When someone asks me to help out on a concert or entertainment, I just can't refuse."

But the Days of '47 concerts are just a part of Mr. Jelesnik's busy schedule these days. From his office in the Newhouse Hotel crowded with sheet music, records, pictures of celebrities, and telephones he is setting up his *Celebrity Artists Series* for next fall and winter in Salt Lake City. Mr. Jelesnik is arranging bookings for Utah appearances with agents and other impresarios from New York to Los Angeles. He has five telephones to handle the calls on everything from circuses to solo harpsichordists.

In addition, Mr. Jelesnik and his wife operate Gold Leaf Records Co., which he uses to help Utah talent. The Jelesniks also have a television program in the wintertime, and he plays his violin at a Salt Lake restaurant—as well as for conventions and meetings of various groups throughout the year.

A very busy life, but "this is the way I like to work," said Mr. Jelesnik.

From the time that he was first tempted to run off with the Gypsies and join the circus, Eugene was always fascinated by the world of the circus performer. Over most of his professional career he had followed a lifestyle akin to that of an itinerant juggler. His work ethic also owed something to the circus acrobat or trapeze artist: the training and practice, the long hours of rehearsal, and the uncompromising dedication to perfection. Once, during the early fifties, he had helped bring Ringling Brothers Barnum & Bailey Circus to the Utah State Fairgrounds. This was the circus of the "Big Top" and the sideshow, the carnival and the roustabout. By the mid-nineteen fifties, Barnum & Bailey had abandoned the huge expense of the world's largest tents in favor of using arenas to stage its shows. They did so to focus on the quality of their acts and to better care for their performers and animals. In the years that followed, the move was hailed by many as the salvation of the American circus, but others saw it as its death blow. In 1964, it was not certain which position was correct. Revenues had been steadily declining for several years. The huge growth of professional sports had something to do with the falling gate, as did television and other new entertainment mediums such as rock concerts. Some said that the circus was a thing of the past. Even its most ardent supporters had to admit that the future of the circus was in doubt.

Eugene Jelesnik could not imagine a world in which there was no circus. For Eugene, "The Greatest Show on Earth" was just that, and no possible substitute could take its place. If he had anything to say about it, the circus would live on forever. In 1964, Eugene began an association with Ringling Brothers Barnum & Bailey Circus. The circus people recognized immediately that Jelesnik was no common "jossler or gilley,"[1] but was a true afficionado of the art form. The professional arrangement between Ringling Brothers and Jelesnik would last for more than three decades. In addition to his many other jobs and obligations, Eugene would see to it that the circus always came to Salt Lake City. He would do everything necessary to make certain that it did. He would act as advance man, promoter, "street worker,"[2] and resident "diddy"[3] if he had to, but for Eugene, the circus was always going to come to town.

In addition to Maurice Abravanel, there were a few other musicians in town who believed that Eugene was doing far too much. Generally they wished that Jelesnik would spread the work around a bit more. But in fact, Eugene was doing just that. When he began bringing in the Ringling Brothers Barnum & Bailey Circus to Salt Lake, he hired local musicians to fill out the orchestra. When performers in his *Celebrity Artists Series* needed backups or larger ensembles, it was Eugene Jelesnik who insisted that they hire local talent. When the rodeos, ice shows, fairs, hotels, and clubs needed musicians, they turned to Eugene Jelesnik, and Jelesnik turned to the local musicians union. Eugene created many events specifically to employ local musicians; and all the while, he was scouting for talent and sending the best off to New York so the rest of the nation could see them as well. No agency of government made possible as many jobs for musicians as did Jelesnik, and Local No. 104 of the Salt Lake Federated Musicians Union never had a better friend. But even if he had employed everyone in the state all the time, there would still be those who would be disparaging of his efforts—those who Jelesnik could never please. Their motivations had nothing to do with anything but their own prejudice.

But all else aside, nothing inflames resentment like success, and there was little doubt that some were openly resentful of the Maestro's ubiquitous activities. His *Celebrity Concert Series* in particular had raised a few eyebrows. If Eugene Jelesnik could bring in celebrity stars and make a fortune, well others could too, or so they thought. Jelesnik had in fact created a market that had not existed before, and markets have a way of fostering competition. In 1964, TV personality Art Linkletter and several local investors opened the Valley Music Hall in North Salt Lake. The advance publicity for the hall said that the owners intended to bring the finest nationally known artists to a facility "worthy of the growing Salt Lake metropolitan area." For its time, the Valley Music Hall was a first-rate venue with one of the largest seating capacities of any performance space outside of the Mormon Tabernacle. The Hall—which had the added novelty of seating in the round— also had all the latest technical innovations. Eugene could see instantly that the ancient Coliseum at the state fairgrounds could never compete with such a facility. But none of his other performance venues (Highland High School, Kingsbury Hall, and the Rainbow Rendezvous) could compete with it either. For nine years

Eugene had brought some of the greatest performing artists of the day to appreciative Salt Lake audiences. He had brought in touring theatrical productions and Broadway shows such as *The Music Man; Mary, Mary;* and *Carnival.* He had spotlighted great classical artists like Mischa Elman and Jose Iturbi. He had brought in Ferrante and Teicher, Roger Williams, Mort Sahl, Shelley Berman, Frank Sinatra, Liberace, and a host of others. He had done it at a minimal cost to the public, and at great financial risk to himself. But he believed it had been more than worthwhile from the standpoint of personal satisfaction, if not profit. He also believed that he had performed a service to the citizens of Salt Lake City. But if others thought they could do it better, they were welcome to it. It was time to shift his energies to something else. To Eugene's distress, and Virginia's relief, the *Celebrity Concert Series* was discontinued after the 1964 season.

Because Eugene believed that any disruption in the cash flow might have dire consequences, he quickly filled his time with new projects, bookings, and enterprises. On 22 December 1964, he signed a six-month contract with a new sponsor for his long-running TV show: *Talent Showcase.* Southeast Furniture Company was to be the sole sponsor, an arrangement that was said to be unusual for local television programming. The newspapers said that Christmas had come early for the Jelesniks, implying that the new contract was a financial improvement on what he had been receiving. The program would air weekly under the new sponsor beginning on 17 January 1965. In signing the contract with Jelesnik, Horace A. Sorensen, president and general manager of the Sugarhouse furniture store, was quoted as saying, "My brothers and I are proud to team up with Eugene Jelesnik in presenting this weekly hunt for talent as a service to the community."[4] Southeast Furniture would continue to sponsor Jelesnik for decades to come.

The hunt for talent was always the big attraction of the program and was the basis of the show's steady performance in the local ratings. Hundreds of talented hopefuls, stage-door mothers, and starstruck teens dreamed of the day that Eugene Jelesnik would discover them and send them off to a life of fame and fortune. Among those hoping for stardom was comedienne Roseanne Barr. Roseanne was twelve or thirteen years old when she made her debut for Eugene Jelesnik, but unlike any of the other hopefuls, Barr did not make her audition on *Talent Showcase* but on Main Street, in front of the Continental Bank building. Barr described her encounter with Jelesnik in her memoir, *My Life As a Woman:*

> There was a talent contest show in SLC, which was on TV every Sunday afternoon, and you could go on there and if you won, and were good enough, you could eventually go to New York to be on the Ed Sullivan show.[5] The show was hosted by another Jewish person in Utah, Eugene Jelesnik, a fat little man with a bald head and huge nose. Each week, they would showcase four or five people and then the audience would pick the winner. I used to ride my bike downtown, or take a bus, and wait to be discovered by Eugene Jelesnik. I knew that his TV show was broadcast from downtown, and I was sure I would bump into him and that he would discover me.
>
> One day I was riding around with my girlfriend, and who should appear but Mr. TV himself, looking thinner and younger in person I might add. When I saw him I went berserk, screaming, "Mr. Jelesnik, Eugene, my name is Roseanne Barr, and you should discover me, discover me, Mr. Jelesnik!" But he just kept walking, like he couldn't hear me. I followed close behind and even beside him for a few blocks, singing and dancing and trying to tell jokes, but alas I was not married yet, and had not hit on the eventual winning combination of myself-and-husband jokes. He continued to stride away from me, and I was shattered; I was too young then to realize that he would merely be the first of many talent-spotting persons to whom I was invisible.
>
> When I met him a few years ago after headlining my own show in SLC, I reminded him of that little girl a long time ago, and he said he couldn't remember anything like that and then he apologized. I forgave him, too, as I always try to do, when someone says they're sorry and were indeed wrong. Never having been wrong myself, it is definitely a trait I admire most in mortals.

Roseanne had made the audition process much more difficult than it needed to have been. All it would have taken was a simple postcard sent to the TV station, and the future national sensation could have arranged for an audition in the studio.

If fame and fortune were not enough to offer the *Showcase* contestants, there were other incentives. The weekly winners not only received prizes but were automatically entered in the grand finals, which were held every May in Salt Lake City. Ted Mack, the host of *The Original Amateur Hour,* was usually on hand for the program. The grand winner (or winners in the case of a group) was given an all-expense-paid trip to New York City to audition for the Ted Mack show. The alternate winner received a vacation at the Stardust Hotel in Las Vegas. Every year Eugene took the winning contestants to New York and frequently escorted them around his old hometown. For those with the most potential, he would do even more, including introducing them to the people who could most help their careers. The winners of *Talent Showcase* routinely did well on the *Amateur Hour.*

The job of prescreening most of the acts for *Talent Showcase* fell to Eugene's wife, Virginia. Unlike Eugene, who could be abrupt in dismissing a poor performance, Virginia had a way of softening the blow. She had a special knack of letting the hopeful singer with the tin ear or the dancing disaster "down easy." She also knew exactly what Eugene liked and didn't like. She knew his whims and blind spots better than he did himself. As did Eugene, Virginia had a good head for organization. Having run her own businesses in Hollywood, she also had a sixth sense for publicity and was a whiz at handling a myriad of details from costumes to contracts. For the previous quarter century she had also been Eugene's number one audience member, promoter, and full-time friendly critic. She was also his partner in every sense of the word. It was little wonder that Virginia Washburn Jelesnik was also the associate producer of *Talent Showcase.*

One hopeful who auditioned for Virginia was an LDS mother of four from Bountiful, Utah: Carleen Hall Brown. Carleen had a long history of performing locally. When she was growing up in Bear River City during World War II, she had frequently performed for soldiers who passed through the area. She danced tap at fairs and pageants and sang for anyone who would listen. With her golden ringlets and bright eyes she had been northern Utah's own version of Shirley Temple. When she called to audition for *Talent Showcase* she billed herself as a singer and arranged to meet Virginia at the Jelesnik home on Coatsville Avenue.

Carleen never forgot her first meeting with Mrs. Jelesnik. For the young Mormon mother, Virginia was something of a shock. When she opened the door she was wearing a long caftan and house slippers. She had a cigarette in one hand, and her other hand was firmly on her hip. She looked Carleen over and sized her up before speaking: "Well," she said. "you at least *look* like a singer." Then Virginia turned from the door and walked back into her living room. "Come on in," she called over her shoulder after she had reentered the house.

The audition began with a long interview on the particulars of Carleen's life, focusing on her background, education, and training more than her talent. Carleen had been raised in a traditional LDS family in Bear River, Utah. She was married and at that time had four children. It was obvious to Virginia that Carleen would never be able to pursue a career in music, but she was curious to know why she wanted to try. Gradually, Virginia elicited from Carleen the story of her life. As Virginia listened, she recognized that the woman felt trapped by both her marriage and her children. She told Carleen that she had talent, but she discouraged her from pursuing it. Unlike the agent or scout, Virginia had broader scope and interests than music. She told Carleen that there was more desperation than ambition behind her desire to appear on *Talent Showcase*. In short, she told the woman she was trying to escape. Though this may have been obvious to Virginia, it was a revelation to Carleen who recognized in an instant that it was true. Virginia never minced her words and spoke exactly what was on her mind. She was a great talker and Carleen was a great listener. The two women spent the entire afternoon together and were soon fast friends. While Carleen did not sing for Virginia that day, as things later turned out, she had auditioned for Eugene Jelesnik all the same. The role that she would eventually be given would surprise everyone, most especially Carleen herself.

Over the next twenty years, Virginia would be Carleen's

closest confidant. There was no subject that was taboo between the two women. They would discuss the origins of music, psychology, philosophy, art, and religion. As her letters to Carleen testify, Virginia would advise her friend on the most personal matters affecting her life, including finances, raising of her children, and advice on saving Carleen's failing marriage. For a long time they talked daily on the telephone. When Eugene was out of town, Carleen would occasionally help Virginia with *Talent Showcase* auditions and would also help with various errands. Though she met Eugene early on, she saw much more of Virginia than of the Maestro. She would later say: "I was always around but in the shadows."

In early 1965 Eugene took a job for a short time directing the orchestra aboard the SS *Atlantic* for a ten-day Caribbean cruise. In March of 1965 Eugene added yet another task to his ever-lengthening list of duties by getting himself appointed as "Entertainment Director of the Utah State Fair." The appointment by Utah's Governor Calvin Rampton was submitted to the State Fair Board's entertainment committee for approval. The vote was unanimous. Eugene had another job. The position would give him the opportunity of becoming acquainted with a whole range of country-western stars, including Crystal Gayle, the Gatlin Brothers, and Minnie Pearl. He co-hosted the *Talent Showcase* finals in May and directed a special pops concert benefit for the Order of the Eastern Star Home for the Aged. The concert featured Billie Loukas and tenor Theron Nay who had performed with Spike Jones and the City Slickers. In July, Eugene directed his annual Days of '47 Pops Concert. Also, he was not finished tinkering with *Talent Showcase*. The program was originally broadcast in 1955 by Channel 2. In 1958 it moved to Channel 4, and in the summer of 1965 it moved again, this time to KSL Channel 5, where it would remain for the next twenty-one years. In September came the Utah State Fair, and Eugene handled all the entertainment arrangements. And so it went, week after week, and month after month, job after job after job. By the fall of 1965, Eugene must have needed a break from his busy and demanding schedule. He signed up for another USO tour, this time to Europe. Perhaps he thought he needed a rest.

Eugene's fourth USO tour was billed as "Holiday Kapers" and featured the talents of ventriloquist Sammy King, tap dancer Barbara Stalzle, vocalist Meri Kayne, and musicians Chuck Burgess on piano and Tommy Shields on electric bass. Jelesnik was tour manager, featured violinist, and master of ceremonies. Once again this was a Bert Wishnew production. The tour would last four and a half months and would give performances at U. S. military bases and installations in Spain, Morocco, Italy, and Germany. Before Eugene left Salt Lake, Utah's Governor Calvin Rampton conferred on Jelesnik the honorary title of "Utah's Ambassador to the Armed Forces." In a story by United Press International correspondent Don Reed, Jelesnik explained why he was going on yet another USO tour: "It may sound corny, but it isn't easy to repay this nation for the privilege of being an American. The USO tours and the 'JFK March,' which I composed for the late President Kennedy, are just token repayments when I think of the opportunity this country has extended to me."

On the eve of his departure from the East Coast, 13 October 1965, Jelesnik told United Press International writer Frederick M. Winship in a New York City-datelined article that: "President Lyndon Johnson has more or less put the USO back on a wartime basis." The quote was foreboding. While the situation in Vietnam was indeed heating up, the country was officially at peace. If the entertainers of the USO were being put on a wartime footing, then what might be next? Was Johnson going to call up the National Guard?

Eugene had never been to Spain or Morocco and so his trips there—while brief—were filled with exotic sights and sounds he had never encountered before. He spent as much time as his schedule would allow sight-seeing. Of course, he was familiar with Italy. While Rome, Venice, and Naples were much as he remembered them, Italy was not the same as it had been when he toured there with the 10th Mountain Division in 1944 and 1945. The grinding poverty and near starvation was gone, and the food was almost as good as the Cinegrill's.

Jelesnik arrived in Germany on November 4th. The first leg of the German USO tour took him to the port of Bremerhaven where he had set sail for America more than forty years earlier. Nothing looked familiar. He then went to Bremen where he, his mother, and Aunt Ruth had lived following their escape from Russia. He tried to find the buildings where the family had been housed, but he could not. Then he remembered the address of the Gymnasium where he had first attended formal school, "Number 12 Zwingliestrassr." It was there that his teacher, Mr. Richard Feller, had given him his first lessons on the violin. But the address no longer existed. As was the case with most German cities, Bremen had been largely destroyed during the war. The only thing that seemed at all familiar was the little lake in Berger Park, but he could not be certain. On 20 December 1965, Eugene's unit arrived in Würzburg, and he got the surprise of his life. The Third Infantry Division Band greeted Jelesnik and his troupe by performing the "JFK March." Jelesnik was quoted by UPI as saying it was the greatest Christmas present he had ever had.

While Jelesnik was in Germany, Virginia received news from Ted Mack that many of Eugene's proteges from *Talent Showcase* had been invited to perform on a special edition of *The Amateur Hour,* which was to be taped in Hollywood, California. Virginia had conducted the auditions for the show back on December 3rd. She had made all the arrangements, including securing the sponsorship of the Sorensens and Southeast Furniture. Originally the program was to be a regional production, but the talent had been so good that Mack decided on an all-Utah show. The lucky winners included Meteliko Tuiasoa, a Tonganese guitarist from Brigham Young University; the Salt Flats, a Salt Lake barbershop quartet; Doug McKendricks, from the University of Utah department of ballet; Sharlimar Carter, a Salt Lake soprano; four trumpet players, students of Faye Hansen at Weber State College; Axel Myerberg, a Salt Lake saw player; the Five Singing Strings, a Magna string band; and once again, the Terry Sisters. The program was to be taped in late January for airing nationwide in April. Since Eugene was out of town, Virginia had to produce the entire program as well as escort the performers to Los Angeles on a

Greyhound bus. Many of the performers were young and "rambunctious," and Virginia also had to act as the chaperone. Though the taping went well and the program later received high praise, Virginia had had enough of being nursemaid to young performers. Her only comment after she returned to Salt Lake was, "Never again!"

Eugene's USO tour lasted until mid-March. The troupe gave 132 performances for an estimated 30,000 military and civilian personnel. In Stuttgart, Germany, Jelesnik met Carlos Alexander, who had directed the Utah Opera Workshop and who had also worked with Eugene on several pops concerts. Jelesnik told the UPI that he had not seen the Utah baritone since he had left Utah in 1954. When Eugene visited Alexander, Carlos was performing with the Stuttgart Opera Company. Of the tour Eugene was quoted as saying:

> It is very gratifying, although we have had a constant battle with the weather. I would like to stress the wonderful feeling we here in the USO have for the loyal people who are representing us in the U. S. armed forces. And they have expressed so much appreciation for the shows which are sent from the U. S. for their enjoyment.
>
> The smallest group for which we performed was 20 at a missile site in Germany 20 miles from the Russian border. The largest was about 750 in Spain. We were well-received everywhere we went. It was a real thrill for all of us to make the appearances. It was a memorable experience. I visited the Dachau concentration camp near Munich where 70,000 were killed by the Nazis. It is a real grim reminder of the terror of war and dictatorship.

During his tour of Europe, Eugene realized how much he loved traveling and how much he had missed performing for the appreciative military audiences. He even found that the hectic work load and heavy travel schedule were part of the appeal. He loved the excitement of arriving at military bases, and the special treatment that the military always extended him. The tribute that he received at Würzburg, Germany, with the performance of the "JFK March" was not the only time that he was similarly honored.

Every place the tour went, they were treated like visiting royalty. On occasion, it reminded him of the way his father had been treated by the waiters in Alexandrovsk. Eugene loved meeting ranking officers and important political figures. He loved the attention, the smiles, and the applause. But even more than the V.I.P. treatment, Eugene loved the USO because it made him feel as though he were making a real contribution to the country. He liked everything about the tours, even when the schedule was brutal, the food was poor, the lodgings inadequate, and the weather atrocious. He loved the tours because they gave him the immense satisfaction of knowing that he was doing something important. Before his German tour was half over, he sent a request to Bert Wishnew asking to be sent to Vietnam as soon as possible, as early as that summer if it could be arranged.

From 1965 to 1980, the USO would dominate Eugene's life and his career. Though he would continue to work in Salt Lake City for the State Fair, the Days of '47, *Talent Showcase,* and the Salt Lake Philharmonic, a substantial portion of his time was now committed to entertaining troops overseas. Over the next sixteen years, Eugene would take fifteen more USO tours. He would travel to nearly every part of the globe to entertain United States troops wherever they were stationed, including three tours to the battlefields of Vietnam.

Beginning in August of 1966, Eugene began holding special auditions in Salt Lake City for the USO. He initially confined his talent search to previous winners of *Talent Showcase.* He hoped to be able to attract enough talent that an entire USO tour could be auditioned, cast, and mounted from Utah. Bert Wishnew was skeptical of the whole idea but flew out to Utah to see the finals. Eugene arranged to have the auditions staged at the Crystal Heights Ward meetinghouse of The Church of Jesus Christ of Latter-day Saints. The first local winners selected in the competition were Salt Lake ventriloquist Roy Baumbart; Deanne Johnsen, a pianist-composer-singer from Logan; and The Terry Sisters—Carla and Becky—who were now eighteen and seventeen years old. The Terrys had graduated from Jelesnik's "Harvest Days" television show to the concert opening the amphitheater at Zion

National Park and to appearances on Ted Mack's coast-to-coast
Amateur Hour. Like many of Jelesnik's performers, they would
serve a hitch with the USO. While the local winners would not be
asked to go on tour that year, the audition demonstrated to
Wishnew that Eugene's idea wasn't completely mad.

Eugene's fifth USO tour was not to Vietnam but once again to
Germany. It was less than seven months since his last tour ended,
but by 18 October 1966, he was back in Europe and not with his
Utah performers but with a group of Irish singers from Belfast
called The Witnesses. Writing for *Stars and Stripes,* Bill Collins
called Mr. Jelesnik "The GI's favorite fiddler" and the eight singers
of The Witnesses "one of the best acts that we've ever had here."
For Jelesnik the music must have been familiar. He had toured
Italy during World War II with a singer of Irish ballads, Bob
Gilchrist.

On 12 June 1967, Jelesnik had his second USO *Talent Showcase*
audition finals in Salt Lake. On hand again was Bert Wishnew,
joined by Maj. Gen. Michael B. Kauffman, Chairman, Utah USO,
and H. C. Shoemaker, a local USO official. The first made-in-Utah
USO tour was a nineteen-week trek to Alaskan and Pacific bases,
including Vietnam. The tour ran from 4 September 1967 through
January 1968. Joining Jelesnik on the 50,000-mile trip through
Alaska, Taiwan, the Philippines, Japan, Okinawa, Thailand,
and Vietnam were the Terry Sisters, Las Vegas-based dancer/
comedienne Betty Jo Houston, pianist and Miss Utah contestant
Lenora Ford, musical theater performer Sandra Defa of Salt Lake,
and musical duo Aggie Lee and Ray Ball. The performers gave up
both Thanksgiving and Christmas at home to entertain American
troops overseas. They performed in jungles, in cities, on remote
islands, at hospitals, air bases, and radar stations. At the beginning
of the tour, in Alaska, Rebecca Terry became ill. By the time the
troupe arrived in Japan, she had to be hospitalized. She would
remain there for more than two weeks. Rebecca remembered that
Eugene, who apparently never got sick himself, was disappointed
in her that she had.

She recalls that he was a real trouper. "The guy would get out
there and play with all the emotion and feeling he had no matter if

there were just a couple of guys in a jeep or thousands in a stadium." Both Terry sisters would say they were changed by the tour. They felt they had embarked as naive little girls and had come back as seasoned performers. Rebecca in particular saw herself from then on as a show girl. In all, excellent training for the future "Saliva Sister."

In Vietnam, the troupe crossed paths with other USO performers, including comedienne Martha Raye. The troupe met many military and civilian leaders, including General William Westmorland who commanded all U. S. forces in Vietnam. Near the end of the grueling tour Eugene described the spirit and pluck of the performers for *Deseret News* television editor Howard Pearson: "They were incredible. They put on two shows a day for eight days straight in Vietnam. This is a rough schedule. It means getting up at five o'clock each morning, traveling, meeting people, performing, traveling, meeting people, performing, meeting more people, and—finally—turning in late at night. Believe me, they might not get the publicity of Bob Hope, but they work hard to bring some of home to the troops."

Among the hardships that the Utah performers had to endure in Vietnam was the necessity of having to stop the show repeatedly to sweep a four-inch-deep layer of exotic bugs off the stage. Without the periodic sweeping the dancers would slip on "squashed bug juices." Jelesnik said that because of the delays it took three hours to perform a 90-minute program. A news story featuring the troupe was datelined Bien Hoa, Vietnam, on 16 January 1968:

VIETNAM, SCENE OF *TALENT SHOWCASE* REUNION

The world became a little smaller recently for local talent scout, entertainer Eugene Jelesnik. Jelesnik is in Vietnam as manager and MC of an 8-member USO group now touring for our servicemen in the Far East. "Utah Showtime" features Jelesnik, the singing Terry Sisters of St. George, Utah, dancer Betty Houston, local vocalist Sandra Defa, the musical comedy act of Ray Ball and Aggie Lee, pianist Lenora Ford.

In Bien Hoa, Vietnam, for an afternoon show at the camp Zinn headquarters of the 7th Battalion, 8th Artillery, Jelesnik was greeted by PFC Gregory J. Allen of Huntsville, Utah. Allen, the son of Mr. and Mrs. Dean Allen, appeared on Jelesnik's *Talent Showcase* TV program in July, 1966.

Jelesnik was continually running into former *Talent Showcase* contestants everyplace he went, and invariably they seemed to be the losers. It was almost impossible to avoid them. By 1968 there were already several thousand, and it made him doubly appreciative of Virginia's efforts to placate those who did not get their chance at stardom, particularly since so many of the former contestants were now carrying guns.

Eugene couldn't understand the attitude of the Americans back home who opposed the war in Vietnam. Jelesnik's own experience with communists had been firsthand, and he had no doubts about why the war was being fought. The "domino theory" was still intact, and the specter of monolithic communism was very real at the time. Neither the political nor military leaders of that day seemed to know that the enemy was motivated as much by fervent nationalism as communist ideology. It was a misunderstanding that would lead to catastrophe, but whatever the reasons for the war, it was increasingly clear that the United States was losing. Jelesnik may not have been party to the inner conferences of President Lyndon Johnson's cabinet, MacNamara's "war room debates," or the speculations of Nixon's inner circle, but he knew instinctively that a divided country could never win.

Shortly after Nixon was elected President in 1968, Jelesnik saw a news broadcast where someone in the crowd called out to the President-elect, "Bring us together again." Jelesnik thought about the comment for several weeks before composing a song of the same name, which he debuted at the annual Pops Concert. Because this piece was dedicated to President Nixon, it showed that the same Eugene Jelesnik who composed the "JFK March" could embrace a very wide political spectrum. Republican Representative Laurence J. Burton had the song printed in the *Congressional Record* along with a tribute to Jelesnik. It was the third time he was so honored by the U. S. Congress. In his speech Representative Burton told his colleagues: "Eugene Jelesnik is a

man who speaks with his heart; he is a man whose personal ideology reflects his deep feelings for all mankind."

Eugene's routine began to take on a pattern of annual activities that would prevail through the next decade. When he wasn't
touring with the USO or running his weekly *Talent Showcase* television program, the cadence of his life ran with the seasons. The
Philharmonic usually presented a pops concert every spring. In
May came the annual finals of *Talent Showcase*. In June were the
auditions for the USO. July was taken up by the annual Days of
'47 concert and rodeo. In August and September came the circus,
the Labor Day Pops Concert, and the Utah State Fair. By late
October, Eugene was usually headed overseas with the USO. He
was never home for the Holidays.

Eugene's 1968–69 USO tour was called "Utah Varieties." The
performers included Jelesnik's longtime Pops Concert soprano
Billie Loukas; jazz/ballet dancer Sharon Foulger of Murray; Larry
Banks, a 16-year-old guitarist from Granger, Utah; Idaho
folksingers Mike Wendling and Diana Hopperstad; and pianist
Marilyn Laughlin of Salt Lake City. Hopperstad was a former Miss
Idaho. The troupe embarked on 29 November 1968, and returned
in mid-January. This was not the most hospitable time of year to
visit remote bases in Alaska. Every time they stepped out of the
plane they were slapped with temperatures that hovered around
45-degrees below zero. Nor were the rigors confined to freezing.
The troupe was snowed-in for four days at Unalakleet, Alaska,
and the airplane sent to bring the performers out had to turn back
because of engine failure. The general consensus was that it would
have been more efficient to have traveled by dogsled. The final
performance in Anchorage was beamed live to forty stations on
the Armed Forces Radio Network. It was the first USO show to be
broadcast since a Bob Hope program nine years earlier. The forty-
nine day tour had covered more than 20,000 miles.

Nineteen sixty-nine was very special home season for Jelesnik.
In addition to his usual routine, he conducted a performance of the
Salt Lake Philharmonic for the grand opening and dedicatory
ceremonies of the new Salt Palace Arena. The concert took
place before a select audience of community leaders who were

instrumental in seeing the facility constructed. Jelesnik took great satisfaction in providing the music for the event. It was not only a great honor, but he suspected the new facility might probably put the Valley Music Hall out of business.

During the fall of 1969, Eugene led two separate USO tours. The first, "Mirth, Magic, and Music," began in September. This was a thirty-five-day tour through Vietnam and Thailand. Diana Hopperstad again joined the tour along with another Miss Idaho, Karen Ryder. Utah pianist Brent Johnston took the first of three tours with Jelesnik. The "Mirth" tour was followed by a *Utah Showcase* production, which also visited the Pacific bases.

The *Utah Showcase* performers included guitarist Larry Banks, on his second USO trip with Jelesnik; country-western duo John and Darlene Clayton; and once again, pianist Marilyn Laughlin. While the tour was billed as a *Utah Talent Showcase,* in fact a number of the performers were national winners of Ted Mack's *Amateur Hour* competition, including dancer/musician Linda Flitton of Calgary, Alberta, Canada; vocalist Claudia Soelberg of Idaho Falls; and tap dancer/juggler Carolyn Stockton of San Diego, California. If Jelesnik stretched the borders of the state to include the performers in *Utah Showcase,* it was still true that most of the performers were "Beehive State natives."

While the troupe was in Korea, Eugene appeared on that country's most popular TV show with Korean comedian Kwak Kyu-Suk. On Nationalist Chinese Taiwan they gave a "command performance" for Chinese officers and troops on the eve of a birthday observance for Dr. Sun Yat-Sen, founder of the Republic of China. The show was held in the theater of the high security compound of the Taipei Military Arsenal. So many Korean leaders were in attendance that authorities feared that the show invited assassination or worse. The performance was so exclusive that it was held in secret. Public mention of the event was withheld from the Taiwanese press until several days later, when the nationalist government authorized the publication of stories about the concert.

One serviceman stationed in Asia at the time was Sgt. Lyle J. Gurney of Big Piney, Wyoming, who said in a letter to the *Deseret*

News that he had seen the *Utah Showcase* troupe twice: "The same enthusiasm marks their performances, whether they are playing to several hundred or only a few. We in the military appreciate these troupes from home, even if the visits do make us homesick. They fill the void. One thing about troupes like this is they appear in places the groups headed by celebrities don't visit."

Each of the USO tours was unique. The circumstances of time and place were always different, and the individual performers made each tour special. But the travel was numbing, and Jelesnik's tours were so many and so frequent that they also began to blur together. Still there was something about each tour—an incident or a personality—that made it completely different from all the rest. Sometimes a tour was remembered for a celebrity or important personage who might have been encountered. Sometimes it was memorable because of a hardship or perhaps a special honor.

In 1970, Jelesnik headed up two more USO tours back-to-back. "Utah Showtime," an ensemble—with Brent Johnston, Diana Hopperstad, Ray Ball & Aggie Lee, Claudia Soelberg, and Shirley Stringham—spent ten weeks in the Mediterranean and Europe, from 20 July through 5 October. The European tour turned out to be one of the more difficult due to frequent schedule changes caused by aircraft breakdowns. At one point, a scheduled flight into Turkey had been canceled due to mechanical problems. The performers were flown to their next destination in a general's plane that happened to be piloted by Brigham Young University graduate Major William Hyde. Everywhere that Eugene went he kept running into Utahns, and like the fictional Forrest Gump, everyone seemed to know him. Many of these chance meetings were with *Talent Showcase* losing participants as well as the sons and daughters of people he knew in Salt Lake. "We played to 20,000 Dutch, Belgian, British, Canadian, German, Greek, and Turkish troops. We traveled 30,000 miles and gave 45 performances, many to isolated units. Since I returned, I have been busy calling parents and families of Utahns we met on the trip."[6]

One of the servicemen who Eugene met was an appreciative *Showcase* winner, Seaman Douglas McKendrick of Salt Lake City. Eugene was so relieved that Douglas was not another disappointed contestant that he got special permission from McKendrick's commanding officer to let him appear with Jelesnik in the shows. It was proof to everyone that *Showcase* winners actually existed in the military. McKendrick was assigned to the U. S. Naval Station in Rota, Spain, and while Eugene's USO unit was in the area, he made several appearances with the troupe in a comedy sketch.

No sooner had Eugene returned to the States than he began preparing for his next USO show, another 30,000-mile, five-week tour of Thailand and Vietnam. The show was once again dubbed "Mirth, Magic, and Melody," but it might just as well have been called "mud, misery, and mayhem." Johnston, Hopperstad, Karen Ryder, and Loya Bigler joined the tour. It would rival his experiences in Italy for danger. The tour took place during Vietnam's monsoon season, and the unit had to travel from base to base by helicopter. By 1970 all of Vietnam was a war zone, and any helicopter might become the target of hostile fire. On one occasion, the company was on its way to a performance when they found themselves in the middle of a typhoon. The helicopter was buffeted by high winds and the passengers were all terrified. They ended up being blown far off course and had to land at a forward position to wait out the storm. When the wind subsided, the chopper took off again, but they had to fly through another heavy rain squall to reach the place of their performance. The pilot later told Eugene that he believed they had also been fired on by the VC. Pianist Brent Johnston, formerly of Clinton, Utah, and by then the veteran of two previous USO tours, also recalled the helicopter experience, if not the enemy attack: "We waited for one and a half hours for the wind to die down," he told Howard Pearson in a *Deseret News* article published on 19 November 1970. "The craft was battered, but the men helped us put on three shows that day."

It rained through that entire tour, and the performers were so heavily scheduled there was no time to properly dry clothing or costumes, and both became mildewed from the damp. In his extensive collection of USO memorabilia, a series of photos show Jelesnik and Johnston busily sweeping water from their tent. In a personal letter from Jelesnik to Howard Pearson, excerpts of which were printed in the *Deseret News* on 9 November 1970, Eugene wrote: "We got caught in some rains. The water came into the building where I was sleeping and almost came up to the top of my bed. . . . About 3 A.M. I gave up and got permission to sleep outside in a truck."

Jelesnik and his "Mirth, Magic and Melody" tour were honored by the supreme commander of U. S. Armed Forces in Vietnam, General Creighton Abrams. The General entertained the performers in his villa in Siagon with a special four-hour dinner. At a time when Americans at home were protesting the war in Vietnam by the millions, the appearance of congenial civilians at the front was a welcome surprise, and Abrams heaped praise on the entertainers for the patriotic duty they were performing. Eugene's father would have loved the treatment. The servers and attendants waited on the diners hand and foot. General Abrams was added to Eugene's list of unlikely friends. The performers later received special citations from the General at a ceremony held before the troupe returned to the States.

Eugene scheduled two more back-to-back tours in 1971. Ever since he had trailed Marilyn Monroe's USO company in Korea back in 1953, he had known what GIs really wanted in a USO troupe. With the exception of Jelesnik, the "Utah Showtime" junket of 1971 was all-female. The tour visited widely scattered Pacific bases from 10 September through 2 December. Major Alfred C. Fisher, special services officer for the U. S. Eighth Army, reported how enthusiastically American servicemen and others received the mostly female troupe. "I can say, without hesitation, that this was the best show to tour Korea in a long, long time." Eugene's assessment of the soldiers taste in entertainment had been correct all along.

The tour attracted unusual attention from Korean officials. The opening show in Seoul was debuted in a special "Utah Showtime Six Star Salute" in the Chosun Hotel. The party was attended by South Korean President Park Chung-Hee and Gen. John H. Michaels, commander-in-chief of U. S. forces in Korea. Again, Eugene felt like he was visiting royalty. He obviously found this kind of treatment addicting. No sooner had the tour ended than he was back with another "Talent Showcase" company for a thirty-five-day trip to Vietnam and Thailand. In a little over one month they gave seventy-three performances for an estimated 35,000 servicemen. On several occasions in Vietnam the performers were traveling in military convoys that were halted for several hours by "VC activity up ahead." At the end of the tour, Eugene and his fellow entertainers received Bronze Service Medals and ribbons from the Republic of Vietnam, along with special certificates from the Department of Defense, which cosponsored the tour.

In October of 1971, Eugene brought Virginia to Tokyo for a short family reunion. The two toured the sights and took in a Kubuki play. They were only together for short periods of time, since Eugene was performing in the Tokyo area daily, and Virginia was only on a twenty-one-day packaged tour.

Eugene's 15th USO tour was inspired by the same sense of impeccable casting as "Utah Showtime." It also harkened back to Eugene's first marquee at the Hollywood Restaurant, thirty-seven years before. The all-female troupe was called "Girls, Girls, Girls!" The official USO shows announcement described the show as "a groovy variety show from Utah," although once again Eugene reached outside the state's borders. Though three of the five girls were from Utah, the other two were from Missouri and Arizona. The tour lasted seventeen weeks, from 28 September 1972, through the end of January. Members of this troupe were acrobatic contortionist Linda Almstedt of Salt Lake City; pianist/singer Connie Sommercorn, also of Salt Lake; pianist/vocalist Julia West of Nephi, Utah; baton twirler/singer/drummer Terri Ellen of St. Louis, Missouri; and guitarist/singer Sharon Tenney, who was a disc jockey at Ricks College. Almstedt and Sommercorn returned with Jelesnik the following year as part of "Utah Sunshine," a forty-two-day USO tour to the Pacific. Although this tour had been scheduled to end on 22 November, Eugene offered to extend the show a few weeks longer after he learned that no other USO shows had been booked in Korea and Japan during Christmas.

On 30 November 1972, the *Deseret News* published a short article about Eugene extending his tour. A reporter called Eugene's wife, Virginia, to ask her what she thought of the development. Her reply was revealing: "Eugene and I have had one Christmas and one Thanksgiving together in the past thirty-five years, but I am happy to have him entertain our servicemen if they are made happy, and I know they are because we have received many 'thank-you' letters."

To Carleen Hall, Virginia was more frank: "Eugene has his life, and I have mine."

Not all of Eugene's USO tours involved leading his musicians and performers into snow-covered Alaskan wastelands or sweltering, bug-infested Asian jungles. In July 1974, he led a small troupe of three performers (Linda Almstedt, Susan Ericksen, and Connie Sommercorn) on a twenty-one-day tour of the Caribbean. The tour included America's forty-four-square-mile bastion of Guantanamo on the communist island of Cuba. There were also stops at the exotic Caribbean ports in the British West Indies, Grand Turk Island, Antigua, and Camp Garcia at Vieques (Crab) Island. During the twenty-one-day excursion, the ensemble performed for 6,000 troops, including stops at seabee encampments, hospitals, and marine stations. This trip also earned the participants a "Certificate of Esteem" from the Department of Defense and a letter of commendation from Howard H. Callaway, Secretary of the Army.

Shortly after the tour ended, Jelesnik was honored on the steps of the United States Capitol building, where he was presented a special commendation by Senator Jennings Randolph of West Virginia as a highlight of the 1974 USO Shows committee meeting held in Washington, D.C.

In 1974, Jelesnik, Sommercorn, and Almstedt, along with USO newcomer Lisa MacGregor, took a sixty-three-day "Utah Sunshine" tour to military bases in Australia and across the Pacific. As he had before his first USO tour, Eugene also took the troupe to Veterans Administration hospitals in the San Francisco Bay area. In October of 1975, Jelesnik and three former USO tour comrades—Billie Loukas, Susan Ericksen, and Brent Johnston—were joined by another newcomer, Liz Fertitta, for a forty-six-day USO entertainment trip to Germany, Italy, and Iceland. With overseas military involvement winding down, Jelesnik took his next-to-last USO tour, dubbed "Mr. J's Jamboree," on a forty-two-day tour of American military bases in Korea, Japan, the Marshall Islands, and Hawaii. Pianist Brent Johnston, who probably accompanied Jelesnik on as many tours as any other single performer, was along once again, with Susan Ericksen, also a USO veteran, and three newcomers: dancer Bernice Santiago and pop music duo, Jackie Wood and Margie Christensen.

For this tour, the Jelesniks received one of the finest awards ever presented to them. This one was a special plaque for Jelesnik's wife, Virginia, "for your support of your husband's USO projects and for being so gracious in allowing him to make the tours."

Eugene Jelesnik's final USO tour, which also traveled under the title of "Mr. J's Jamboree," was a fifty-two-day tour (2 October to 22 November 1979) throughout the Pacific. This all-new, all-girl company took Jelesnik and his troupe on a 25,000-mile journey through Japan, Korea, Okinawa, the Marshall Islands, Midway, and Eniwetok Island. Performers on this landmark tour were pianist Jolene Dalton, dancer Shelly Cordova, vocalist Tammy Renstrom, and guitarist-singer Janet Love. Among the highlights of this tour was a stopover at the Fifth Air Force Headquarters at Yokota Air Base in Japan, where Jelesnik—usually on the receiving end of USO awards—presented a silver tray from the USO to Jimmie Fukuzaki, entertainment coordinator for U. S. forces in Japan. During Eugene's last tour of Korea, South Korean President, Park Chung Hee, was assassinated. President Park had been in attendance at a party in Seoul honoring Jelesnik's "Utah Showtime" tour back in 1971. The rest of the Korean tour was canceled.

On the return trip, Jelesnik and his troupe performed before one of the smallest audiences in his long history of mounting shows. There were only twenty-eight Coast Guard members at Loran Communications Station in the Marquis Islands. It took seven hours of flying just to reach the isolated base. There were actually forty-eight people in the audience. Twenty of them were Japanese personnel stationed there to assist the Coast Guard. "Mr. J's Jamboree" gave its farewell performance at the island of Eniwetok. Jelesnik was told that this would be the final performance by a USO troupe there. A few months later, possession of the island reverted to the natives.

Through sixteen consecutive years of touring for the USO, Jelesnik received hundreds of awards, plaques, certificates, medals, and letters of commendation. Almost every unit he performed for gave him something to remember them by. In 1973, Jelesnik received a Distinguished Service Award from the USO, as a way of honoring him for twenty-nine years of USO work. In 1974 Jelesnik was made a member of the USO's National Board of Governors, and later in the same year he was appointed chairman of the National USO Shows Committee. In 1974 the Department of the Army also honored the Maestro:

June 19, 1974

Dear Mr. Jelesnik:

I take great pleasure in transmitting to you the enclosed Certificate of Esteem which has been awarded you by the Department of Defense. This certificate is presented in gratitude for your entertainment tour of Armed Forces installations in the Pacific.

Entertainment from home is extremely popular with our servicemen and women throughout the world and is among the most effective of the recreational programs designed to stimulate and maintain high morale in the Armed Services.

It is hoped that this Certificate of Esteem will serve in some measure to express the deep appreciation of the Department of Defense for your generous contribution to this important program.

Sincerely yours,
Howard H. Callaway
Secretary of the Army

The Department of Defense
Presents This
Certificate of Esteem
to Eugene Jelesnik
Member of
"Utah Sunshine"
for Patriotic Service in Providing Entertainment

to Members of the Armed Forces in
the Pacific
During the Period
October 1973–January 1974

In 1978 Jelesnik received a National Council Special Award from the USO during the organization's national convention in San Antonio, Texas. He was named the recipient due to his "outstanding contributions to the cause of USO and for distinguished service to the men and women of the armed forces." The award was a national honor and was signed by President Jimmy Carter. It also gave Eugene some much-needed "local" recognition:

Dear Friend:

I was pleased to note you were honored by President Carter at the White House last week for your most outstanding work with the USO. This is a well deserved honor, and it is good to see this recognition come to you.

The festivities in Washington sounded exciting, and I certainly hope you enjoyed being there.

All of us at Bonneville International Corporation send best wishes to you and Virginia for continuing success and happiness.

Cordially,
Bonneville International Corporation
Arch L. Madsen, President

On 11 February 1980, the United States Congress granted a Congressional Charter to the USO. It was only the third charter Congress had granted any independent agency in the previous ten years and was a testament to the stature that the organization had achieved. Much of the credit went to Eugene Jelesnik. In recognition of his efforts, Jelesnik was awarded the USO's National Council Special Award for his thirty-four years of service.

Jelesnik's USO troupes spanned three major wars and more than three decades, bringing local and national talent to active servicemen stationed everywhere from European foxholes to sweltering Asian jungles and frigid Alaskan outposts. The exact numbers he entertained is unknown and the miles he traveled impossible to compute, but Jelesnik racked up more USO miles than Bob Hope and/or any other big-name celebrity. Furthermore, Jelesnik was not reluctant to trek into the hinterlands. Many of the more famous performers would visit the major bases, but not the small, out-of-the-way sites. No post or encampment was too small or too remote for Jelesnik and his troupers, who brought a little bit of "home" to lonely military personnel.

In addition to the many ribbons and medals from both houses of Congress and the various branches of the military, Eugene received special recognition on the occasion of the USO's 40ᵗʰ anniversary. A story by United Press International writer Peter Gillins, filed on 4 February 1981, opened with the following: "Entertainment provided by the USO isn't always Bob Hope and pretty girls singing and dancing on the flight deck of an aircraft carrier. Sometimes it's Eugene Jelesnik and his violin, entertaining half a dozen airmen in a radar dome in the wilds of Alaska."

The story recapped Eugene's entire career with the USO, including his encounter with the minefield in Italy and his tours to Korea and Vietnam. The story appeared in 110 newspapers in twenty-nine states.

One of Eugene Jelesnik's friends and colleagues during his long association with USO was Josie Morse, a Filipina, who helped coordinate all of the logistics involved with moving USO troupes around the vast Pacific command. "The troops just loved him especially when he played something classical then went into the 'Orange Blossom Special.'" She said that Jelesnik's shows would not only hit the major posts, but could also be sent to small, isolated islands and onto ships deployed in the Indian Ocean. Josie first met Eugene in 1964, and they maintained a friendship long after Jelesnik's USO touring days were over. Her most vivid memory of Jelesnik was also the most touching: "I would stop at his dressing room and find him with the case of his treasured Amati violin open. There was a photograph of his dear Virginia glued to the inside of the case, and Eugene would talk to her photograph before every performance."

HONOR, TRIUMPH, AND TRAGEDY

From the time that Eugene Jelesnik first arrived in the Salt Lake Valley, he had enjoyed a close relationship with the leaders of The Church of Jesus Christ of Latter-day Saints. The first serving President he met was Heber J. Grant who was introduced to Eugene by Guy Toombes at the Hotel Utah in 1939. From 1947 on, Eugene's work on the annual Days of '47 celebration gave him the opportunity of meeting many Church leaders. Through the years, LDS Presidents were frequently called upon to deliver prayers or appear at important Days of '47 events, and Eugene was invariably on the podium.

Over the years Jelesnik had also lent his talents to many events in the Church's behalf. In 1951 he produced a variety show as a benefit fund-raiser for the 15th Ward.[1] The proceeds went to purchase a new carpet for the ward's chapel. He would perform for many such events through the years, both for charity fund-raisers and other Church-sponsored causes. He collected many letters from Church leaders thanking him for his help. His Salt Lake Philharmonic Pops Concerts usually kicked off the public celebration of the Days of '47, and LDS Church leaders were routinely in attendance. President George Albert Smith, who headed the Church from 1945 to 1951, attended Jelesnik's concerts at the Assembly Hall on Temple Square.[2] Eugene worked closely with President Smith's daughter for several years in charity drives for the polio foundation, and Eugene remembers meeting the President many times, once with many members of the Smith family at a reception in his daughter's home following one of the fund-raisers.

But it was President Smith's successor, David O. McKay, who would first befriend the Jewish maestro. President McKay had once been a musician himself. As a young man he had studied the piano and had even performed with his hometown orchestra in Huntsville, Utah.[3] He also enjoyed singing and all forms of orchestral and choir music. President McKay's keen interest in civic affairs brought him to many events and meetings where Eugene, or his orchestra, provided the music. It was inevitable that the two men would get to know each other. It was during this period that Eugene began putting together special Pops Concerts for LDS conference weekends. In later years Eugene would frequently play his violin for President McKay and the prophet's wife, Emma Ray, at their anniversary celebrations and birthday parties. Jelesnik also met and worked with many of President McKay's counselors. When Eugene and his orchestra performed for the opening of the amphitheater in Zion National Park in 1963, President N. Eldon Tanner gave the dedicatory address.

Jelesnik was also well-acquainted with President McKay's successor, Joseph Fielding Smith. President Smith's wife, Jessie Evans Smith, was a frequent soloist with the Salt Lake Philharmonic Orchestra. In July of 1968, while Joseph Fielding Smith was serving as First Counselor to President David O. McKay, Mrs. Smith sang two songs under Eugene's direction: "Let There Be Peace on Earth," and "Such Lovely Things." Three years later, after her husband had received the mantle of the Presidency, she sang the songs again for the Pops Concert on 13 July 1971. It was most unusual for the wife of a serving Prophet to perform in public, outside of religious services, and Eugene felt doubly honored by her return appearance. But even Eugene was startled when at the Days of '47 concert at Highland High School, Jessie brought the President on stage to sing with her.

Jelesnik also got to meet many future LDS leaders during this time, including Elders Harold B. Lee, Spencer W. Kimball, and Gordon B. Hinckley, who would all become close friends of Eugene's. He also met future President Ezra Taft Benson at various governmental functions and patriotic events during the time when Benson was serving as Secretary of Agriculture in the

Eisenhower cabinet. He, too, attended Days of '47 Pops Concerts and rodeos. President Benson's daughter Barbara, a professional singer, made several guest appearances on Eugene's television shows.

Jelesnik recalled one specific occasion when President Spencer W. Kimball called Eugene up personally and requested that Jelesnik come play for his birthday party as he had for President McKay's. This was a command performance, and Eugene considered it a great honor. The party was held at President Kimball's home, and Eugene spent an entire afternoon with the Kimball family as the President and his wife greeted guests.[4]

Eugene's relationship with the leaders of The Church of Jesus Christ of Latter-day Saints has been lengthy and somewhat unique. Through his community involvement there have been many occasions when he has shared the podium or otherwise been involved with the Presidents of the Church and other General Authorities. Eugene is a sentimental and loyal man—traits that make him easy to know and to like, and his dealings with the LDS leaders have been marked by mutual respect and genuine friendship.

In an interview with *Deseret News* writer Ivan Lincoln, Ringling Brothers Barnum & Bailey Circus managing director and publicist Bill Powell told the story of his first encounter with the man who seemed to have access to the Church office building.[5]

"The year was 1977, and the circus was performing at the Salt Palace. Several LDS performers were with Ringling Brothers at the time, including Ringmaster, Tim Holst, and a girl in 'clown alley,' Peggy Williams. These performers called me and told me that since they were going to be in Salt Lake they would like to arrange a tour of the Tabernacle and the Church Office Building if that was at all possible. They said that there were other LDS members with the circus and since they would be in the 'Mormon Mecca' for several days, they wondered if some kind of brief tour could be arranged. Jelesnik, who handled the music for the circus at that time, had told me, 'If there is anything you need, anything at all, you call me first!'

"So I called Eugene to see if Jelesnik knew what the procedures were for taking tours of the Tabernacle and the Church

Office Building. I was just calling to get the number of someone to call and I fully expected to make the arrangements myself.

Powell remembered what happened next: "Eugene said: 'Bill, why do you need to call anybody? I'll take care of it. It's done!' I said, 'I really don't expect you to set all of this up. There's probably going to be six or seven people at least who will want to go.' 'No, no, no. No worry, no worry. It's done, It's done. What day do you guys want to go see it?'

"I told him the days that the circus would be there, but I said, 'Listen, they may be busy over there, and may have certain days for tours.' He said, 'You tell me what day you want to go and it's done.' So I said, 'Okay, let's try Friday morning.' And he said, 'Now, you want to meet President Kimball, right?' And I laughed and said, 'Well, I don't really think they expect anything like that.' 'It's done, believe me. He'll see you,' Eugene said. I said, 'Okay.'

"I called back to the performers and got a hold of Tim, and I said, 'Hey, they've got this tour arranged. It's for Friday morning, and you're going to meet over at the old Church Office Building. You go there. There's a reception desk to the right, and we'll be escorted back to see President Kimball.' And he said, 'What? We're going to see the Prophet?' And I said, 'Yeah, according to the guy who set it up. It's been arranged.' (Powell was beginning to think that he had been fed a line and began to hedge his bets.)

"I told him, 'Now I don't know if this guy was boasting or not, but I'm sure you'll be able to get into the Office Building and have a tour there at least.' And Tim said, 'Oh, this is great,' and they were all elated. So, sure enough, Friday morning, we get up and we go over there. And we go into this office building, and I remember there is this little reception area over to the right. And I remember distinctly there were some guys with little things in their ears like security radios. And then this gentleman comes out, very nice, greets everyone and says, 'Come back with me and we'll start our tour.'

"And so we get up to follow him and we're going down corridors and hallways and we get sort of in the back corner of the building, and there's a long hallway and there was this little door at the end of the hallway. And it was open and there stands this little elderly guy in his late seventies with white hair. And Tim and Peggy were, like, almost trembling to tears. And I knew something major was happening with them. We proceeded on in, and Eugene was at the front of the line, and all of a sudden, President Kimball said, 'Eugene! How are you doing?' And Eugene walks up there and they embrace and hug and kiss each other on the cheek. And President Kimball says, 'Eugene, you never call me. How come I hear from you so little?' And he starts talking about a party where Eugene played the violin for his daughter. He said, 'You know, my daughter loved the piece. We really do want you to come back in a couple of weeks for something else. And it really was delightful. But you know, you really have to keep in touch with me more often. I just like to hear from you.'

"So by now I'm going, my gosh, this is tremendous. And so Eugene waves us in and we have this very gracious visit, and Tim Holst and Peggy were so elated, and I remember that President Kimball had these huge elephant tusks in his office that were given to him by Church members from Africa. And he went over to them and explained everything about all the gifts that have been given to him from people around the world. And we stayed there for, I would say, forty-five minutes. And he asked everyone with our group what they did and how they came to work for the circus and what they liked about it—just a very warm and nice visit. Then we get up and our visit is over and we get ready to go and he shakes everybody's hand, very cordial. Eugene was at the end of the line, and he grabs Eugene and he hugs him and kisses him again. And he says, 'Now don't you be so scarce. You should call me more often.'"[6]

The Presidents of the LDS Church were not the only ones who thought Jelesnik was special. In 1982 he was honored by the Valley Forge Freedoms Foundation who awarded him the George Washington Medal for Achievement. In May of 1983, the Exchange Club awarded him its highest honor, The Golden Deeds Award for "Entertaining servicemen, for his patriotism, and for working with youth through *Talent Showcase*." In November of the same year, the Salt Lake Valley Convention and Visitors Bureau gave him a special award "for his many years of dedicated service to the youth of Salt Lake City." In 1985, in a surprise presentation at the April 5th Pops Concert, Eugene was presented with a crystal statue by the Z.C.M.I. Merchants Association and Zions Security Corporation. The certificate, which accompanied the statue, read: "In recognition of your many years of service to the community and to the state." Eugene was not only collecting awards and honors, but he was also getting an enormous amount of publicity. A full page article by *Deseret News* drama critic and entertainment editor Howard Pearson on 23 January 1981, painted an endearing picture of one of Utah's most recognizable characters.

> He can walk a block on Main Street and have twenty out of twenty-two persons he passes shout hello. He can walk down State Street on his way home and a bus will pull over to an empty spot in the middle of a block so he can catch a ride. Experimental television programming started forty-seven years ago. He has been a performer on the tube for almost forty-seven years.
>
> The man is Eugene Jelesnik—impresario, promoter, violinist, orchestra conductor, television producer, performer, and well-known man about town.
>
> The bus incident comes about because he doesn't drive. He never has. He rides buses a lot. Most of the drivers on his route know him. If the traffic isn't heavy and they see him walking south on State about Fourth South, they will pull over and he then becomes a paying customer. He also rides taxicabs quite often and when he calls a cab to his home, he usually gets one within five or ten minutes.
>
> The reason he doesn't drive dates back to his childhood. When he started taking violin lessons, when he was nine or ten years old, his parents told him not to drive a car because he might injure his hands. They also told him not to play baseball because he might break his fingers. "I kept the warnings in my head," he says. "I just never had a desire to drive a car and I didn't care if I ever played baseball. When I got married in my early 20s, my bride drove, so I had no desire nor urge to drive. She tried to teach me to drive once, but decided it would be better if I carried the thing no further."

While Pearson heaped praise on Eugene for his many contributions to Salt Lake City, he did not forget Virginia. The article not

only outlined Eugene's life and career but duly credited Virginia
for her contribution:

> With his marriage to Virginia, he changed twenty-four years
> of being dominated by his mother to forty-two years of being
> dominated by his wife, according to Virginia.
>
> Just how much of a part she plays in his life is shown by the
> fact that they pay cash for everything they buy. "I used to not
> budget money or worry about it," Gene says. "Virginia has
> made me conscious of money. The only thing we didn't pay
> cash for was our home on Coatsville Avenue. When we bought
> the house, Virginia said we were not to take a pleasure trip until
> it was paid for. We didn't, not even as far as Murray."
>
> Virginia has always assisted him with bookings, at concerts,
> and with his television programs, for which she is his
> accompanist. The association between the two apparently has
> been ideal. For their 25th wedding anniversary, he turned over
> the keys for a new car for her as a present in a ceremony we
> attended at the Cinegrill. She knows where he is every hour.
> "I'm not being an interfering wife," she says, and he agrees.
> "His business connections and calls make this necessary."
>
> Gene calls Virginia "Muggsy," the reason for which, he says,
> is lost in time.[7]

The evening before their 44th wedding anniversary, 4 July 1982,
"Muggsy" wrote Eugene a long letter celebrating their life
together. In it she described in detail their long love affair, their difficult early days, and her hopes for the future. It had been a continuous struggle, but it was clear that she didn't regret any of it."[8]

> . . . Eugene, I wonder how much of our years come back to
> you as you recall your US tour, meeting Sid Fox, meeting Peg,
> meeting Uncle Grover, and packing your bags for an overseas
> tour, your fall in the Excelsior Hotel, your return to New York,
> your trip to Utah. After 37 years here it's not easy to wonder
> how we landed and we have been in this home 32 years. The
> day before July 4, 1982, we have a small leak in the bathroom.
> I'm sure you could say our personal problems are few,
> considering we have money to pay our bills.
>
> I thought of Frances Orlob, alone in a rented apartment. We
> must be thinking of our years ahead, deeply, well-planned and
> knowing we cannot count on anyone but ourselves. All I ask is

that I can stay here for a while to hold down the routine. I know you will think and plan your days and save your energies so you can have another good concert and carry out your commitments we have scheduled until October.

I hope we can rest, keep cool, and get this place in order so you'll be organized for September and get your county fair job over, and most of all plan a vacation at home. Dull as it may seem, I can not think of a better place to relax. We may have time to think, recount our affairs, and make a safe plan for our years ahead. Slow down when you can realize how hard we have worked to get this far. Forty-four years is a lot of time and experience.

It's getting late now, 5:30 A.M. I awakened at three. It's been a nice visit and a good recall. When you remember Arthur Weiner and Rudy Van Gelder, Dorothy and Bert Wishnew, Sid Fox, Horace Sorensen, Grant McFarlane, and of course our mothers, your aunt, and Louise, Mimi, Dad, my brother Ed, Rolland, and Chris and realize we are still here, still alive and have so much more to do.

Be thankful for all the good people that you have for friends, Arch Madsen, all the people at KSL, Art Jones, Barbara Busby, and the people you count on to help you make this year's responsibilities the easiest, and the smoothest.

Go to Vegas, see what you can do about that change.

Be thankful for your health and take care to keep that blood pressure under control. I will enjoy the day of July 5, 1982 knowing all is well here if we determine to accept our ages and take life in stride.

I look forward to a year at a time from now on. Let's keep well and be happy. I love you and appreciate that you have been recognized for your best efforts to make a good honest living.

Make the most of your years ahead, stay well, and keep aware and remember the price we paid to be us. Love to you and my deepest thoughts on our 44th Anniversary and my 77th year, Wow!

What more can we expect?

Love, Mugs.

Virginia's letter was ten pages long. In addition to her pleas that Eugene take better care of himself and watch his blood pressure, she also touched on her own recent health problems. Virginia had trouble with her back and her legs for many years. She had always attributed the onset of her back pain to the incident when she was run down by a reckless bicyclist in the Wyoming town shortly after they were married. But Virginia also had trouble with the circulation in her legs and feet. In 1973 she was given emergency femoral bypass surgery. The procedure was not entirely successful and after that her mobility was restricted. She also suffered from the onset of osteoporosis. She had been hospitalized after a bad fall in 1978, and at the time she wrote the anniversary letter to Eugene four years later, she was still recovering. One line is particularly telling: "All I ask is that I can stay here for a while to hold down the routine." Virginia was very much afraid of being sent to the hospital, and was letting her husband know it. But Virginia's bones were so fragile that she might break them with the slightest strain. In a letter to Carleen Hall, written about the same time, Virginia complained that her back and legs hurt so much that she was hardly able to function. She wrote: "My windows are a disgrace, but I can no longer do much housework."

In April of 1984, Jelesnik was the subject of a special program on KSL Channel 5's *Prime Time Access* with Bruce Lindsay. The entire half-hour program was dedicated to his life and career. Lindsay not only put the spotlight on Eugene, but paid special tribute to Virginia. In an article about the program, Howard Pearson of the *Deseret News* wrote:

> Virginia has been his "woman Friday" through most of his entertainment work. She has kept track of his goings and comings and knows where he is at nearly every moment. He carries a beeper so she can get in touch with him. Even when he walks downtown streets at too fast a pace for others to follow him, Virginia is able to contact him to let him know so-and-so is on the telephone or that a producer will call him at a particular time. Virginia also has shown up at most of the programs for which Eugene has been sponsor and made sure everything in the seating area was in good shape. She is also the accompanist for his talent search shows.

Lindsay's *Prime Time Access* program featured many highlights from Eugene's thirty-two years with the Days of '47. The program also presented scenes from Eugene's early days in television, including a segment from *Music Hall Varieties*, which Lindsay said "proved Jelesnik had invented music video." While the claim was tongue-in-cheek, the program was a loving tribute to Eugene's fifty-two years of work in television and showed scenes from Jelesnik's appearance on Kate Smith's national broadcast and scenes from *Talent Showcase* and *Ted Mack's Original Amateur Hour*.

In September of 1984, Eugene's good friend and most recent publicist Howard Pearson of the *Deseret News* died. At the funeral, Eugene played some of Pearson's favorite selections from "The Sound of Music." The heartfelt performance was cathartic for all the mourners, including Jelesnik, who wept openly. In attendance at the funeral was President Thomas S. Monson. President Monson was deeply moved by Eugene's playing and noted the similar effect that his performance had on the Pearson family. After the service was over, he introduced himself to Eugene and told him how much he appreciated his playing. The two men had known each other from a distance for some time, but afterward were very close friends. Years later in a fete honoring Jelesnik, President Monson would recall that day: "He notices the unnoticed, and he befriends those who really need friends. I think he never does so well with his violin as when he's honoring someone who has passed away, when he conveys his condolences to the family through the medium of music.

"I heard him play for the funeral services for Howard Pearson, his long-time friend. And he had tears in his eyes when he said 'Howard loved "The Sound of Music."'" And then Eugene played a medley from the musical. And I think it brought as much comfort to that family as any spoken word. God in his heaven seemed particularly close that day." President Monson concluded his remarks by reciting these lines:

> *How far is heaven?*
> *It's not very far.*
> *For people like Gene,*
> *It's right where you are.*[9]

In the mid 1980s, Jelesnik used his Days of '47 Pops Concerts to highlight the music of Rubens Marshall, a black immigrant composer and pianist from Brazil. Rubens had been blind since birth, and the story of his life and his struggle to escape the poverty of his native province of Minas Gerais and the slums of São Paulo moved Jelesnik deeply. Like Marshall, Jelesnik was an immigrant, and like the Brazilian composer, Eugene had endured much in his youth. But Eugene couldn't imagine what it would be like to be afflicted with blindness as well. One of Marshall's compositions, "I Am Now an American Citizen," was composed as a tribute to his adopted country, to Ellis Island, and to the Statue of Liberty. Jelesnik enthusiastically took on the project of scoring the composition for the Salt Lake Philharmonic. "I Am Now an American Citizen" was performed at the Salt Palace during the Days of '47 Pops Concert on 10 July 1985 and 9 July 1986. The narration was written by Gerald McDonough, and was read by Art Lund in 1985 and by Utah's Governor Norman Bangerter in 1986.

Jelesnik continued to garner awards and honors, but the 1980s were a period of transition for the Maestro. In October of 1986, after a thirty-one-year run, *Talent Showcase* aired for the last time. It was the longest running locally originated entertainment program in television history. In making the announcement, William R. Murdoch, vice president and general manager of KSL, pointed out that more that 10,000 performers had appeared on the program over the years. Although Jelesnik's weekly time slot was gone, he continued his association with KSL. Murdoch simultaneously announced that "Jelesnik will assume expanded responsibilities as the station's musical director and talent coordinator of KSL. For some time the station has been planning projects to enhance its role in the community. Because of his years of experience as a musician, composer, conductor, and producer, Mr. Jelesnik's role in these plans is considered invaluable."

The Days of '47 celebration was also going through changes. Big-name country stars who had been the centerpiece for the rodeo—including such Nashville celebrities as Rex Allen Jr., Dottie West, and Judy Lynn—now preferred performing in a full-fledged concert to merely working an intermission break between the

Brahma bull riding and steer wrestling events. It was getting more difficult to bring big stars to the celebration. Those who did come often did so only because of Eugene Jelesnik. Over the previous forty years he had served as energetic supporter, volunteer, committee member, board member, and first vice president of Utah's biggest celebration. It would not have been much of a party without Jelesnik's help, and this was increasingly clear to everyone, including Utah's politicians.

On Friday, 17 March 1989, Utah Governor Norman Bangerter formally rechristened that St. Patrick's Day as "Eugene Jelesnik Day in Utah." The proclamation was the third such honor that Eugene had been given by a Utah governor. Following the reading of the proclamation, Jelesnik was given a special reception in KSL Television, Studio A. Maestro Jelesnik was lauded as "a paragon of the State of Utah." The news broadcast that day said: "This special day was declared to honor KSL's talent show host for his long and devoted contribution to the State of Utah and to Mountain America's field of television." Don Glen, KSL television commentator, read the Governor's proclamation at the KSL reception.

The commendation spoke of Jelesnik's *Talent Showcase* production, which had provided opportunities to talented youngsters for over thirty-one years. The proclamation said in part: "The Jelesniks have offered Utah's youngsters opportunities they might have otherwise never experienced." KSL Vice President, William R. Murdoch, presented Eugene with a plaque commemorating his work at KSL. In addition, the Maestro was honored for reaching another milestone in his personal life. The 19th of March was his 75th birthday. During the reception Jelesnik was congratulated by many dignitaries, including: President Monson, Mr. and Mrs. Arch Madsen of Bonneville International, and Ron Brady and Bill Murdoch of KSL-TV. Tributes included seventy-five balloons from Bill Powell, director of public relations for the Ringling Brothers Barnum and Bailey Circus, as well as cards, cakes, and gifts from a large number of well-wishers. There was even a box of succulent beef fillets. The plaque presented to Eugene from KSL-TV read: "To Maestro Eugene Jelesnik, one of Utah's natural treasures. In appreciation of your many years of unselfish service to Mountain America and KSL-TV. Happy 75th Birthday."

On 15 April 1990, *The Salt Lake Tribune* announced that Eugene Jelesnik was being honored again. The paper reported that he was to be the recipient of the prestigious "Honors in the Arts Award" given by the Salt Lake Chamber of Commerce. Others honored included Joseph Silverstein, conductor of the Utah Symphony, Ed Gryska, founder of the Salt Lake Acting Company, and Delmont Oswald, director of the Utah Humanities Council. Jelesnik's citation read in part: "[He] is one of the state's most celebrated and decorated citizens, one who has enhanced the arts in Utah for generations. The Russian-born musician is permanent conductor of the Salt Lake Philharmonic Orchestra. He also is credited for starting hundreds of Utah entertainers on their show business careers through his efforts on KSL's *Talent Showcase.* Under Jelesnik's direction, the Salt Lake Philharmonic Orchestra presents pops concerts free of charge to the general public as a way for Utahns to experience the joy of music without financial restraints."

Virginia took another bad fall in 1987, and this time she became completely bedridden. It now seems likely that she may have fractured her hip. But having already been told that the brittleness of her bones would preclude further operations, Virginia refused to have anyone come in to look at her. While she continued for a time to act as Eugene's answering service, she began to withdraw from the world beyond the walls of the house on Coatsville Avenue. She wrote Carleen Hall that she was "in bed trying to rest my back." She usually closed her letters to her friend with a personal note, but this time it ended with a certain finality: "I am as always thinking of you, Love always, Virginia."

In one of her last telephone conversations with Carleen she said: "Don't let just anybody get their clutches on Eugene. They'll kill him." Shortly after that she abruptly ended the relationship, and Carleen didn't know why. But it was the beginning of a pattern. Virginia soon severed her social contacts with everyone she had known. Eugene remembered that she had lost circulation in one leg and was afraid that the doctors might amputate it. She was also terrified that she might be put in a rest home. Leaving the house that she had called home for more than thirty-seven years was unthinkable. As with all aged, there was always the dread that the ride to the rest home would be her last. Whatever her fears, she refused to see a doctor or anyone who might take her from her home. She controlled her pain without drugs and with no more anesthetic than her considerable powers of mind and determination.

From 1987 through August 1992, Virginia did not leave her bed. She steadfastly refused to see a doctor and would not have a nurse or anyone else brought in the house to care for her. This meant that her husband who was nine years younger would have to do all the nursing. During that five- or six-year period of time, Eugene supplied her every need. Most of the year he was able to care for her with twice daily trips back home, but once a year Eugene had to attend a three-day talent convention in Las Vegas to book performers for the Utah State Fair. During these periods he flew to Nevada in the morning, flew back again at night, and repeated the long-distance commute the following day and then the next. While he was gone he left four electric coffee pots brewing beside the bed as well as a generous supply of cookies, cheese, and other snacks. It is hard to imagine the conditions in which the Jelesniks were living, and harder still to comprehend why they did not seek outside help. Carleen Hall, who was shut off from the Jelesniks during this period, believed that Virginia just didn't want anyone to see her in her final decline. But the ordeal would last for five difficult years. Of that period Carleen would later say in amazement: "Virginia wasn't just bedridden part of the time! She didn't get out of that bed, period! You can't imagine in your worst nightmares what it must have been like caring for her like that. What they must have endured together. All her personal needs, her food, toilet, everything. Its unimaginable that he could do it for a few months. But this went for five years!"

Carleen could not understand any of it. But for Eugene, the obligation to care for Virginia according to her wishes was more important than his own comfort. He had learned from an early age the necessity of enduring the unendurable. The two years he spent living in the tiny darkened room in Alexandrovsk with his mother and aunt had taught him that suffering and endurance went hand in hand. From the first decade of his life he had also learned that survival was often a matter of self-reliance, and self-reliance was something that Virginia insisted upon. Carleen Hall once said that she had never witnessed a man and woman treat each other with the degree of mutual respect and dignity as did the Jelesniks. They had vowed to care for each other in sickness and in health, for better and for worse. For Eugene it was time to show that those vows were not merely words.

As he had his entire life, Eugene kept his mind focused on the tasks that had to be done. There was no longer any time to plan very far ahead. The immediate needs of Virginia took every free moment of the present. Less important things would just have to be set aside. But there was a price to pay for this increasingly demanding concession to immediate necessity. Specifically, since neither Eugene nor Virginia ever threw anything out, the past was quickly catching up with him and was overtaking the present. The piles of USO plaques, the awards, certificates, and framed letters of appreciation, the performance contracts, record albums, concert programs, and pile after pile of Eugene's orchestrations and music gradually filled room after room until, near the end, they had swallowed up every conceivable foot of usable floor space. There was literally no place to stand or to sit, and Eugene was eventually relegated to sleeping in a tiny corner of his bed.

Virginia Belle Washburn Jelesnik died the morning of 31 August 1992. The funeral was held on Friday, September 4th at the Salt Lake Mausoleum overlooking 11th Avenue, on the city's north bench. The service was conducted by Eugene's great friend Floyd "Flip" Harmon, who had served with Eugene on the Days of '47 committee for decades. Speakers included clothier Mac Christensen and President Thomas S. Monson. Billie Loukas sang at the service. She was accompanied by pianist Bob Davis. Virginia's obituary noted that she had been a constant companion to her husband for fifty-three years and had worked side by side with him in all his endeavors, including his musical and theatrical presentations. At the time of her death, Virginia was eighty-seven years old.

After Virginia's death, Eugene tried to recover some of the ground he had lost over the previous five years. As he had following the death of his mother, he threw himself into his work with renewed ardor, as if ceaseless activity was the antidote to grief. The first concert after Virginia died was the annual Holiday Pops, which in 1992 was held at the Marriott Hotel the day after Thanksgiving. On the holiday itself Eugene had played the violin for four hours straight at the University Park Hotel. The following morning he went to the Marriott Hotel and spent the entire day setting up sound, lights, and staging for the concert he would conduct in the evening. Eugene was long accustomed to booking himself into such schedules. But he was no longer the young man that he used to be, and the strain was beginning to take its toll. Eugene always put a lot of physical energy into his conducting and that evening he pushed himself to the limit. Carleen Hall attended the concert and noted that Eugene seemed at the brink of exhaustion. After the show was over she went up to the Maestro and told him she enjoyed the concert, but she also told him that he didn't look well, and asked him, "Eugene, how is your blood pressure?"

The inquiry was met with an instant rebuff. "What do you know about my blood pressure?" he said and then walked off in a huff. Jelesnik had no idea what his blood pressure was, but he did know that Carleen was right about one thing, he was not well. That evening he was so tired after the show that he couldn't even make it to his driver's car to get home. He got a room in the hotel and collapsed onto the bed. He would stay at the hotel until he was strong enough to go home.

Within a few weeks Jelesnik was back to his heavy schedule. He kept all of his commitments and gave close attention to his new duties at KSL. All the while the honors and awards continued to roll in. On 1 February 1993, the Utah State Legislature passed a resolution honoring Eugene, noting he has made "incalculable contributions to the musical culture of the State of Utah and its citizens, and remains a warm, active, and kind friend of Utah and its people." The resolution praised "his decades of service—enriching the lives of Utahns through his love of music." He was cited for "his tireless contribution of music to the people of Utah."

The three and a half pages of text filled with "whereas's" applauded Jelesnik for his compositions, his concerts with the Salt Lake Philharmonic Orchestra, his forty-six years of Utah television programs, his nineteen USO tours, and the aid he had given to thousands of aspiring entertainers over the thirty-one-year run of *Talent Showcase*. The ceremonies were held on the Senate floor during a regular morning session. One of the sidelights was a brief speech by Senator Delpha Baird who rose and claimed the right of personal privilege to say: "I must confess that almost forty years ago I was a contestant on Eugene Jelesnik's *Talent Showcase*." The main speech of the day was given by Eugene's friend President Thomas S. Monson, who said in part:

> President [Arnold] Christensen and distinguished senators. I'm honored today to be in this historic chamber and add my voice to your resolution and to the expressions others have given pertaining to Eugene Jelesnik. I've know Eugene for many years, and whether he's wearing that big ten-gallon hat for the Days of '47 celebration, or his coat of many colors when he performs on stage with the baton in his hand, he is truly loved by this community and all who have had an opportunity to interface with him. As I think of you, Eugene, I think of the expression given of Jesus of Nazareth when it was said of him— "He went about doing good." Eugene Jelesnik goes about "doing good," in every climate, in every season, and I would like you, Eugene, to know that we all appreciate you and your talents. But more particularly, the manner in which you serve others. I know that if others in this community could stand here they would join me in an expression of gratitude to you for your selfless devotion. You are truly a state treasure. And I feel I speak in behalf of Virginia, your companion who passed away last year, . . . and all with whom you've associated through the years. This is a wonderful honor accorded to you, Eugene, by the Utah Senate, and I thank them for it, and I thank heaven above for you and your service.[10]

On 12 July 1993, Eugene Jelesnik and the Salt Lake Philharmonic Orchestra presented its final Pops Concert at the Salt Palace. The concert paid tribute to the community leaders who had been instrumental in getting the facility built, including Jack

Gallivan, James E. Hogle, Gus Backman, and President David O. McKay. The project had been bitterly opposed by some, including J. Bracken Lee, but without the Salt Palace there would have been no Utah Stars professional basketball franchise, no Golden Eagles, no Utah Jazz, and perhaps no suitable venue for Jelesnik's Pop Concerts. Salt Lake City would have been culturally impoverished and a much different place without it. Jelesnik recognized the incredibly important role that the Salt Palace had played in the cultural life of the community. He felt an urgency to honor the people who had been responsible for it before they were gone and before the structure itself was torn down. A quarter of a century earlier, Jelesnik and his Philharmonic musicians performed for a grand opening banquet in what was then considered to be a state-of-the-art arena. By the early 1990s, the building had become obsolete and inadequate and was seismically unstable. The decision to build the larger Delta Center meant that the Salt Palace was destined for the wrecking ball. But the Salt Palace would not be torn down without an appropriate send-off.

Jelesnik put in long hours on the program. He once again engaged Gerald McDonough to work the script and brought in Utah Jazz coach and team president Frank Layden to deliver the narration. Guest artists included longtime Philharmonic soloists Billie Loukas and local baritone Cliff Cole. The concert also featured headliner artists Jack Imel, formerly of the *Lawrence Welk Show,* and Dolores Park who had performed with Bob Hope. In addition to the Salt Lake Philharmonic, the program included a performance by Jerry Floor's "Touch of Greece Combo." The program was exceptionally hard to mount and provided the added headache of a complicated slide show. Eugene had always burned the candle at both ends, but his schedule that week was particularly taxing. Carleen Hall had been hospitalized with food poisoning earlier in the week, and he had visited her repeatedly in the hospital. There were problems with the sound and lighting systems, and the dress rehearsal was a nightmare. The day of the concert, he had gone to the airport to meet friends and performers who were flying in for the show that evening. The plane was late and there were delays in getting the baggage. The show was scheduled to start in less than three hours, and he still hadn't picked up his costume or made the final sound checks. Still, he took his friends to dinner before returning to the Salt Palace. This time he was trying to do too much. The last hour before the show was hectic even for Jelesnik and everyone noticed the strain. But somehow, as always, he pulled it off, and the concert was a huge success. When it was over, Carleen Hall brought Eugene a large bouquet of roses. His response was almost as abrupt as it had been when she asked him about his blood pressure six months before: "What are you doing here?" he asked.[11]

In the hallway near his dressing room after the concert, an exhausted Eugene Jelesnik was talking with Carleen Hall and Billie Loukas when he suddenly dropped to the floor. The women called for help, but Eugene revived and was quickly back on his feet. The women were holding him—one on each arm—when it happened again. Carleen said: "I thought I had hold of him, but he just dropped to the floor." Again the women yelled for help and again Eugene revived. He said he was just tired and wanted to rest for a while. The women helped him to his dressing room and he sat down in a chair. He said he was fine and asked everyone to leave. But while he was just sitting there, he passed out again and slid to the floor. By this time the paramedics were on their way. Jelesnik did not want to go to the hospital and told everyone to leave him alone, but his fourth fainting spell in less than ten minutes finally convinced him that there was more wrong with him than just "being tired." When they got him to the hospital, they found that his blood pressure "had gone through the roof."[12] Carleen Hall had been worried about Eugene's blood pressure for more than six months. At the hospital she remembered that Virginia had told her to "keep an eye on Eugene," and she realized then that she must have also meant, "After I'm gone." She knew, too, that she had not kept her unspoken promise.

After Eugene's release from the hospital Carleen began to look after him. She made sure that he took his blood pressure medicine and avoided overtaxing himself. She acted for a time as his chauffeur and drove him wherever he needed to go: Mr. Mac's, KSL, the grocery store, and other places around town where Eugene regularly shopped. Carleen found that they were retracing the same routes several times a day and finally said, "Why don't you do the things you need to do at this end of town all at once?" It was then that she realized another reason why Eugene didn't drive: "He had no conception of where anything in town was or how far away things really were, nor did he care."

It wasn't long before Carleen discovered the conditions that Eugene was living under at Coatsville Avenue. When she finally saw where Eugene had been sleeping, she couldn't believe her eyes. The place was piled up waist-high with papers, programs, and music. Eugene apologized for the mess and told her, "I'm sorry, but this is the way it is." Carleen then heard for the first time the full, sad story of the last five years of Virginia's illness. It was clear to Carleen that Eugene could not stay any longer at the house on Coatsville Avenue. Until other arrangements could be made, Carleen would care for Jelesnik in her condominium near downtown Salt Lake.

Eugene could not believe the view from Carleen's sixth-floor apartment. All during his recuperation he stared out the window and would periodically sob at the view. It was the same reaction that he had the first time he set eyes on the Wasatch range of mountains. Over and over again Eugene would say, "Only in Switzerland could you see such a view." Eugene asked Carleen who owned the condominium next door to hers. He found out that the owner had moved to New Jersey several years before, and since then had been leasing the apartment out. Eugene made an offer to buy the place. Initially the man refused, but Eugene was insistent, and it wasn't long before he and Carleen Hall Brown were neighbors. Jelesnik had his condominium decorated exactly like Carleen's.[13]

March 19th of 1994 was Eugene's 80th birthday and for months before the event his friends had been plotting a surprise party for him. The party was thrown at Marianne's Delicatessen, and the owners, Horst and Marianne Young, had schemed with Flip and Lois Harmon to make the party a big event. Over forty of Eugene's closest and dearest friends would be in attendance. Mrs. Young catered the entire event with the exception of the birthday cake—a special "Black Forest" cherry-chocolate cake, which was prepared by the head pastry chef of the Red Lion Hotel. The huge cake was shaped like a violin. Carleen Hall came up with the idea of presenting Eugene a special quilt with the photographs of all his friends silk-screened onto it. It took months of quiet, behind-the-scenes maneuvering to acquire quilt blocks for a huge, king-size quilt that Lois Harmon pieced together. Each block on the quilt was created using a process in which photographs were transferred to the quilt material. Featured were photographs of everyone from President Thomas S. Monson and his wife to local entertainers and KSL personalities. Assembling the quilt and keeping the project a secret took all the planning and guile of a military campaign.

On the day of the party, Flip Harmon called a special emergency meeting of the Days of '47 executive committee, and Eugene of course showed up to find out what was so urgent. Harmon and several members of the committee took Eugene out to a shed in Tooele County where they showed Jelesnik a pile of dirt. "Eugene," Harmon announced in a gravely serious tone, "if anything should happen to me, you must promise me that you will see to it that this pile of dirt gets transported to the rodeo arena. The whole show depends upon it." Eugene knew everything about the music for the rodeo but nothing about "rodeo dirt" or how it got into the arena. Still he knew that this was obviously a serious matter. "I'll handle it," Eugene said. "Are you certain?" Harmon asked. "Don't worry, it's done, it's done," said Jelesnik.

After their trip to the dirt pile, Flip Harmon told Eugene he was hungry, and they pulled up in front of Marianne's Deli. As they walked into the back of the restaurant, Jelesnik recognized Doug and Barbara Smith, Bob Davis, the Monsons, and a number of other friends. When he saw Carleen he said, "What are you doing here?" He did not realize that it was a surprise party until he saw Ivan Lincoln of the *Deseret News*. After the group sang "Happy Birthday," Harmon told the assembled crowd of the trip to the dirt pile and how Eugene had vowed to take care of it. "It's done, it's done!" Harmon said, mimicking Eugene, and the party erupted in laughter.[14]

There was a certain inevitability to the next bit of transition in Eugene's life. Virginia's last instructions to Carleen were to watch over Eugene and "make sure that not just anyone gets their clutches on him." Gradually it became clear to both Carleen and Eugene that Virginia had auditioned Carleen many years before for the role she was about to undertake. Both Carleen and Eugene believed that Virginia intended they would end up together. In 1994, little over two years after Virginia's death, Eugene Jelesnik and Carleen Hall Brown were married, on Monday, the 24th of October, at two-thirty in the afternoon in Suite 1507 of the Marriott Hotel. With the marriage to Carleen, Eugene found that he suddenly had a very large extended family. In addition to being the stepfather to Carleen's six children, there were daughters- and sons-in-law and a host of offspring. By March of 1997, the Jelesniks would have thirteen grandchildren and nine great-grandchildren.[15]

In April of 1993, Eugene Jelesnik was awarded the highest honor of his career—The Presidential Citation of Brigham Young University. The award was given during the 118th Spring Commencement Exercises. The Presidential Citation and Medal, which were presented by President Thomas S. Monson, were accompanied by a lengthy tribute. It said in part:

> Brigham Young University is proud to honor Eugene Jelesnik with this Presidential Citation and medallion for his love of Utah and his selfless efforts in recognizing and developing the musical talent and appreciation of its citizens.
>
> Eugene gave patriotic service because he felt he owed a debt for the privilege of being an American. As permanent conductor for the Salt Lake Philharmonic Orchestra for more than forty years he continues to lead his musicians in annual free pops concerts for audiences numbering sometimes as many as ten thousand people, celebrating seasonal events such as LDS general conference, the 24th of July, Labor Day, and Thanksgiving. Brigham Young University is proud to honor Eugene Jelesnik with this Presidential Citation and medallion.[16]

Jelesnik never passed by an opportunity to play his violin for anyone who would listen. He had volunteered his talents countless times over the years to a variety of causes from "Uncle

Robert" Spiro's "Parents Day" to fund-raisers for the Cancer Society, the Polio Foundation, and wardhouse chapel carpets. Of his volunteer efforts in Salt Lake City, Don Reed of the Associated Press wrote:

> Of all his musical activities, the "volunteer" roles are the ones which Jelesnik enjoys the most in his adopted land. The conductorship of the Philharmonic is certainly a high spot. But, it's at the Yule season that Jelesnik waves his baton or plays the violin with the greatest gusto. "Traditionally, many of us in the orchestra take a week-long tour of the hospitals at Christmas time to play for the patients," he says. "It's the greatest thing I've been involved in and I'd feel bad if I couldn't do it."

The very first concerts that Eugene heard as a young boy were the Christmas concerts in Alexandrovsk. The first music that he played on the violin was "Silent Night" and "Oh, Christmas Tree." For more than sixty years he had given his professional time and talent to entertaining "Gentiles" on their most important holiday.

Jelesnik's most appreciative audiences were those who were the least able to pay for his services: the frail, the sick, and the elderly. Eugene did not gauge his success in Salt Lake on the amount of money he earned, or even on the number of people he reached. For Jelesnik, the achievement and satisfaction of his work was never calculated with reference to the size of the gate or the volume of the applause. Whether the audience was a sick child at Primary Children's Hospital, a young couple having dinner at the Cinegrill, a wounded soldier in Vietnam, or 7,000 senior citizens at the "always free" Pops Concerts didn't matter. His greatest joy was the simple act of sharing his music with others.

Considering all the honors and awards he received over the years, one moment stands out. Ringling Brothers Barnum and Bailey Circus was performing at the new Delta Center. It was Channel 5 Night at the circus, and a number of KSL personalities and officials and their families were present, including Al Henderson, president of KSL-TV. The grand entrance had been made and all the costumed performers, elephants, tigers, and clowns were in the arena. Suddenly the Delta Center went completely dark and a single blue spotlight picked up Steve Linsley, the vice president and general manager of KSL Television, who delivered the following address:

> The man I am about to introduce has received many honors over the years for his contribution to this city and to the state of Utah. You may recognize him as . . . the man who organized and led USO tours of entertainers to front-line areas during three wars in order to build the morale of U. S. military personnel. You may recognize him as the man who conducted the Salt Lake Philharmonic Orchestra for more than 40 years and presented free pops concerts to the public throughout those years. You may recognize him as the man whose weekly program *Talent Showcase* ran for more than three decades on KSL-TV and showcased over 10,000 talented Utahns. But tonight we would like to recognize him as the man who has worked with the circus in Salt Lake City for thirty years. You know him as "The Maestro." We know him simply as *Eugene*. Ladies and gentlemen, please help us honor Eugene Jelesnik, one of this state's most valued treasures.[17]

Another spot went up on Eugene Jelesnik, resplendent in a gold embroidered jacket. The audience broke into thunderous applause, and the house lights came up slowly to reveal the entire circus family clapping and cheering for Eugene Jelesnik. The clowns all stood at attention, and the elephants bowed in homage. Nearly eighty years after Shurachka Yakovlevich Zheleznykov had first set out to join the circus, he was finally in the center ring.

SUMMARY

This book was primarily written as a personal favor to my friend Eugene Jelesnik. It was also written for those who ever found him a little strange and mysterious or wondered what he was about or what he was doing in Salt Lake City. What was it that motivated him? The answer to all these questions is surprisingly simple. Eugene Jelesnik was motivated by one driving passion, gratitude—gratitude for his life, gratitude for his talent, and gratitude to the country that extended him refuge and then sustained him.

Gerald M. McDonough

THE LAST WORD

It is 18 February 1997, and as I have been relating the story of my life to my friend Gerald McDonough, I am still alive and well. I am eighty-three years old. I just wanted to pause a moment and tell my thousands of friends here in Utah and around the world, and especially the six children of my wife, Carleen, that I am the most fortunate man alive. Carleen Hall of Bear River City, Utah, became my wife on the 24th of October, 1994. We were married at the Presidential Suite of the Salt Lake Marriott Hotel. The ceremony was performed by Rabbi Fred Wenger and Judge Ray Uno.

Were it not for Carleen's loyalty, compassion, and understanding, I would not have been alive to tell this story.

Eugene Jelesnik

ENDNOTES

NOTES TO CHAPTER ONE

1. All documents, dates, and personal data relating to Eugene Jelesnik are taken from newspaper articles, archival documents (such as concert programs), and materials in the Eugene Jelesnik "Family Study," a series of documents prepared by the Family History Library of The Church of Jesus Christ of Latter-day Saints. Much of the material is from Mr. Ivan Lincoln who made extensive preparations for writing this biography before this author was engaged. Unless otherwise noted, all other materials come from interviews with Mr. Jelesnik conducted by the author between September 1996 and February 1997. Sources identified in the text are not cited in the notes. Many newspaper clippings are from Eugene Jelesnik's scrapbooks. Many are not identified by name of paper or date. Other materials can be found in the Eugene Jelesnik Archive, housed at the Utah State Historical Society.

2. Jacob's second name, Israelevitch, Son of Israel, actually derives from the fact that his father's name was Israel.

3. Rapoport, p. 2.

4. Gitelman, Introduction, xiii.

5. Ibid.

6. Interview with Eugene Jelesnik.

7. From "Zheleznykov Family Study," prepared by the Languages Department, Brigham Young University (hereafter, JFS/BYU).

8. Gitelman, p. 78.

9. Ibid., xiii.

10. Ibid., xv.

11. Ibid., pp. 2–3.

12. Ibid., p. 13.

13. Yarmolinsky, p. 250. (See also Gitelman, p. 13.)

14. Ibid., p. 5.

15. Statistics quoted from Gitelman, p. 39.

16. Property deeds and other papers from JFS/BYU.

17. JFS/BYU and interviews with Eugene Jelesnik.

18. Gitelman, pp. 38–59.

19. All the material on the Rothaus family is from JFS/BYU.

20. Interview with Eugene Jelesnik and materials in Jelesnik family photo albums.

21. Chumak, p. 314.

22. See Crimean travel server on the Internet, http://www.elis.crimea.ua/CTS/CTS.html.

23. Gray, pp. 51–52.

24. JFS/BYU, marriage documents, Jelesnik family history.

25. Gray, p. 52.

26. Jelesnik family album.

27. Interview with Eugene Jelesnik, September 1996.

28. Elman, pp. 2–3.

29. Sachar, p. 366.

30. Interview with Eugene Jelesnik, September 1996.

31. Sachar, p. 367.

32. Bachmann, p. 365.

33. Interview with Eugene Jelesnik, September 1996.

34. Ibid.

35. Gitelman, pp. 5–7.

36. Ibid., pp. 123–24.

37. Interview with Eugene Jelesnik, September 1996. See also *Deseret News*, 12 December 1954.

38. Ibid.

39. Collier's Encyclopedia, "World War I," Vol. 23, pp. 593–604.

40. For a thorough discussion, see Chamberlin, Vol. 1, *"The Autocracy Collapses,"* p. 73.

41. Gitelman, pp. 96–108.

42. Chamberlin, Vol. 1, p. 158.

43. Channon, p. 103.

44. Ibid.

45. Chamberlin, Vol. 1, pp. 348–50.

46. Ibid., p. 375.

47. Ibid., p. 509. (Documents in Appendix.)

48. Chamberlin, Vol. 2, p. 67.

49. From Russian language documents translated by Brigham Young University, September 1996.

50. Chumak, pp. 309–11.

51. For a history of the Zaporozhian Cossacks, see Seaton, pp. 34–59.

52. Chamberlin, Vol. 2, p. 126.

NOTES TO CHAPTER TWO

1. Massie, pp. 1–6.

2. Detailed descriptions of the Civil War in the Ukraine can be found in Chamberlin's excellent, two-volume history *The Russian Revolution*.

3. Ibid., Vol. 1, p. 504. (Appendix of documents.)

4. Ibid., p. 506.

5. Rapoport, p. 31.

6. Chamberlin, Vol. 2, pp. 66–67.

7. Channon, p. 103.

8. Chamberlin, "Chronological Table of Events," Vol. 2, pp. 529–34.

9. Ibid., and pp. 229–35.

10. Gitelman, pp. 96–107.

11. Rapoport, p. 32.

12. Chamberlin, Vol. 2, pp. 227–31.

13. Sanders, pp. 328–36.

14. Chamberlin, Vol. 2, pp. 229–32.

15. Sanders, pp. 343–46.

16. Gitelman, pp. 98–108.

17. Chamberlin, Vol. 2, pp. 216–17.

18. Gitelman, p. 108. See Chamberlin for estimates of deaths, Vol. 2, p. 240, Note 8.

19. All details of Yakov (Jacob) Zheleznykov's will are taken from the actual document as translated by Brigham Young University Languages Department, September 1996.

20. Chamberlin, Vol. 2, p. 230.

21. Ibid., pp. 232–34, description of Nestor Makhno. See also Gitelman, p. 102.

22. Chamberlin, Vol. 2, p. 235.

23. Ibid., p. 236.

24. Ibid., pp. 286–87.

25. Ibid., p. 319.

26. Ibid., pp. 322–23.

27. Ibid., p. 238.

28. Ibid., pp. 232–33.

29. Ibid., p. 494. Appendix document.

30. Ibid., p. 495. Appendix document.

31. JFS/BYU.

32. Interview with Eugene Jelesnik, September 1996.

33. Ibid.

34. Ibid.

35. Ibid.

36. Chamberlin, Vol. 2, pp. 107–9.

37. Channon, pp. 104–5.

38. Sanders on HSIAS, pp. 367–79.

39. Interview with Eugene Jelesnik, September 1996.

40. Ibid.

41. See Hammond, "World History Atlas," Section H, p. 37. See also Channon, maps of the Ukraine, 1914–26.

42. Mellor, p. 242.

43. Zaporotzhe State University home page, on the Internet. Address: Hpop Internet Gmbh, Hannover Germany. www.hpop.de/zsu.

44. Ibid.

45. Klein, pp. 284–85.

46. Sanders, p. 380.

47. Ibid.

48. Rapoport, pp. 5–6.

49. Sanders, pp. 381–82.

50. Ibid., p. 383.

51. Ibid., p. 386.

52. Ibid., p. 387.

53. Ibid.

54. Interview with Eugene Jelesnik, September 1996.

55. Ibid.

56. Elman, p. 171.

57. Interview with Eugene Jelesnik, September 1996.

NOTES TO CHAPTER THREE

1. Dunne, pp. 31–32.

2. JFS/BYU, immigration forms.

3. Unless otherwise noted, the information in this chapter comes from interviews with Eugene Jelesnik conducted in October of 1996.

4. Dunne, p. 49.

5. Ibid., p. 51.

6. A photograph of the mural as it appeared in 1970 is found in Dunne—fifth photo from the end of the book.

7. JFS/BYU, immigration forms.

8. Ibid.

9. Sanders, p. 394.

10. Interviews with Eugene Jelesnik, October 1996.

11. Franck, p. 104.

12. Jelesnik scrapbooks/clippings.

13. Stein, p. 335.

14. Interviews with Eugene Jelesnik, October 1996.

15. Stein, p. 337.

16. Ibid., p. 376.

17. *New York Times,* Jelesnik clipping file.

18. From program schedules in Jelesnik archive.

19. From "A History of Television."

20. Jelesnik scrapbooks.

21. Tucker biography.

22. Bourgoin, pp. 250–52.

23. Jelesnik scrapbook.

NOTES TO CHAPTER FOUR

1. Most of the material in this chapter comes from interviews with Eugene Jelesnik conducted in late October of 1996. Newspapers and other sources quoted in the text are not generally cited in the notes. Many clippings in the scrapbooks are undated.

2. Jelesnik photo album.

3. Clipping in Jelesnik scrapbook.

4. Ibid.

5. Interview with Jelesnik.

6. Newspaper clippings from scrapbooks.

7. Jelesnik archive.

8. Newspaper photo in scrapbooks.

9. Ibid.

10. Clipping in Jelesnik scrapbook.

11. Interview with Eugene Jelesnik, October 1996.

12. Moquin, pp. 54–62.

13. Ibid., pp. 170–71.

14. Ibid.

15. Ibid.

16. Ibid.

17. See *New York Times*, 23 October 1935, p. 3. See also *New York Times*, 24 October 1935, p. 9/ 25 October 1935, p. 20.

18. Ibid., 26 October 1935, p. 6.

19. Flyer in Jelesnik scrapbook.

NOTES TO CHAPTER FIVE

1. Jelesnik scrapbooks and interviews.

2. Opening night program in Jelesnik archive.

3. Interview with Eugene Jelesnik, November 1996.

4. From flyer for Vanezia Restaurant in Eugene Jelesnik archive.

5. Telegram collection in Jelesnik archive.

6. Interview with Eugene Jelesnik, November 1996.

NOTES TO CHAPTER SIX

1. Steorts, pp. 1–10. See also *Deseret News*, 12 July 1911.

2. Arrington, pp. 1–3; 24–35.

3. Steorts, pp. 11–13.

4. Arrington, pp. 35–39.

5. Ibid., p. 35.

6. Description of Hotel Utah in Arrington vii–viii. See also lobby photos, p. 2, 33.

7. Ibid.

8. Details of the Hotel Utah booking come from interviews with Eugene Jelesnik conducted in November of 1996. Also from scrapbook clippings, publicity flyers, and concert programs.

9. Jelesnik archive.

10. *Variety* clipping from scrapbook, spring 1935.

11. Photo, Jelesnik album.

12. Information of the Washburn family and the history of Mulberry Grove, Illinois, taken from privately published notes in Jelesnik archive.

13. Interview with Eugene Jelesnik and Carleen Brown Jelesnik.

14. Interview with Carleen Brown Jelesnik, December 1996.

15. Letter to Eugene dated 4 July 1984, in Jelesnik archive.
16. Ibid.
17. Material on Eugene's television career comes from a variety of sources in the archive including programs, clippings, and promotional flyers.
18. Columbus *Post Dispatch* article in Jelesnik scrapbook.

NOTES TO CHAPTER SEVEN

1. Advertisement for Bal Tabarin in Jelesnik archive.
2. Promotional materials in Jelesnik archive.
3. From album covers of "Nodocky Polka" and interviews with Eugene Jelesnik conducted in December of 1996.
4. For material on the early career of Frank Sinatra see *Frank Sinatra, My Father* by Nancy Sinatra, pp. 55–83 and *An American Legend*, 63–79.
5. Ibid.
6. Complete records of Jelesnik's USO tours including itineraries are found in the archive.
7. Photo of Skelton's send-off for Eugene is found in Jelesnik photo album. See photo 34, this book.
8. From USO promotional materials in archive.
9. Ibid. Also *Stars and Stripes*, January 1945.
10. The forgotten front.
11. *Life Magazine*, March 1945.
12. For a more complete discussion of the Italian campaign and the 10th Mountain Division's part in the fighting, see Wallace, pp. 179–202.
13. *Stars and Stripes*, 15 March 1945/ Italian campaign edition. Jelesnik archive.
14. Letters are found in Jelesnik archive: "USO TOUR ITALY."
15. Ibid.
16. Though a lot of previously published material exists on Eugene's encounter with the minefield, this version is based on an interview conducted with Mr. Jelesnik in December of 1996.
17. Wallace, pp. 185–86.
18. Ibid.
19. Ibid., p. 188.
20. I am indebted to my friend Bob Woody, a veteran of the 10th Mountain Division, for this account of the final assault on the German lines.
21. Interview with Eugene Jelesnik, December 1996.
22. For a discussion of Italian art under the Fascists, see Hulten and Celant, pp. 86–88, 130–32, 209–10.
23. Photos of Silvers and Sinatra's USO tour of Italy are found in the Jelesnik archive. Also see *Frank Sinatra, My Father* by Nancy Sinatra, p. 100, for photo of Jelesnik, Sinatra, and Silvers in June of 1945. See photo 39, this book.
24. Nancy Sinatra, *An American Legend*, p. 67.
25. Incident with Sinatra from interviews with Jelesnik conducted in December 1996.
26. Letter in Jelesnik archive.
27. Interview with Eugene Jelesnik, December 1996.

NOTES TO CHAPTER EIGHT

1. *Salt Lake Telegram* article, 22 August 1945.
2. Ads, *Salt Lake Tribune* and *Telegram,* clipping file, Jelesnik archive.
3. Interview with John W. Gallivan, *Salt Lake Tribune* publisher.
4. Article and photograph, *Salt Lake Tribune,* Jelesnik scrapbook.
5. *Salt Lake Tribune,* 23 December 1945.
6. Interview with Eugene Jelesnik, December 1996.
7. Ibid.
8. Ibid.
9. Salt Lake Philharmonic history from concert program collection, Jelesnik archive.
10. *Salt Lake Tribune,* Jelesnik clipping file.
11. *Deseret News* article, Jelesnik scrapbook.
12. ASCAP artist directory, Jelesnik archive.
13. Undated *Deseret News* article in Jelesnik clipping file.
14. Undated article in Jelesnik clipping file.
15. Photograph of marquee in Jelesnik scrapbook.
16. Undated article in Jelesnik clipping file.
17. Interview with Eugene Jelesnik, December 1996.
18. Biographical sheet, KDYL-Television, Jelesnik archive.
19. Interview with Eugene Jelesnik, December 1996.
20. See *Dictionary of American Biography.*
21. Biographical sheet, Jelesnik archive.
22. Interview with Eugene Jelesnik, December 1996.
23. Undated clippings, Jelesnik scrapbook.
24. Information on Sid Fox from interview with Eugene Jelesnik, December 1996.
25. Ibid.
26. Clipping, *Salt Lake Tribune,* 1 April 1953.

NOTES TO CHAPTER NINE

1. Clipping file, Jelesnik archive.
2. Interview with Eugene Jelesnik, January 1997.
3. USO Press releases, Jelesnik archive.
4. USO itineraries, Jelesnik archive.
5. Clipping from *Stars and Stripes,* December 1953.
6. *Stars and Stripes.*
7. See Collier's Encyclopedia, Vol. 23, p. 247.
8. Ibid., p. 246.
9. Jelesnik photo album.
10. Interview with Eugene Jelesnik, January 1997.
11. Undated clipping from *Stars and Stripes,* Jelesnik's USO files.
12. Jelesnik letter file.
13. Most of the information on Ed Allem comes from his sister, Jenny Boyer, interviewed January 1997.

14. Cinegrill menus, Jelesnik archives.

15. Jenny Boyer interview.

16. Ibid.

17. Ibid.

18. Information of *Talent Showcase* is from materials in the Jelesnik archive, KSL Television clippings and publicity releases and from interviews with Eugene Jelesnik.

19. Interview with Rebecca Terry Heal, February 1997.

20. Ibid.

21. Ibid.

22. Interview with Heller, January 1997.

23. Interview with Eugene Jelesnik, December 1996.

24. Clipping file, Jelesnik archive.

25. Transcript of program courtesy of KSL-TV.

NOTES TO CHAPTER TEN

1. A "jossler" in circus language is a member of the general public. A "gilley" is an outsider. See Croft-Cooke, p. 186.

2. A "cerb hawker" or "floor salesman" sells circus merchandise.

3. A Gypsy who travels with the circus, often performing odd jobs.

4. *Deseret News*, 22 December 1964.

5. Barr was mistaken. Contestants were sent to the *Ted Mack Show*.

6. *Deseret News*, 5 October 1970.

NOTES TO CHAPTER ELEVEN

1. Flyer for "Rug Benefit" is in Jelesnik archive.

2. Photos and programs of concerts in Jelesnik archive.

3. LDS Presidents "Home Page" on World Wide Web/ Brigham Young University.

4. Interview with Eugene Jelesnik, February 1997.

5. Cited in Spring Commencement exercises program, Brigham Young University, 22 April 1993, p. 10.

6. Ivan Lincoln interview with Powell (tape and notes).

7. *Deseret News*, 23 January 1981.

8. Letter file, Jelesnik archive.

9. Speech delivered by President Monson/Jelesnik archive.

10. Speech recorded on KSL-TV.

11. Interview with Carleen Hall, January 1997.

12. Ibid.

13. Ibid.

14. Interview with Carleen Hall, February 1997.

15. Ibid.

16. Commencement Program, Jelesnik archive.

17. Text of speech courtesy of KSL-TV.

BIBLIOGRAPHY

BOOKS

Altman, Jack. *Discover Germany,* 2nd Edition. New York-Oxford: Berlitz Publishing Co., 1995.

Arrington, Leonard J. & Swinton, Heidi S. *The Hotel.* Salt Lake City: Privately published, 1986.

Bachmann, Alberto, *An Encyclopedia of the Violin.* New York: D. Appleton and Company, 1926.

Bilmanis, Alfred. *A History of Latvia.* Westport, Connecticut: Greenwood Publishers, 1951.

Bourgoin, Susan M., ed. *Contemporary Musicians.* Detroit: Gale Research, Inc., 1994.

Chamberlin, William Henry. *The Russian Revolution: Vols. 1 & 2.* Princeton, New Jersey, Princeton University Press, 1987.

Channon, John and Robert Hudson. *The Punguin Historical Atlas of Russia.* London: Penguin Books, 1995.

Chumak, George & Hodges, Linda. *Ukraine.* New York: Hippocrene Books, 1994.

Croft-Cook, Rupert & Cotes, Peter. *Circus: A World History.* New York: Macmillian Publishing Company, 1976.

Crankshaw, Edward. *Shadow of the Winter Palace.* New York: Viking Press, 1976.

Cook, Fred J. *Mob, Inc.* New York: Franklin Watts, 1977.

Dunne, Thomas & Tifft, Wilton. *Ellis Island.* New York: W. W. Norton and Company Inc., 1971.

Elman, Saul. *Memoirs.* New York: Privately published, 1933.

Feingold, Henry L. *A Time for Searching: Entering the Mainstream, 1920–1945.* Baltimore: John Hopkins University Press, 1992.

Freedland, Michael. *Sophie: The Sophie Tucker Story.* Woburn Press, 1978.

Gitelman, Zvi Y. *A Century of Ambivalence: The Jews of Russia and the Soviet Union, 1881 to the Present.* New York: Schocken Books, 1988.

Gosnell, Kelvin. *Belarus, Ukraine, and Moldova.* Brookfield, Connecticut: Millbrook Press, 1992.

Gray, Bettyanne. *Manya's Story.* Minneapolis: Lerner Publications Company, 1978.

Hammond World Atlas: Medallion Edition. Maplewood, New Jersey: Hammond, 1986.

Hardy, Phil & Lang, Dave. *Faber Companion to Popular Music.* Faber and Faber, 1990.

Howe, Irving & Libo, Kenneth. *How We Lived: A History of Immigrant Jews in America*. New York: Richard Marek Publishers, 1979.

Hulten, Pontus & Germano, Celant. *Italian Art: 1900–1945*. New York: Rizzoli International Publications, Inc., 1989.

Klein, Wilhelm. *Insight Guides: The New Soviet Union*. Singapore: APA Publications, Ltd., 1991.

Lyman, Susan E. *The Story of New York*. New York: Crown Publishers Inc., 1964.

Masie, Robert K. *The Romanovs: The Final Chapter*. New York: Random House, 1995.

Mayer, Martin. *The Met: One Hundred Years of Grand Opera*. New York: Simon and Schuster, 1983.

McDonough, Gerald. *The Hogles*. Salt Lake City: McMurrin-Henriksen Books, 1988.

Mellor, R. E. H. *Geography of the U. S. S. R.* London: Macmillan and Company, Ltd., 1964.

Moquin, Wayne & Van Doren, Charles, eds. *The American Way of Crime*. New York: Praeger Publishers, Inc., 1976.

Nash, Jay Robert. *Bloodletters and Badmen: A Narrative Encyclopedia of American Criminals from the Pilgrims to the Present*. New York: M. Evans and Company, Inc., 1995.

Neville, Peter. *A Traveler's History of Russia and the USSR*. Brooklyn, N. Y.: Interlink Books, 1990.

Oparenko, Christina. *The Ukraine*. New York: Chelsea House, 1988.

Radzinsky, Edvard. *The Last Tsar: The Life and Death of Nicholas II*. (Translated by Marian Schwartz). New York: Doubleday, 1992.

Rapoport, Louis. *Stalin's War against the Jews: The Doctor's Plot and the Soviet Solution*. New York: The Free Press, 1990.

Robbins, Jhan. *Inka Dinka Doo: The Life of Jimmy Durante*. New York: Paragon House, 1991.

Robinson, Harlow. *The Last Impresario: The Life, Times, and Legacy of Sol Hurok*. New York: Penguin Books, 1994.

Sachar, Howard M. *A History of the Jews in America*. New York: Alfred A. Knopf, 1992.

Sanders, Ronald. *Shores of Refuge: A Hundred Years of Jewish Emigration*. New York: Henry Holt and Company, 1988.

Seaton, Albert. *The Horsemen of the Steppes: The Story of the Cossacks*. New York: Hippocrene Books, 1985.

Shoener, Allon. *Portal to America*. New York: Holt, Rinehart, and Winston, 1967.

Sinatra, Nancy. *Frank Sinatra*. Santa Monica, California: General Publishing Group, 1995.

Sinatra, Nancy. *My Father, Frank Sinatra*. Garden City, New York: Doubleday and Co., 1985.

Slide, Anthony. *The Vaudevillians*. Westport, Connecticut: Arlington House, 1981.

Smith, Dennis Mack. *Mussolini*. New York: Alfred A. Knopf, 1982.

Stein, Charles W. *American Vaudeville*. New York: Alfred A. Knopf, 1984.

Steorts, Phyllis L. *Remember When: A Personal History of the Hotel Utah*. Salt Lake City: Privately published, 1986.

Turkus, Burton B. & Feder, Sid. *Murder, Inc: The Story of "The Syndicate."* New York: Da Capo Press, 1992.

Wallace, Robert. *World War II: The Italian Campaign.* Alexandria, Virginia: Time-Life Books, 1978.

Yarmolinsky, *The Road to Revolution.* New York: Macmilliam, 1959.

NEWSPAPERS & MAGAZINES

Albany Times Union, Albany, New York.

Atlantic Evening News, Atlantic City, N. J.

The Daily Mirror.

Variety.

The Sunday Mirror.

New York News, N. Y. C.

LIFE Magazine.

Columbus Post Dispatch, Columbus, Ohio.

Oakland Post Inquirer.

The Long Island Daily Star.

The Salt Lake Tribune, Salt Lake City, Utah.

The *Deseret News,* Salt Lake City, Utah.

The *Salt Lake Evening Telegram,* Salt Lake City, Utah.

The New York Journal.

The New York Times, New York City, N. Y.

Stars and Stripes, United States Armed Forces.

Salt Lake City Magazine, Salt Lake, Utah Partners Publishing.

DOCUMENTS

The Jelesnik Archive, housed at the Utah State Historical Society in Salt Lake City, Utah, consists of the following:

> Eight scrapbooks containing photographs and newspaper clippings.
> Concert programs (more than 1,000).
> USO tour memorabilia, plaques, letters, schedules, photos, and certificates sorted by tour.
> Several large boxes containing correspondence, newspaper press releases, clippings, and unsorted files of programs and advertisements grouped as follows: Days of '47/USO/*Talent Showcase*/Pops Concerts/Salt Lake Philharmonics/KSL/Rodeo/Ringling Brothers Circus/Utah State Fair/*Celebrity Series*

INDEX